The Language Imperative

Other books by Suzette Haden Elgin, Ph.D.

The Gentle Art of Verbal Self-Defense
More on the Gentle Art of Verbal Self-Defense
The Last Word on the Gentle Art of Verbal Self-Defense
Genderspeak
Success with the Gentle Art of Verbal Self-Defense
The Grandmother Principles
You Can't SAY That to Me!
Try to Feel It My Way
How to Disagree Without Being Disagreeable

the
LANGUAGE
IMPERATIVE

SUZETTE HADEN ELGIN, PH.D.

PERSEUS PUBLISHING
Cambridge, Massachusetts

Many of the designations used by manufacturers and sellers to distinguish their products are claimed as trademarks. Where those designations appear in this book and Perseus Publishing was aware of a trademark claim, the designations have been printed in initial capital letters.

CIP information for this book is available from the Library of Congress
ISBN: 0-7382-0428-5

Perseus Publishing is a member of the Perseus Books Group

Text design by Jeff Williams
Set in 11-point Minion by the Perseus Books Group

1 2 3 4 5 6 7 8 9 10—03 02 01 00
First paperback printing, December 2000

Perseus Publishing books are available at special discounts for bulk purchases in the U.S. by corporations, institutions, and other organizations. For more information, please contact the Special Markets Department at HarperCollins Publishers, 10 East 53rd Street, New York, NY 10022, or call 1–212–207–7528.

Find us on the World Wide Web at http://www.perseuspublishing.com

Contents

Preface

According to Chomsky, a Martian sent to Earth would conclude we speak a variety of dialects with mutually unintelligible vocabularies—but dialects, nonetheless, of a single Earthish tongue.

(Kalbfleisch 1994)

Could this be true? Could it be that—in spite of the seeming multitude of differences between English and Kwakiutl, Navajo and Japanese, Albanian and Hawaiian—every human being could accurately say, "I speak a dialect of Earthish"?

Let's assume for a moment, for purposes of discussion, that it's true; let's suppose there is in fact a language that we could (a bit more gracefully) call "Terran." What might that mean for humankind? Does it matter? Would it be important and significant, or would it only qualify as a tidbit of information to include in trivia contests?

If it's true, we clearly need the answers to a number of other questions. For example:

- Does it matter which of these Terran dialects is your own native tongue? Are some of the Terran dialects *better* than others—more useful, more beautiful, more powerful, or in some other way more desirable?
- If you happen to have native or near-native fluency in more than one "dialect" of Terran, are you blessed, or burdened, or neither? That is, do bilingualism and multilingualism have

significant effects on human minds and lives, and if so, what are their consequences?

- Are there good reasons to work toward *eliminating* many of these language differences? Should we perhaps try to get rid of the hundreds of varieties now spoken only by very small populations—so that we humans could communicate with fewer of the cumbersome systems and devices now required for translating and interpreting all over the world? Or would that be a mistake?

These questions aren't trivial. We're forever hearing people say, "Oh, it's only talk!" and "Oh, we were only talking!" As if speech were some minor phenomenon of human life, something we all do but not something that deserves much of our attention. If it's "only" talk, we could save very substantial amounts of energy and time and money by stamping out most of our baroque array of ways of speaking. On the other hand, if languages are powerful and important, perhaps we should be more careful with them than we are. Perhaps we should be worried about losing *any* of our ways of speaking. Surely we ought to know more about what we're doing before we make decisions in this area of our lives.

We understand what it means to know *one* language—a single native language. Having a native language is to the definition of "a human being" what "feathered" is to the definition of "a bird." There are other creatures that are mammals, that can walk upright on two legs, that have opposable thumbs, and so on; other creatures able to communicate limited sets of messages to one another exist on this earth. But only human beings, so far as we have yet been able to determine, have native languages. Language is so important to us that the loss of the ability to use language (or the very rare failure to acquire that ability) is perceived as one of the worst of all possible catastrophes; we say of persons without language that they are "trapped" inside their bodies.

By contrast, we know astonishingly little about what it means to know more than one language, whether natively or simply fluently, and our understanding of the little we do know is limited. We don't know what adding another language *means* for a human being.

Opinions (even among those who don't actually *disapprove* of multi-lingualism) range along a broad continuum. At one extreme is the idea that multilingualism is roughly like knowing how to play two or more musical instruments instead of just one. It has a certain social usefulness, and sometimes professional usefulness—like the situation of someone who learned to play the piano as a tiny child and then learned to play the guitar as well. At the other extreme is the idea that for each language learned, the learner gains another world-view—perhaps even another "personality." Which would mean that the miracle of language is multiplied every time a new tongue is learned, or at least that the miracle grows significantly in power and degree. In between those two extremes lies every sort of variation upon them.

In this book we will consider this issue, and some related issues, from a number of different points of view. To set the stage for our investigation, let's look at half a dozen brief scenarios, set in today's United States and based on my own experience with languages and the human beings who speak them.

- Jack grinned at the relatives crowding his living room and shook his head at them in mock despair. He'd known they would find his bragging hard to believe; he'd been prepared for resistance. "I'm not kidding you!" he insisted. "I bought that Spanish computer program for Jennifer, and in two months—*two months*—she was rattling off Spanish like a native! And we're talking about a three-year-old *kid* here! I'm going to get her the French program next!"

- Thomas was determined not to lose his temper with the kids again, but he couldn't keep the sternness out of his voice as he spoke. *They're not stupid!* he thought. *What do I have to say to get them to pay attention?* "Listen to me, you two!" he said urgently. "Haven't I told you, over and over, not to let me hear you talking Tagalog? Haven't I? Hasn't your mother told you the same thing? What's the *matter* with you, you want to spend your whole life on welfare? You speak English, you hear me? Don't make me have to tell you *again!*"

- When Barbara got home from work she was in a good mood. It had been such luck that she'd still remembered enough from her years in China to be able to interpret for the patient and Dr. Gales! There could have been serious misunderstandings if she hadn't been there—and she'd saved the hospital the cost of a Chinese interpreter, too. But when she told her husband about it, he frowned at her. "I don't know if that was such a good idea," Jim said slowly. "Don't you think the other nurses may resent the way you were showing off?"

- Philip didn't like having to talk to Anna's mother about this subject; he was very worried about hurting her feelings. But it was his duty to the child, and he was determined to get it done. "Mrs. Kolyoff," he said carefully, "I'm really sorry to have to say this. Russia is a great country; I know that. It has a wonderful history of music and art and literature and scientific discovery. I'm glad that Anna can speak Russian; that's terrific. But you have to realize that it's holding her back. If you want her to go on to fourth grade, ma'am, you're going to have to convince her to speak English!"

- Greg nodded his agreement to what the others were saying about their colleague: Harold Fleming was a top-notch lawyer, no question about it!
  "But I keep wondering," Greg cut in. "How long are we going to be able to keep Hal in the firm? Did you know that he speaks four languages fluently? Including Japanese? He can write his own ticket, you know? He could get a top position *any*where. I just hope we can hang *on* to him a while, myself!"

- Janet sighed, looking at the gloomy faces around the table; it wasn't easy being a school principal in times like these. "All right then," she said wearily, "we all hate to do it, but we don't really have any choice. The only way to find the money is to get rid of the frills, and that means dropping French and Spanish. Not that foreign languages aren't a good thing, mind you! If we had unlimited funds I'm sure we'd all be solidly behind having them in our curriculum. But they're not important the way football and math are important, and that's all there is to it. They've got to go!"

These six incidents are typical of the confusion in our attitudes about the power and importance of languages. Is it a good or a bad idea for people in this country to have command of two languages, or of more than two languages? What does it mean, for them and for others and for society? Is the learning of languages a luxury that should only be pursued by those rich enough to afford it on their own, like horseback riding, or should it be a goal of our public educational system, paid for with our hard-earned tax dollars? Should we have an international language, or is that a silly (or perhaps dangerous) idea? Do languages have the power to shape our lives as individuals and as a nation? If they do, what are the implications of the decisions we make about which languages we favor and which we ignore? Obviously, we haven't yet made up our minds.

Attitudes about languages have changed over the past three decades, sometimes for the better. I don't believe that any employer today would tell me, as did a man who was my boss in the 1950s, that he'd fire me if he ever saw me studying a Russian grammar during my lunch hour again. "What on earth will our customers *think* if they see you doing that?" he demanded. "What are you trying to do, destroy my *business??*" I'm sure that today, when people hear tales of high school superintendents who insist that "If English was good enough for Jesus Christ, it's good enough for our students!" they know that they're hearing a joke.

However, the U.S. government and some state governments are now working seriously to establish "English Only" laws that would drastically restrict the use of foreign languages in the United States. Isn't it a bit strange to spend tax money for classes to teach Spanish to English-speaking students in our schools, while at the same time making it difficult (or illegal) for Spanish-speaking individuals to use Spanish there? This is just one of many curiosities resulting from the current confusion about language and languages.

Some accounts give the impression that general agreement now exists on multilingualism and that language policy decisions about it in the United States are made on the basis of firm knowledge and solid science. I wish that were true; it's not. Our feelings about bilingualism and multilingualism are a dense thicket of muddles and contradictions. As the six incidents on pp. ix–xi show, there is no one attitude that represents a national consensus, or even a national majority opinion. Our decisions with regard to language issues such as multilingualism, most of the time, are based not on scientific facts but on folklore and politics and emotion and expediency. We can't allow this to go on. In a world that is so rapidly becoming a global society, we have to do better.

About This Book

My intention in this book is to take some useful steps toward sorting out this linguistic turmoil and laying a foundation upon which others can build to carry the improvement forward. Because there are so many differences of opinion, and because those differences are as likely to come from scholars and experts as from the general population, I won't be able to provide all the missing answers that would be needed for a rational and practical language policy. However, I will do my best to . . .

- Set out the questions that must be answered with regard to the power of language in human life, especially in the areas of public policy and in education.
- Establish the *importance* of multilingualism within the context of the larger topic of the power of language.
- Explain why there is so much confusion and contradiction about multilingualism and about language learning as a whole.
- Provide a fair hearing for both (or all) sides of the major controversies.
- Present the basic facts, when they are available.
- Discuss the possible effects of multilingualism in some major areas of human life.
- Present useful information gathered from speakers of two or more languages about their personal perceptions of, and experiences with, multilingualism.

- Help make possible the building of a consensus for or against multilingualism that is based on scientific information and real-world facts.
- Outline possible directions for further research.

We will be focusing on seven questions—quite broad questions. They were chosen because I believe that the search for their answers will help us find ways of thinking about multilingualism and human language abilities that are more appropriate for today's world. They are:

1. What is multilingualism?
2. What is the link between languages and cultures?
3. What effect, if any, do languages have on human perceptions of reality?
4. What are some consequences of multilingualism in a few representative areas of human life (for example, medicine, business, and family life)?
5. Should we have a single language that *everybody* learns, worldwide, with which to carry on international communication? What effects might that have on our lives?
6. How do people become multilingual, and what happens in their minds and/or brains when they do? Is this good or bad?
7. What does all this information tell us about the power of human language?

A distinction is usually made between "bilingualism" and "multilingualism" when such questions are discussed. The reason for that distinction is not that we know the two "isms" differ in some significant and relevant way; we make the distinction only because it's traditional. It's also a nuisance. It's a nuisance to keep specifying whether we're talking about two languages or more than two. In this book the term "multilingual" will be assumed to include everyone with a command of more than one language, however many that may be, unless there's a good reason to give the exact number.

We will also be concentrating on spoken language, for the most part, although the many different situations among my respondents with regard to literacy in their various languages deserve a book of their own. (For example, one of my Latvian respondents—who has asked to remain anonymous—writes that the only way she can understand written Latvian is to read it out loud. When she *hears* it, she understands what she has said as she was reading it, but she can't read it just by looking at it.) Reading and writing are important in multilingualism, and will be brought up where directly relevant, but they're not our primary concern.

While writing this book, I have done the things any researcher and writer does in the course of writing nonfiction. I've read stacks of books and academic journals and newspaper stories; I've spent endless hours reading on the Internet. I've consulted with scholars and experts in the academic and scientific fields concerned with language learning, multilingualism, and related topics, and have profited greatly by their counsel.

In addition to doing that necessary groundwork, I have collected lengthy questionnaires from multilinguals all over the world who have graciously and generously given of their time and energy to help me with my task. Their questionnaires form a valuable database that is a window on the world of language as multilinguals perceive it. Each of my respondents speaks English plus at least one other language; sixty-nine speak English plus two or more. Altogether they represent fifty-five different languages—or dialects of Terran—from Afrikaans and Arabic to Xhosa and Zulu. (You'll find the complete list of languages on page 249–250.) Certainly it's important to know what scientists and scholars and medical experts think about the questions we are investigating here; it's equally important to listen to the ideas and opinions of people who have intimate personal knowledge about those matters.

Full Disclosure

Multilingualism is an issue about which such intense passions exist that I am reminded more than anything else of the uproar over the theory of evolution. People don't just have opinions about it, they hold those opinions *devoutly*. We haven't yet seen headlines about factions demanding the teaching and maintenance of multilingualism on religious grounds, in spite of the biblical story of the Tower of Babel—but I can easily imagine that happening. We've seen plenty of headlines about the scientific controversies and the political ones; those stories have been sensational, even inflammatory, and, far too often, misleading. Multilingualism is what's known as "a hot topic."

In the interests of fairness and full disclosure, therefore, I have to tell you where my own convictions lie with regard to the major controversies we'll be examining. I want to set out my own positions for you here so that I don't have to try your patience by coming back to them over and over again later in the book. And I want to acknowledge, in advance, that many important and distinguished scholars and scientists disagree with me. Here is my personal list of carefully considered conclusions, for your reference:

- I am convinced that Chomsky is correct in his claim that human infants are born with some innate capacity for learning human languages.
- I am convinced that there is a core of elements common to all human languages, usually referred to as universal grammar but more accurately global grammar.
- I am convinced that the link between language and culture is so strong that loss of a language inevitably means loss of the associated culture as well, and I consider such losses tragic.
- I am convinced that human languages (and dialects of human languages) do structure and constrain human perceptions of reality in significant and interesting ways.
- Finally, I am convinced that multilingualism is desirable for humankind and should be encouraged in every way possible.

Acknowledgments

I am indebted to so many people for this book that it's impossible to list them all. I would have to begin by listing the thousands of scholars who have built the foundation of knowledge on which I have had the privilege to stand as I wrote. I would have to list every teacher who encouraged my love for languages (and later, my love for linguistic science), and every speaker of a foreign language who was patient with my attempts to speak one. The lists would be endless, the task impossible. I will therefore mention only a few of those to whom I am deeply grateful, with the understanding that I'm well aware I'm only scratching the surface. My respectful thanks, then:

To Leonard Newmark, who showed me how to teach not only languages but a love for learning. To Amanda Cook, my editor, who has been a constant source of support and information. To my literary agent, Jeff McCartney, whose comments and insights as I worked through the many drafts and revisions have been invaluable to me. To my daughter and colleague, Rebecca Haden Chomphosy, who has been my research and fieldwork associate. To my multilingualism questionnaire respondents, without whom this would have been only half a book. To my colleagues in linguistics who have put up with my endless questions and shared their knowledge unstintingly when I needed it, even when they profoundly disagreed with me. And to my long-suffering family, who as always has had to endure the burdens that are inherent in living with someone who is With Book.

All of these persons—and the many others I have not identified here—are entitled to much credit and much gratitude; none of them is responsible in any way for my errors or omissions.

Suzette Haden Elgin, Ph.D.
PO Box 1137
Huntsville, Arkansas 72740–1137
ocls@ipa.net
http://www.sfwa.org/members/elgin

The Language Imperative

Introduction

What Is Multilingualism?

*Despite bilingual nannies, tapes, picture books, and even sending
their kids abroad for the summer, bilingual parents in this
country are losing the battle to maintain their children's grasp of
a foreign language. . . . The challenge to raise a child bilingually
becomes even more difficult for languages of lesser prevalence.*

(Mireya Navarro, quoted in Landers 1996, page 5)

The quotation above describes a reality very unlike the one we ordinarily see described and discussed in the mainstream media. How
could it be a challenge to raise a child bilingually or multilingually,
as Navarro claims? All the news stories and editorials are about the
dangers of multilingualism in the United States and the need for de-
fensive strategies against it, as if American English might vanish at
any moment! With the single exception of documentaries about Native Americans, we see no news reports in which parents are lament-
ing the fact that—despite their best efforts—their children speak
only English.

We need to know which version of reality is accurate, and we need
to find out how and why two such wildly differing portraits of our
language environment can exist simultaneously. We can be reasonably sure that a communication breakdown like this one occurs only
when two or more groups of people are using the same words and

phrases but aren't giving them the same meanings. These situations, which I call "reality gaps," can go on for many years without anyone who is involved even being aware that they exist; meanwhile, the problems they create are blamed on all sorts of irrelevant factors.

Our first and most basic question is: What do we mean when we say that someone is multilingual? And our first and most typical reaction to that question is of course that it's absurdly easy to answer. After all, aren't we're just talking about people who know more than one language? Isn't the meaning obvious?

The question *isn't* easily answered, and the meaning is anything but obvious. This is because we can't define "multilingual" or "multilingualism" until we have agreed on the meaning of that phrase, *"know more than one language."* No real consensus exists, you see, on what it means to "know" a language, or on precisely what a "language" is. We are well and truly stuck at this point, and the lack of agreement has created a seething broil of controversies. Controversies that can lead to the spending or withholding of many millions of dollars; controversies whose consequences can be as trivial as a bumper sticker—and as grave, even tragic, as civil disorder, terrorism, and civil war.

Defining "Multilingualism"—What It Means to "Know" More than One Language

David Crystal (1992, page 259) defines multilingualism as the ability to "make use of" more than one language. By this definition I am multilingual; I can "make use of" quite a number of languages. My *Webster's* has no entry for multilingualism, but defines *bi*lingualism as someone's ability to use "two languages with equal or nearly equal facility." By this definition I fail to qualify, because although I speak French very comfortably, I certainly don't use both English and French (or English and any other language) with "equal or nearly equal facility." In *Mirror of Language: The Debate on Bilingualism* (1986), Kenji Hakuta tells us on page 4 that "very few people who would be considered bilingual have anything resembling native-like control of both languages." The lack of native control he refers to will only increase as the number of languages increases. Francois Grosjean writes that it is "perfectly normal to find bilinguals who can only read and write one of their languages, who have reduced speaking fluency in a language they only use with a limited number of people, or who can only speak about a particular subject in one of their languages"(Grosjean 1994, page 1656). It's common for multilinguals in my database to judge their own language proficiencies in ways that reflect this confusion; for example, Karen Arouca writes that her oral fluency in Spanish is "not very good," but notes that when traveling in Argentina and Uruguay she is "sometimes taken for a native." How are we to make sense of all this?

The simplest way I know to clarify matters is to compare the language skills of my first husband (Peter Haden) with my own. His mother was French and his father was an American diplomat. Peter grew up in France and Switzerland in the international diplomatic community, a language environment where multilinguals were as ordinary as pondwater. It is an ordinary event in Switzerland for conversations to go on among three or four people, each of whom is speaking a different language, without anyone seeming to notice; such conversations are common on Swiss television. Peter learned both French and English from birth and had native fluency in both; the only difference he was ever able to identify for me was that he found it a little bit easier to do math in French.

As for me, I began studying French in high school and continued at the University of Chicago (where I met Peter), and I always got As. After we married, we spent some months living with his family in Geneva and in the south of France, speaking almost exclusively French during all that time. I have a bachelor's degree in French, and a high school teaching credential for it; I've taught French at both the high school and the university level. I worked as a French translator for a time in Washington, D.C. And Peter and I spoke French in our home after we returned to the United States. Does this mean that the one word "multilingual" can be used to describe both of us?

Well, it depends on how we define our terms, bringing us right back to where we began. Peter spoke both English and French as flawlessly as anyone speaks a native language. I speak English as a native, but my French is barbaric. I make grammar errors constantly. I use constructions that no native French speaker would ever choose, because they let me avoid some of the parts of French that I find difficult. My accent is an indescribably odd mixture of the French of Toulouse, the French of Geneva, and the French taught in Missouri's small-town schools in the 1950s. Nevertheless, if I were suddenly teleported into a community where French was the only language spoken, I could manage perfectly well. I am at ease carrying on conversations and handling daily affairs in French; I could teach in French without feeling uncomfortable. Perhaps most important of all, when I don't know how to say something in French, or don't understand something, I know what to say to repair the deficiency on the spot.

Peter and I are perfect examples of the two extremes of multilingualism. The linguistic difference between us should serve to make a point that is crucial to this book and must be understood: *Statistics about exactly how many multilinguals there are in a given location are almost always meaningless.* When Cambridge University Press announced the launching of a new journal (*Bilingualism: Language and Cognition*) on the Internet on March 24, 1997, its claim was that "more than half of the world's population use two or more languages in their everyday lives, and may therefore be defined as bilingual" (multilingual, in our terms). I welcome the journal, but I would have to ask: "Bilingual in what way? The way my husband was bilingual, or the way I am, or something in between?"

At the University of California–San Diego, where I taught in the French section of the foreign language program, it wasn't grades that got students through the classes. A perfect accent and flawless grammar wouldn't do it, nor would top scores on written exams. To satisfy the foreign language requirement for graduation, our students had to survive an exit interview—a ten- to fifteen-minute conversation—with two native speakers of the foreign language. The two interviewers had to agree that the student "knew" the language and knew it well enough to participate in that conversation with ease. Otherwise, the student—no matter what his or her grades were—did not pass the course and could not graduate. (Yes, many students did find this requirement almost impossible to believe, since grades are the measure by which most educational institutions decide whether people "know" a language.) By the UCSD standard, even if my interviewers had spent the fifteen minutes hilarious with laughter at my French, I would meet the definition of multilingualism.

Respondent Fran Stallings (English/Japanese) had an experience that casts a good deal of light on the difference between knowing a language in the sense of being able to use it in the real world and knowing a language in the sense of being able to pass tests. She was touring the United States with a Japanese scholar, and was asked (by the Japanese teachers at a training institute) whether she spoke Japanese. She demonstrated that she was fluent in the real-world sense of that word by answering with the standard phrase a native Japanese speaker would have used, a phrase that means "Just a few words." A teacher on the American team immediately demonstrated his own fixation on the "test-passing" sense of the word by a rude challenge: How, he wanted to know, could she possibly serve as the Japanese scholar's tour manager and translator, if her Japanese was no better than that? Dr. Stallings knew Japanese: her challenger only knew the answers to test questions.

Defining "Language"—What It Means to Know "a Language"

There is also no exact definition of "a language." The number of languages existing on Earth today is either roughly 6,000 or roughly 10,000 or roughly a figure somewhere in between those two. Depending. Barbara Grimes' *Languages of the World* (twelfth edition, 1992), a respected scholarly source, sets the number at 6,528. David Dalby, who directs the Observatoire Linguistique (a team working on a directory of the world's languages for the United Nations), announced in the July 29, 1997, *London Guardian* that the number of Earth languages is more than 10,000. This is a very large difference indeed, even for scholars. How are we to explain it? The cliché among linguists (usually credited to Max Weinreich) is that a language is a dialect with an army and a navy; that may be overstated, but it's true that the line is frequently drawn for political rather than linguistic reasons.

According to Jared Diamond, all of Europe has "only about 63 native languages," while New Guinea is at the opposite extreme with "about 1000 languages—yes, 1,000 mutually unintelligible languages" (Diamond 1997, page 544). The reason the word "about" appears in both those statistics is that other people might draw the lines between the languages and dialects differently.

I've worked as a linguist with both Navajo and Apache, and I would consider them dialects of a single language; I would consider a person who spoke both Navajo and Apache multidialectal, not multilingual. But neither Navajos nor Apaches, in my experience, would accept that judgment. Some linguists consider the variety of Laotian spoken by my son-in-law to be a dialect of the Thai language; but Bounlieng, who speaks both Lao and Thai, finds that idea unacceptable. No one (except perhaps the hypothetical Martian linguist mentioned in the preface) disagrees with the statement that Chinese and English are two different languages, but for many thousands of other "manners of speaking" on this earth it's impossible to draw the line that clearly.

Does it matter? Most people believe that it does. It makes us uneasy to think that we can't know with reasonable accuracy how many languages our planet shelters. Few of us view it with the concern felt by those peoples of the northwest Amazon who consider marriage between native speakers of the same language to be incest, but it matters a great deal nonetheless. I will be discussing ways we can be certain that it matters (as well as many ways that it *might* matter) as we go along in this book.

At this point it will be clear that there's only one sensible way for us to proceed. Our definitions of multilingualism are far too *vague*. Nevertheless, even though we have no solid definition for what it is to "know" more than one language, whatever "a language" may turn out to be, we have to keep moving. There's no other way to broaden our knowledge base and make progress.

How *Many* Different Languages Could One Person "Know?"

Suppose that we use our terms loosely (as they are most commonly used) so that by "knowing a language" we mean something like "being able to carry on conversations with other speakers of the language easily and comfortably." Put that way, how many languages might a single individual know?

Theoretically, as long as the languages are learned in infancy and early childhood, no upper limit exists. In practical terms, however, even if a child lived in a giant commune with native speakers of fifty different languages, it probably wouldn't be possible for the child to learn all fifty. There aren't hours enough in the day for adequate exposure to that many languages. And in practical terms, most human households even in societies where multilingualism is routine are composed of native speakers of only a few languages. Still, if someone Iearns "a few" as a child and goes on adding more as an adult, where is the upper limit?

We don't know. A recent discussion of this question on the Internet list for linguists had anecdotes about persons alleged to know sixty or more languages, but without any way to verify those numbers or know just what they might mean. A story by William H. Honan in the *New York Times* for December 31, 1997, titled "To Masters of Language, A Long Overdue Toast," began as follows:

> Each vocation or avocation has its Babe Ruths and Baryshnikovs, and so it is with the Linguistic Society of America. The champion is Francis E. Sommer, fluent in 94 languages. . . . There were no Olympic medals or Nobel prizes for him, but that is a mistake that should be rectified, said scholars coming to New York City . . . for the annual convention of the Linguistic Society of America.

But suppose we accept on faith the claim that Francis E. Sommer was fluent in ninety-four languages. We have no way to be certain what that would mean. As Dorian (1982, page 33) says:

At the lower levels of semispeaker proficiency there are some individuals who actually say very little yet continue to interact in a highly successful fashion with fluent speakers. Thanks to their superb passive bilingualism they follow all verbal interactions without any difficulty, and . . . they can participate for years in a linguistic network without anyone paying much attention to the assymetric nature of their interactions, or even to their flawed productions.

I see nothing unreasonable, based either on the scholarly literature or my own experience, about the idea that people might be comfortable with scores of languages in the fashion that Dorian calls "passive" multilingualism—that is, able to function and carry on their daily lives in an area where any one of those scores of languages is spoken. If you and I are having a conversation and it seems to us that we understand each other, if neither of us is stopping every few minutes to ask what a word means or complain of being unable to keep up, it's very unlikely that either of us will issue some challenge that would require proof of fluency in the language. That happens only in special situations where professional services are being rendered, as when a teacher says to a student, or a lawyer says to a client, "Now, tell me what I just said, please, so that I can be sure you understood." Our foreign language examiners at UCSD all agreed that one of the most important demonstrations of "knowing a language" was that a student laughed in all the right places—a skill that has little to do with accent or verb endings.

In many parts of the United States people tend to look upon multilingualism as something strange and exotic. Unless they work in a field where multiple languages are a standard professional requirement, they may not know personally even one person who speaks more than one language. They are likely to assume that because this is true of their personal language environment it represents what is usual and normal everywhere. Their assumption would be incorrect; in much of the world, it's *mono*lingualism that's unusual, not multilingualism.

James Geary writes that it's common for many Africans "to speak five or six tribal languages in addition to their own mother tongue"

(Geary 1997, page 6). One of my husband's relatives was fluent in seven languages, as a result of having spent his childhood in a missionary compound where all seven were spoken. In the foreign language program at UCSD it wasn't unusual for people to be very fluent in four or five languages; one of my associates there was fluent in fourteen.

In my database of multilinguals, people who claim to be able to get by comfortably in four or more languages are common—and many take their expertise with English so much for granted that they didn't even list English as one of their languages when they filled out my questionnaire in English. If I were to create a sort of "Prototype Multilingual" from that database, the linguistic life story would go something like this:

> My father spoke Polish and my mother was Italian, and we spoke both of those languages at home because my grandmother lived with us and her only language was Italian. Then when I was three years old we moved to France, and it took me about six months to learn French, which was the language all my friends spoke. I started taking English in school when I was ten, and then we moved again, this time to Turkey, and so I learned Turkish. My first job was with a company that sent me to Japan, and so I learned Japanese when I was in my early twenties. Somewhere along the way I picked up German—I don't really remember when—and although my Russian certainly isn't native I can get by well enough for social and business conversation in that language as well.

How *Hard* Is It to Become Multilingual?

We have more than enough evidence that it's no real stretch for tiny kids to learn half a dozen languages natively if they're regularly exposed to all of them; the number that they can learn easily may be much higher than that. Matters are different for adults, whose language learning performance tends to vary widely, but we can be reasonably certain of a few basic items:

- The hardest foreign language for an adult to learn will be the first one learned, all else being equal.
- Each tongue learned thereafter from the same language family will be easier to learn than the first foreign language was.
- Even languages from different language families—for example, Spanish and Japanese—will be easier to learn after a few other languages have been mastered.
- So far as we know, and so far as time allows, any number of languages can be learned over a lifetime; no evidence exists to support any upper limit.
- With rare exceptions, none of the languages learned as an adult will be learned with *native* fluency.

When linguists are faced with the need to learn a new language, they're not alarmed, even when it's a language for which no written form exists. It's not just that practice makes perfect. It's that the characteristics of human languages, in spite of their unarguable differences, are a relatively limited set. Writing of Noam Chomsky, David Berreby (1994, page 49) tells us that

> he likens language to an elaborately wired box of switches —root concepts and grammatical principles—set in one position or another by experience. Chinese sets the switches in one pattern, English in another. But the fundamental conceptual framework of how concepts and syntax interlock is the same.

Theoretically, any sound a human being can make could be part of a human language. Why not? In actual practice, however, all languages choose their sounds from the same set of possibilities, a set containing somewhere around seventy to eighty sounds. Nothing logically—or physiologically—prevents a language from having words that begin with a sound made by touching the upper lip to the lower teeth. Many languages have sounds made with the *upper* teeth touching the *lower* lip, like English "F" and "V." But no language uses that other option. A language could, logically, include as one of its sounds the sound of the hands clapping, or the nose sniffing; no languages take advantage of those possibilities. Two languages may be separated in time and space by vast distances; nevertheless, they will confine their choices of meaningful sounds to the basic human set.

In the same way, nothing prevents a language theoretically from having any grammar rule the human mind can imagine. However, all human languages use only four kinds of grammar rules:

- *Rules that delete something.* (We can say either "You eat your peas!" or "Eat your peas!")
- *Rules that insert something.* (We say, "It's raining," although there is no "it" that rains.)
- *Rules that substitute one thing for another.* (Instead of "I was looking for the book about Indo-European languages and I found the book about Indo-European languages," we ordinarily say, "I was looking for the book about Indo-European languages and I found it.")
- *Rules that move things from one place to another.* (We can say either "I hate eggplant" or "Eggplant, I hate.")

You can reduce that to *three* kinds of rules if you define deletion as the *substitution* of zero.

Within that set, we can think of an infinite number of things—sounds, words, parts of sentences, and more—to delete or insert or substitute or move, and we're fully capable of using all sorts of curious rules about those processes. Just consider the many "secret languages" that human children all over the world are so fond of, like English pig Latin.

There's no logical reason why a language couldn't make a sentence negative by repeating every word it contained. That would be an insertion rule, easy to understand and easy to use: "After each word, insert a copy of that word." If English did that, the negative of "The kids ate pizza" would not be "The kids didn't eat pizza," but "The the kids kids ate ate pizza pizza." No problem! But no language uses that option, and no language has a rule that repeats every word in the sentence, not for any purpose.

Because the characteristics of human languages are limited in this way, the more languages you learn, the more items from the set of possible characteristics you will already have come across in some other language. French forms its negative sentences using two separate chunks, "ne" and (among other things) "pas." When I studied Navajo, which is about as unrelated to French as a language could be and still be Terran, it was easy for me to get the hang of the Navajo two-part negative formed with "doo" and "da." I was already familiar with that way of doing things from French, and it came as no surprise. As you add languages, you think, "Oh yeah! They do that in Kwakiutl!" and "Sure, I get it—it works like Korean." When you approach a language that has never been written down before, as linguists are trained to do, you already know many many things about it in advance, simply because they are things that are true of every human language.

When science fiction writers try to write about extraterrestrial (hereafter, ET) languages, they can throw letters around and create an impression of something truly exotic and different. Some rely on clots of letters and have their ET speakers say things like "Ff't t'qlwx q'wxwxllp!" Some of the science fiction tongues are amazingly ingenious. But when these languages are carefully examined they always turn out to contain only characteristics that can be found in human languages. This isn't because the writers lack skill or imagination. It's because the definition of what counts as a language is part of being human.

How much of language is innate—"hardwired" in the human brain—is a matter of passionate argument; I've only touched on it here. (We'll come back to that argument in Chapter 8.) But there is wide general agreement that the specifications for what can *qualify* as a human language are innate. Presumably you would have to have a nonhuman brain to be able to imagine and describe the characteristics of a truly ET language.

Language Learning in Young Children Versus Language Learning in Adults

Knowing these things should make it easier to understand how tiny kids can learn two or more languages at the same time, a task that most adults would find intimidating. Children are born with the full set of language *possibilities* either hardwired or available to them in some other fashion. As they're exposed to language in their environment, they begin eliminating the possibilities that aren't used in the language they're observing.

Consider what this means in terms of the way languages sound, since sound is so much of what's involved in having a "foreign accent." When babies start babbling they make sounds that occur in some human languages but that don't occur in the speech of the people in their language environment. Babies in an American English household who babble the Spanish "B" sound or the French "R" sound but never hear either one used around them quickly give up making those sounds; if they try to learn Spanish or French as adults, they usually find those two sounds hard to pronounce correctly. Babies in whose surroundings both French and Spanish are spoken, however, will never drop that "B" and "R" from their inventory of sounds that they recognize as worth hanging on to. The closer a child is to babyhood, the more recently foreign sounds will have been discarded; it's not surprising, therefore, that they're easier for young children to learn than for adults.

We don't know what effect it has on tiny kids to be exposed to a language and then have that exposure end very early in life. When my first husband died, my youngest child was only three years old. Her exposure to French in our home ended at that point because I had *no* desire to provide my children with regular exposure to my own peculiar French when no more standard model would be available to them for comparison. When Patricia studied French in college she had to learn it from scratch, but with one somewhat unusual characteristic: French sounds that are almost without exception difficult for English speakers were easy for her, and her accent was excellent from the very beginning. Perhaps this was because hearing French at home during the first three years of her life did have an effect, even though she had no conscious memory of the language; perhaps it was only a coincidence. No evidence is available for choosing between the two possibilities.

At one time we took it for granted that although infants and toddlers could acquire more than one language with ease, it would cause an inevitable delay in their "language development." They would start talking later, we believed. They would mix up their languages. They would put together sentences like the ones that respondent Rhonda Eikamp reports for her three-year-old daughter growing up in the family's English/German household in Germany:

"Ich habe das aufgefinisht." ("I've finished it up.")
"Er supposed das nicht machen." ("He's not supposed to do that.")

The more languages there were involved, the more severe the delays and confusions were expected to be. All this was something "everybody knew." Given the problems most adults in the United States associate with foreign language learning, it all seemed to be self-evident.

Even if the claims had been proved true, I'm not sure they would be anything to worry about. However, dissenting reports have steadily piled up from parents of multilingual children, saying that their kids prove the predictions of language troubles false. It appears that children who have serious or long-lasting problems are the exception rather than the rule. Hakuta tells us : "In most children by the age of three to four, languages are rarely mixed" (Hakuta 1986, page 67). And parents agree: It's unusual for any problems caused by confusion among the languages to last much beyond that age.

One of the most striking things about the information in my database of multilinguals is their relaxed attitude toward their multilingualism. Not a single one complains of having been held back in language development in any way. None report any anxiety about language development in their own children (or look upon mistakes like the ones in the example above as anything serious). And they are unanimous in wanting their own children—existing or potential— to be raised as multilinguals. Typical comments:

"I want them to learn as many languages as they can." (Bertil Eroz, Turkish/English)

"I think children should be exposed to as many languages as
possible and given the opportunity to hear them when they
are still young enough." (Dominique Estival, French/English)

The closest thing to a negative comment about bringing kids up
multilingually comes from Marie Lenstrup (Danish/English/
Swedish/Norwegian, living in Hong Kong), who says, "I'm not sure
that it's such a great idea for little children to have too many languages to choose from." But she goes on to demonstrate that what
she means by "too many languages" is *four or more*, saying, "I would
of course want any children to speak both my language, the language
of their father, and the language of the place we were living in." All
my respondents appear to take it for granted that their children
should learn at least two or three languages, just as the typical U.S.
parent takes it for granted that they should learn to read and write.

Contrast this with the statement from Ruey Brodine (English/Ital-
ian): "The process of learning a new language and a new culture are
so difficult that I can't imagine anyone undertaking it without having to. But if you stick to it, no other learning experience is more en-
riching, in my opinion." Brodine (who lives and works in Italy)
didn't begin learning the Italian language and culture until the age of
twenty-six, by which time it often *is* a formidable project to learn a
first foreign language well. Small children ordinarily react to language learning in this way only when they've been overexposed to
older persons' complaints that the process is something to dread.

The idea that learning a language will always be an ordeal is very
common among native American English speakers in the United
States, even for people who strongly approve of it as a project. Walter
Meyer accurately points out in his wonderful book *Aliens & Linguists*
(1980, page 117) that American science fiction writers will cheerfully
put their characters through almost any imaginable sort of awful ordeal, and some that almost aren't imaginable, with one exception:
Characters are spared the horror of having to learn a foreign language. The *Star Trek* series reflects this attitude by seeing to it that all
potential language problems are settled with a flashlightlike (and extremely improbable) gizmo called a "Universal Translator." If I point

my UT at you and you speak Southern Colloquial Venusian Tqiltqish at me, I will hear American English; and when I answer you in American English, you will hear it as Southern Colloquial Venusian Tqiltqish. This would save huge amounts of money at the United Nations and international gatherings of all kinds, and is without question necessary to keep the filmed stories moving along, but it's fantasy rather than science.

Current Attitudes Toward Multilingualism

Three attitudes toward multilingualism prevail in the United States today. It's not unusual for someone to hold all three of them at once, seemingly without any awareness of what remarkable mental gymnastics that requires. They are:

1. Knowing more than one language is a mark of accomplishment, something to be admired.
2. Knowing more than one language is a *transitional* condition, a burden that has to be put up with until English is learned and the other language(s) can be abandoned.
3. Knowing more than one language is a mark of some sort of deficiency, whether intellectual, educational, social, or other.

Multilingualism Is an Advantage and Should Be Admired

The alleged *benefits* of knowing more than one language, from the point of view of the American English speaker, are well known. Multilingualism broadens the mind; it improves your ability to learn all academic subjects, even those that have little to do with language. It makes you a more well-rounded person; it gives you more than one "worldview." It equips you for success in the same way that any other array of skills does, like the circumstances of the multilingual lawyer on page x whose colleague is afraid of losing him because with fluency in four languages "he can write his own ticket." It is in every way a good thing and will improve your life, goes this school of thinking. So much so that it was once a mark of real wealth: Wealthy families would hire live-in French governesses and Italian tutors for their children so that they could acquire those languages as part of daily life, and they would see to it that their youngsters (at least the boys) were taught Latin and Classical Greek in childhood as a matter of course.

I often talked to my university students (in the 1970s) about this rosy picture of multilingualism. They usually agreed with it; many said they wished they'd had that kind of childhood education themselves. But when I would ask them whether it made a difference *which* foreign languages children learn, they were quick to give me their personal list of languages that *don't* broaden the mind. "Why not?" I would ask them. And they would look at me with surprise and say, "Well, *everybody* knows *that!*"

Multilingualism Is a Burden—
Something to Get Rid of as Quickly as Possible

The alleged burdens are equally familiar. Multilingualism will hold you back in your language development and make it hard for you to succeed in school. It will confuse you and make it impossible for you to fit in with your peers. It will keep you from assimilating to the culture; it will "ghettoize" you and "keep you from becoming an American." You're likely to end up on welfare, or worse. It is in every way a bad thing and will have negative consequences; it may ruin your life. My students were dubious about the evidence for this, but not because they had any evidence against it (although some suggested "the mess that it's made in Canada" as a reason for their feelings). For most, it was once again something that they "just knew."

And how do my multilingual respondents, who presumably would have had to struggle with these burdens, feel about it?

My experience with knowing another language is that the world is much bigger, and more interestingly multifaceted. I know a few multilingual people, and they seem so . . . large (Elisabeth Vonarburg, English/French—both European French and the French of Quebec).

It's like being able to step outside yourself and take a look, or step outside the world and take a look (Rhonda Eikamp).

The more languages a person knows, the more access one has to alternate realities and the more imagination can rove. Multilingualism is always an intellectual advantage (M. J. Hardman, English/Spanish).

None of my respondents complained about multilingualism having held them back, having interfered with their success, or anything remotely of that kind. Where there were complaints, the typical statement was "I only wish I had learned a few more languages." Rebecca Haden Chomphosy has been talking to Thai and Laotian parents here in Arkansas, and they have without exception expressed the wish that their children should grow up speaking Thai (or Lao) in addition to English. None have said that they hoped their children would learn only English because it would be undesirable for them to know both languages.

In the interests of fairness (and science), I have to point out the possibility that when I sent out my call for volunteers to complete the questionnaire, the only people who responded were people who had never found multilingualism a drawback. Maybe there were five times as many who would have taken the opposite position, but none of them offered to participate. (It's not the case that only people with computer skills filled out questionnaires, by the way. Quite a few were passed along to people who filled them out with pen and pencil.) As is typical with preliminary data-gathering research of this kind, there's no way to know whether my group had succeeded because of their multilingualism or in spite of it, or if the two things are totally unrelated; much more research of this kind needs to be done.

It's also important to mention that after M. J. Hardman wrote that multilingualism is "always an intellectual advantage," she added, "This advantage can be, of course, and frequently is, nullified by negative social circumstances (like putting all Spanish speakers in the speech defect class, like they used to do in New Mexico when I lived there in the 50s)."

Multilingualism Is a Deficiency

The third attitude—which as recently as the 1950s was not simply a popular idea but a common official policy in education and social services—is no longer "politically correct" in the United States. It will be worded more subtly when expressed in public today. Still, it continues to thrive in the general population. (Read Hakuta's *The Mirror of Language* for a thorough and detailed historical account of the phenomenon.) When attorney Wendell Gautier was growing up in southwest Louisiana, he and his sisters and brothers were forbidden to speak Cajun French—his parents' native language—at home, because his mother thought "French-speaking children faced disadvantages"(Button 1996, page 82). I've recently read two op-ed pieces in national magazines written by young parents saying that they deliberately use only English around their children because they feel that monolingual English speakers have an advantage. The politicians who are so belligerent with their claims that "*My* ancestors were immigrants, and nobody ever gave *them* any bilingual education classes!" are presumably unaware that many of those same ancestors were labeled mentally deficient at school because they didn't speak English.

However, although the attitude has been toned down a little and is discredited among scholars, it has by no means disappeared from our educational system. Children with nonnative English skills (or whose dialect of English isn't one of the fashionable "Standard" ones) are still being "tracked" into vocational programs instead of being prepared for college. They still are being almost automatically excluded from "gifted and talented" courses and programs. Often the judgments depend on which foreign accent and grammar the child has. French (European French, not Cajun French) is fashionable and a French accent is "charming," but Spanish enjoys no such advantage. The fact that the people making such judgments often have no conscious awareness of what they're basing them on doesn't make the effects on the children any less negative.

Hakuta claims that "a bilingual person must have two parallel systems, one for each language, that must at the same time be interrelated" (Hakuta 1986, page 3). This is, he says, a "packaging puzzle" in which "two language-bounded mental and social systems must be housed in a single mind" (ibid.). And if there are three (or more) languages, we're talking about three (or more) "language-bounded mental and social systems housed in a single mind" (ibid.). It's easy to write that down and read it, but what does it mean? Is it a literal statement or a figure of speech? Does it matter?

Most important of all, should we care? In today's world of huge intractable problems—crime, plague, famine, war—should we bother to explore this question? I strongly believe that we should; I believe it would have critical implications for all of those intractable problems. In today's world, which is fast becoming a global society—perhaps turning from a motley collection of nations into a world called Terra—the most urgent question may well be whether we can afford *not* to care.

Some Necessary Definitions

To avoid confusion as we move on to the next topic for discussion, and to make that discussion less awkward, I want to close this chapter by establishing a few more definitions of terms.

Dialect and Language

When people perceive themselves not only as speaking the same language but as speaking it "the same way," they are using a *dialect*. A *language* is a group of dialects sufficiently alike that all who use them perceive themselves to be speaking the same language, although *not* necessarily in the same way. The exact line between dialect and language, as we have already seen, is difficult to draw. As an example about which there is a general consensus, we would all agree that English is a language, and we would all agree that the typical English of Brooklyn, New York, and the typical English of Little Rock, Arkansas, are two different dialects of English.

Native Language

Usually, the language that someone learns first, in infancy and early childhood, is called the *native* language. In Wolof, the metaphor for a native language is mother's milk; when a Wolof native speaker is asked to identify his or her native tongue, the most typical answer means, literally, "I was nursed on Wolof" (Swigart 1992, page 14).

My database for this book includes a few multilinguals who learned some Language X in this way, but who consider Language Y their native tongue because they abandoned Language X in the first few years of their lives—when their family moved to another country, or they lost the caregiver who spoke Language X, or something of that kind. Mikala Joergensen, for example, writes, "For a period between one and six years I was bilingual in Danish and Greenlandic, but I forgot Greenlandic when my family returned to Denmark when I was six. I no longer speak it." But this is unusual. For most of us, the language we learned first will always be the one we identify as our native language.

The terms "first language," for the native tongue, and "second language" (often used to refer to a third, fourth, and so on) are commonly used in this context, but my respondents objected strongly to that practice. Suppose you are born into a household where your father speaks French and your mother speaks Japanese, with people who speak those two languages coming and going all the time. Suppose you have an Italian nanny who looks after you while your parents are at work. Suppose also that the household is located in Hong Kong, so that as soon as you begin making friends outside your home you learn some variety of Chinese. In such situations, my respondents tell me, assigning labels like "first" and "second" to their languages is impossible. They refused to try. In this book, therefore, we'll confine ourselves to "native"—including circumstances in which more than one language is learned as a native tongue in infancy—and "other."

Pidgin and Creole

When two languages come in contact and their speakers must interact with one another, they sometimes develop a mixed language for that purpose that uses some features from each of the two tongues; such languages are called "pidgins." There may be more than two languages involved. Sheng, a language spoken by young people in Kenya, is a mixture of English, Swahili, German, and Latin—and Swahili itself began as a mixed language. Unfortunately, "pidgin," and often "creole" as well, are terms that have negative connotations for many people. It's important to understand that "pidgin" is a neutral term which is used to refer to "any language that is historically a mixture of two or more languages and that serves as a lingua franca for groups of speakers but is not the first language of any people." (O'Grady et al. 1989, page 344). When children learn a pidgin as their native language, it will begin to develop as any other language does. If it survives, it will then be called a "creole."

Variety

All the usual terms that refer to some "manner of speaking a language" have connotations of one kind or another, often unpleasant. My own native dialect is Ozark English. When people hear the phrase "Ozark English dialect" they think of the *Beverly Hillbillies* television show. They think of those tacky placemats you see in truckstops with the phony "translations" of Ozark speech for tourists. I'm very personally familiar, unpleasantly so, with the negative ideas that are associated with the word "dialect." There are times when we need a term that means, "I am referring to this way of speaking a particular language, and I am making no value judgments of any kind about it when I do so." "Variety" is that term.

Register

Some ways of speaking a language are distinct because they're associated with a particular *role* of the person who's speaking. The way that doctors typically talk while "doctoring" in the United States is an English register often called MDeitySpeak. The child who says, "Bye, Mom!" to his mother and "Goodbye, Mrs. Mason!" to the school principal and "Later, man!" to his friend on the playground is demonstrating command of three registers. The sequence below is a handsome example of Academic Regalian, a register commonly used by college professors:

> Taken literally, the statement "I was wondering if you would be able to drive me to the airport" is a prolix string of incongruities. Why notify me of the contents of your ruminations? (Pinker 1994, page 230)

Sometimes languages themselves become very like registers. In Wales, for example, Welsh is the language of home and church and friendly social situations, while English is the language of government and business. In Maalula, Syria, the language used in schools and public life is Arabic; in the home and on the street, however, people speak Aramaic—the language that Jesus is believed to have spoken. In the United States, the same thing has happened with Mississippi Choctaw and English; Choctaw is the language reserved for private life and Choctaw-community-only events. The technical term for this situation, in which speakers of two languages assign each one to specific roles in life, is "diglossia."

Code Switching

When a multilingual person moves back and forth between two or more languages (or two or more varieties of a language) in a single communication event, that is called "code switching." For example:

> With my fellow Hispanics . . . , I can relax into our *nuevo* creole. (Fernandez 1986)

> "*Maa ngiy à genoux.*" ("I'm on my knees.") (Quoted in Swigart 1992, page 19)

Notice that in the first example we don't consider the word "creole" foreign; it has been borrowed into English and has become part of the English vocabulary. *Nuevo*, on the other hand, is the Spanish word for "new" and is definitely not part of English. In the second example, the speaker starts out in Wolof and ends with the French *à genoux*.

Both of these examples show code switching happening inside a single sentence. It also happens within longer sequences of language, with a sentence or two of one language, a sentence of another, back to the first language, and so on. In multilingual families a child may speak one language to a parent, another to a grandparent, and still another to a sibling; if all are involved in a single conversation, this code switching will go on the entire time. The languages don't have to be of the same language family, nor do their grammars have to be similar; for example, Japanese/English code switching is a common manner of speech in the Japanese community of Toronto.

Two things about code switching need to be kept in mind. First, it doesn't mean that the speaker is making mistakes or has the two languages or varieties mixed up (like the small child on page 14), and it isn't random. There are rules that govern code switching, just as there are rules for the use of a single language or variety. Spanish/English code switching allows "Es muy friendly," in which the Spanish for "very" is followed by an English adjective, but "Es very amable"—English "very" followed by a Spanish adjective—is forbidden. Second, in any multilingual/multicultural society, code switching is a valuable skill; the more codes someone knows, the more choices that person is likely to have in life.

Code switching isn't usually a term applied to the act of moving among various registers of a single language, but it should be. We've all watched doctors on television droning on in the medical register while an interviewer pleads with them to "speak English"; their inability to switch out of a register in which kidney stones are known as nephroliths is a very real handicap. Highly skilled attorneys switch registers at the drop of a hat, to make themselves seem either more or less threatening to those in the courtroom they're speaking to, depending on their strategic need of the moment. The ability to switch from one register to another at will, according to the language environment around you, is like being able to play any instrument in the symphony orchestra; it removes barriers in all directions.

Language Policy

The term "language policy" refers to the official positions that governments take with regard to language use and maintenance, whether supported by actions—laws passed, programs funded, grants made, and the like—or supported only by rhetoric, in speeches and position papers and public statements. At the moment, unfortunately, neither the U.S. government nor any of the governments of the fifty states (with the possible exception of Hawaii) can be described as having a coherent language policy.

1

The Link Between Language and Culture

The most basic reason why linguistic diversity should be preserved is that language helps people to retain their culture.

(Kleiner 1995, page 15)

What new immigrant families across the nation are learning, as their predecessors did before them, is that the power of American culture, and particularly the lure of television, is so strong that it is a challenge to raise a child who can speak a foreign language fluently.

(Navarro 1996, page 5)

A culture is the *sum* of all the things that make up the way a group of people live their lives: how they dress, work, eat, study, raise children, respond to illness, create art, worship, play, argue, make love, function within a family, perceive time and space, and so on. That all peoples have cultures and languages, both of which are of tremendous importance to them, is not a matter of dispute. But there is a debate about whether the language spoken within a culture is just one more element like clothing or housing or music—part of the culture but separable from it—or something quite different and *not* separable.

A common consequence of the idea that language and culture are inseparable is a conviction that any change in the language *threatens* the culture. The French have an official language academy to watch over linguistic developments and try to regulate them. They're so alarmed by what they consider to be the "contamination" of French by foreign tongues (especially American English) that they've resorted to drastic measures. French courts recently overthrew a law that would have "forced private-sector TV stations to eschew borrowed English words—*le weekend, le leader,* and so on—that are sprinkled through every newscast" (Andrews 1995, page 134); the courts ruled the law unconstitutional. That hasn't stopped the language guardians. Their current strategy is to set up for all the mass media obligatory percentages of content created and produced entirely in France—that is, to set up *cultural quotas.*

There's an Internet site called Maison de la Françité (roughly, "House of Frenchness," with a nice pun included) run by le Cercle de qualité du français dynamique (CQFD). Here you can find proposed "pure French" replacements for foreign words, with detailed explanations and justifications. For example, to avoid the potentially contaminating English "flipchart," CQFD proposes *tableau-feuilles.* The stated purpose of CQFD is to watch out for "Anglicisms" and similar language hazards "en vue de contribuer à la qualité de notre langue dans un monde en mutation rapide." (That is, to serve as a kind of quality control for French in a rapidly changing world.)

The French are far from being alone in such practices. Lithuania, for example, has "a force of paralinguists who prowl the streets for illicit phrase pushers. Perpetrators face warnings, fines and humiliation-by-radio" (Newman 1993). We are all familiar with the ongoing controversies in Quebec over laws forbidding English signs and the like.

The United States has no such laws—but not because no one has ever tried to establish them. In 1780, John Adams argued passionately (and unsuccessfully) for the creation of an American language academy to keep American English pure, and proposals for similar measures are a constant feature of editorials and letters to the editor to this day.

The Japanese are an interesting contrast. Despite being one of the world's most conservative cultures, they require their children to begin learning English in elementary school as a matter of course, and they borrow English words with great enthusiasm. They appear to have no fear of "contamination." Perhaps this is because their society is so uniform; perhaps it is because of the well-known Japanese conviction that everything Japanese is inherently superior; perhaps there are other reasons.

The truth can be bluntly stated: *Every attempt to control spoken languages by laws has failed.* If it can be done (and I don't believe that it can), we haven't yet figured out how to go about it. Controlling *written* language is to some extent possible, but all that happens when the written form isn't allowed to change is that the distance between it and the spoken forms of the language grows ever more vast over time.

The ultimate language change is of course its complete replacement by some other language. Our Founding Fathers considered this move shortly after the Declaration of Independence, "when the aversion to all things English extended to the language." They seriously considered making German, French, Greek, Hebrew, or even an artificial language the "official" language of this country. But a careful look at what would be involved led to a change of heart, summed up by Continental Congressman Roger Sherman with "It would be more convenient for us to keep the language as it is and make the English speak Greek" (*Time,* 9/18/96, page 38).

That's a funny story—but not *every* American will find it amusing. Many Native Americans in the United States are trying desperately to keep their languages alive, not only because they cherish their native tongues but also because they're convinced that if the languages die the cultures will die with them.

The state of Oklahoma, with thirty-five native languages and more than 76,000 Native American students, leads the country in this effort, especially for Cherokee, Choctaw, Kiowa, Creek, and Co-manche. "With twenty-two Head Start centers introducing three- and four-year-olds to their native tongue, the Cherokee program has become a model for the entire nation" (Bilger 1994, page 41).

The Keresan speakers of the Cochiti Pueblo in New Mexico are equally concerned about their language, but have taken an unusual path. They are teaching their youngsters Keresan only orally, by the method of total immersion in the language, and will not allow it to be written down for learning. Mary Eunice Romero, who directs their language program, explains that "The language is sacred. One way to protect ourselves is in a sense to be exclusive" (Linthicum 1998). Whether Keresan will survive as an unwritten language in a world where literacy is taken for granted remains to be seen.

On the other hand, there are native peoples who are deeply of-fended by the suggestion that their cultures depend for their exis-tence on the maintenance of their native languages; there are also peoples who are divided on this issue. Navajo Sylvia Wadsworth says, "Our Navajo language is who we are"; but Navajo Byron Charley says, "I think you would still be Navajo even if you're not a Navajo speaker. . . . Being Navajo depends on how you conduct yourself and go about your life"(Cantoni 1996, page 133 and page 135).

Almost all the Navajo children entering kindergarten in the early 1970s spoke Navajo and few spoke any English. Today—despite the fact that the Navajo have created and maintained some of the most highly acclaimed native-language educational programs, including programs at the college level—things have changed drastically. About half of the kindergarteners speak only English, and the status that goes with speaking Navajo has been declining steadily among the younger generations. Whether there is any link between this change and the new epidemic level of violence among young Nava-jos is not known; I would be willing to wager a large sum on the ex-istence of that link. (For a fascinating, and in many ways heartbreaking, account of the attempt to incorporate a Navajo teaching philosophy into the college curriculum, see "Diné College

Struggles to Synthesize Navajo and Western Knowledge," by Paul Willeto, in the Fall 1997 issue of *Tribal College Journal*.)

Politicians in the United States point to examples of turmoil caused by multilingualism elsewhere in the world and demand that every immigrant begin learning English and carrying on daily life in English, if not from Day One then certainly from Day Two. An editorial in the October 22, 1977, *Oakland Tribune* described the situation like this:

> To many, American English fluency is the rite of passage into being an American. To others, who generally agree that the ultimate goal is to be American English fluent, rigid time-tables for learning the language create more harm than good. Wrapped around all this, of course, is what some see as the real fight over preserving a single American culture or fracturing into the kind of multiculturalism that leads to ethnic Balkanization.

Some languages have been so loved or hated as vehicles for culture that they have become a justification for subversion and worse; think of Basque, Irish, and Afrikaans. At the same time, placid little multilingual Switzerland serves as our universal symbol of a peaceful and orderly nation; its languages and cultures appear to coexist and thrive without any serious discord. Clearly, there is no more an international consensus on *this* question than there is on the definition of multilingualism.

When you bring up the hypothesis that losing a language means losing a culture, people typically respond in four very different ways:

1. "Right! And we must not let that happen!"
2. "Right! And the sooner that happens, the better!"
3. "Nonsense. Language is one thing; culture is something entirely different!"
4. "So what?"

Let's consider these responses one at a time.

"Right! And We Must Not Let That Happen!"

When I speak English, I lose in a way part of my Spanish nature.

(Questionnaire respondent)

*I teach language classes, and when I look at the students in there,
I have to think about what we're giving them. We're trying to give
them a language that will allow them to think in certain values,
and certain lifeways that are important to our people.*

(Parris Butler, teacher of the Mojave language, in Hinton 1995)

People who respond this way believe that language and culture are interdependent and inseparable. Many in this camp believe that *every* language and its culture, without exception, are precious and important and should be preserved. Linguist Ken Hale says that languages "embody the intellectual wealth of the people that speak them. Losing any one of them is like dropping a bomb on the Louvre" (in Bilger 1994, page 19). For some this response may well be based only on romanticism; when you get beyond that predictable reflex, the most common justification is based on the comparison of endangered languages with *endangered species*.

Like most metaphors, this one isn't perfect, but it comes very close. We can look at an endangered plant in a rain forest and insist that it must be protected because, for all we know, it's the cure for Down syndrome or the missing link in a scientific problem that will never be solved without it. In the same way, we can look at a language that has only a handful of living speakers, and insist that it must be protected—because, for all we know, it holds the key to ending domestic violence, or is the missing link in some crucial problem in *linguistic* science.

A scientific Foundation for Endangered Languages was founded in 1995. Its members named their newsletter *Iatiku*, after the mother goddess of the Acoma tribe of New Mexico, who "caused people to speak different languages so that it would not be so easy for them to quarrel" (Gill and Sullivan 1992, page 5). The international organization called Terralingua: Partnerships for Biolinguistic Diversity makes the language/biology metaphor explicit. Its mission statement includes, among other things: "To help preserve and perpetuate the world's linguistic diversity in all its variant forms" and "To illuminate the connections between cultural and biological diversity."

In 1997, the Endangered Language Fund (a nonprofit organization whose goal is to preserve languages threatened with extinction) awarded ten grants to projects that they judged likely to contribute to achieving that goal. Among the awards were:

- Funds to produce original television dramas in Choctaw and Creek, to be shown on cable access channels and made available as videotapes to native speakers of these languages in Oklahoma.
- Funds to help a linguist record the last two living speakers of the Klamath language, so that the recordings will be available to the Klamath tribe.
- Funds to buy equipment needed for language immersion programs in the Micmac, Maliseet, and Passamaquoddy languages.
- Funds to help prepare language materials such as textbooks and a dictionary for the Jingulu language of Australia, which now has no more than ten living fluent speakers.

Let's suppose for the moment that this first position is correct and that we therefore really *should* do everything possible to preserve every language and culture. What would that mean, in practical terms? To make the question more manageable in size and scope, let's consider only what it would mean *for the United States.*

American English (by which I mean SAME—Standard American Mainstream English) is not endangered. On the contrary; it's well on its way to taking over the linguistic world. We'll come back to that phenomenon in Chapter 7. But the native peoples who were here before the Europeans arrived had hundreds of different languages, and for them the situation is very grave.

Statistics on the exact number of native languages in the United States today vary (for the reasons set out in the Introduction, as well as because they are dying so quickly); according to linguist Leanne Hinton, there are more than 175. California alone has nearly 50 different Native American languages, and not even one is spoken by children or young people. In 1994, in Oklahoma, the last living speakers of Miami, Peoria, and Quapaw died. James Brooke reports that 55 of the Native American languages are now spoken by fewer than ten elderly persons, and 70 are spoken almost entirely by the elderly; he claims that only 20 languages remain that are spoken by all the generations, with children actually being raised in the language (Brooke 1998). Steven Pinker warns us in the gravest terms that "Languages are perpetuated by the children who learn them. When linguists see a language spoken only by adults, they know it is doomed" (Pinker 1994, page 259).

This information is critically important to our discussion, because the situation of these languages is a special one. Suppose laws forbidding the use of French in the United States were passed; suppose rigorous attempts were made to enforce them. That wouldn't be trivial. The Cajun French culture would suffer negative consequences, for example. But French *itself* would not be extinct. French is spoken all over the world, and children of French ancestry could go to other countries to experience it. This is true for Spanish and the majority of the other European languages, as well as for the native tongues of the multitudes of immigrants who speak languages such as Thai or Cantonese or Farsi.

The Native American languages don't have this advantage, nor do they live on in collections of books and audiotapes and movies. Unlike the case of the Hebrew language of Israel, no ancient books upon which a modern revival could be based exist in these languages. There is literally nowhere on earth the child of Quapaw ancestry can go to find out how his or her ancestors spoke: Quapaw is lost *forever*. If the hypothesis is correct, if losing a language does mean losing a culture, then the Quapaw culture is gone *forever*.

This may or may not trouble you. If you are a supporter of the "survival of the fittest" ethic, you may consider it acceptable. It troubles *me*, and like many others I view it as a tragedy almost beyond comprehension; I know no coherent way to decide what "fittest" means in the context of languages and cultures. But how would we prevent the extinction of languages?

Think what it would cost to train teachers and prepare teaching materials and establish curriculums in nearly 200 different languages, even if roughly adequate grammatical descriptions were already available for them. How would we find those funds in a country where the struggle for education dollars—for instruction in *English*, not to mention Spanish and Cambodian and Chinese and a host of other languages spoken by immigrant schoolchildren—is already deep and bitter?

One obvious solution is to say that clearly we can't save *all* the languages but that we must save *some* of them. (The "fittest" ones, presumably.) But how do we choose which ones to save? What individual or agency would we give the authority to make those choices, and on what basis? We can never be sure in advance which rain forest plant or animal will turn out to be the one that cures a terrible disease, and our scientific foundations for choosing which languages to protect are far shakier than those provided for snail-darters and louseworts by the biological sciences.

Linguist Einar Haugen (Vines 1996, page 27) argues for "thoughtfully planned bilingualism." He wants every single one of us to have a "native, homely, familiar everyday language in which we can live and love" plus another language "of wider communication."(See Chapter 7 for a further discussion of this possibility.) But however attractive that idea might be, the practical problems involved in putting it into practice are so formidable that it's hard even to know where we would begin.

The English Only contingent in Congress seemed for a while to have decided that the proper attitude toward all languages spoken in the United States other than English was "Since we can't save them all, we won't save *any* of them—that's fair!" They had a minor change of heart, later; they did come up with $1 million specifically for preservation of the Native American languages, after the case for their special status was presented.

But the problem still remains: How do we choose which of the Native American languages to give funds to, and on what basis? Who gets the power to make those decisions? One million dollars is a *very* small sum to divide among nearly 200 language preservation programs.

"Right! And the Sooner That Happens, the Better!"

It is absolutely wrong and against American concept to have a bilingual education program that is now openly, admittedly dedicated to preserving the native language and never getting them adequate in English so they can go out into the job market.

(President Ronald Reagan, in Hakuta 1986, page 207)

Winona Simms, a Creek-Yuchi Indian and director of an American Indian program at Stanford, recently told us, "You would think that being bilingual was the equivalent of being learning-disabled." This logic also led an Amarillo judge to tell Martha Loriana two years ago that speaking Spanish to her daughter bordered on child abuse.

(Rodriguez and Gonzales 1997)

Skeptics answer with . . . the Tower of Babel. Just as conflicting languages kept the tower's builders from reaching heaven, they say, language preservation only keeps us further from peace and mutual understanding. With ethnic wars raging across the planet, shouldn't we seek a common tongue to bind us rather than reviving languages to further divide us?

(Bilger 1994, page 38)

That last quotation is particularly instructive in the context of the ethnic wars that have been ravaging the Balkans. Historian Ivo Banac writes (in Woodward 1996), "The fighting may be over, but the successor states of Yugoslavia are waging new wars over words. . . . *'The whole point is to create new differences between Croatia and (Serb-dominated rump) Yugoslavia so that communication between the two is more complicated and the idea of separate identities strengthened.* . . . Croatian authorities are aggressively 'purifying' their country's language by substituting words deemed to be foreign with Croatian words."

Like those who want to preserve and protect languages, those who respond this way believe that the hypothesis itself is correct, and that cultures are lost when languages are lost. But they don't consider that a tragedy or something to be struggled against. On the contrary! Here's Republican Congressman Randy Cunningham of California arguing during a debate for the English Only legislation (a debate that Rep. Pat Williams said was "the most maddening" he'd sat through in his eighteen years in Congress):

> If you want to keep your people in a barrio, if you want to keep them restricted in little tight communities so only you can communicate with them, and we can't in English, then be my guest. But we're going to empower them to get out of that so they can have a piece of the American dream. (Quoted in Schmitt 1996)

Republican Robert Livingston of Louisiana directed his colleagues' attention to the separatist movement in Quebec, predicting that Canada won't last another decade as one country, and said, "We already went through one great civil war. We don't want to go through another" (also in Schmitt 1996).

The English Only law hasn't yet emerged in final form from the congressional sausage grinder, and it keeps changing as it goes along. It looks as though, if it does become law, the Native American languages will be made an exception to at least some parts of it. For a superb and detailed presentation of information about English Only, including copies of all the relevant documents and links to related sites, go to the Language Policy Website maintained by James Crawford at http://ourworld.compuserve.com/homepages/JW-CRAWFORD.

If this second response is the correct one, what would implementing it mean for the United States? One state may already be on the road to finding out.

California has been struggling with the consequences of its new Proposition 227—the antibilingual education initiative called "English for the Children." California's situation is extremely complicated; it has more than 1 million students whose English skills are limited or nonexistent. Their lives will be drastically affected if Proposition 227 remains the law of the state and is enforced. It will forbid almost every use of any language except English for instruction in the state's public schools; it will start the education of all students with limited English by putting them into English immersion programs; and it will severely limit the teaching of foreign languages to English-speaking students. (It doesn't appear to me that anyone is particularly concerned about the effects this will have on the native cultures.)

These drastic measures are entirely consistent with the "Right! And the sooner that happens, the better!" position. People who offer that response feel the same way about attempts to preserve Osage and Kiowa (and Thai or Armenian, in immigrants) that most lumber company executives feel about preserving the spotted owl.

In fairness, however, we need to remember that many who choose this position do so with genuine regret. They're not basing their position on a conviction that multilingualism and multiculturalism are dangerous; rather, they believe that they're luxuries we can't afford. The effects on speakers of languages other than English in the United States are the same, either way.

"Nonsense. Language Is One Thing; Culture Is Another Thing Entirely!"

"If you know your mother and father and family are Navajo, even if you don't speak your language, you're still connected to your culture."

(Claudia Chischilly, in Cantoni 1996, page 136)

This position depends upon the assumption that our original hypothesis is false. It proposes instead that cultures can survive perfectly well without the languages that have been part of them. People who feel this way don't need to take any stand for or against multi-lingualism and multiculturalism. Their only claim is that the two things are for all practical purposes independent, leaving us free to decide for or against the preservation of a language on other grounds.

We have no tidy scientific method for determining whether this response is valid or not; I don't believe that it is. If it could be proved true, it would be a great relief in many ways; it would solve some thorny problems of language policy. But it's difficult to find evidence in its favor. The United States once had waves of immigrants who were Irish and German and Polish and Italian, for example. They arrived speaking only their native tongues and as representatives of their native cultures. No bilingual education was provided for them, and they were granted no linguistic favors whatsoever. Today, with the exception of small isolated neighborhoods (often neighborhoods troubled by severe poverty) in the largest of our cities, it's impossible to tell which of these cultures your neighbors may have come from; they are all undifferentiatedly American. That's what a "melting pot" is supposed to accomplish, and in the past it seems to have done so very well.

It's clear that when these earlier immigrant populations lost their languages, they also lost their native cultures here in the United States. However, this neither proves nor disproves the hypothesis that loss of language means loss of culture. It's an example of correlation, certainly; the two things happened together. But did one necessarily *cause* the other? We don't know the answer to that question, because too many other factors are involved, and we have no way to sort them all out and identify the one (or the ones) that might actually bear responsibility for the loss. Perhaps the cultures were lost because the native languages were lost; perhaps it was because of the geographic isolation of the peoples from their native cultures; perhaps the real cause was poverty so severe that no energy was available for anything more than surviving. I feel strongly that the loss of the language condemned the cultures, but we cannot be certain.

Now we come to the fourth, and to my mind the most astonishing, response to the hypothesis. . . .

"So What?"

So what? "So you lose a culture when you lose a language? So what? Who cares? What difference does it make?"

I can understand the other three responses (and the assortment of possible variations on them) whether I agree with them or not, whether I can find evidence for them or not. If I wanted to argue for or against any one of them, I'd find that doable. The "So what?" response is something else again. This one, it seems to me, when it comes from an adult, can only be described as the position of serene ignorance. "So you lose a culture when you lose a language? So what? Who cares? What difference does it make?"

I wish I could say that this response is rare; it's not. I run into it everywhere I go, and I am as likely to hear it from business executives and doctors and engineers as from a blue- or pink-collar worker. This position represents equal opportunity ignorance. We hear it from Thomas Sowell when he says, "Multiculturalism is one of those affectations that people can indulge in when they are enjoying all the fruits of modern technology and can grandly disdain the processes that produced them" (Sowell 1996, page 82). It will come as no surprise to anyone that the individual almost always considers his or her own native language and culture to be exceptions to the principle, however. The basic position is "So long as there is *one* living language and culture—and so long as that one is my own—that's all we need."

This is deplorable. It's also exactly what we should expect when people can go through twelve years of compulsory public education (plus whatever additional years they can afford and are willing to participate in) without ever having to study even the most basic elements of linguistics. Our educational policy in the United States has been that linguistics is a subject suitable only for specialists at the university level and not for all that many students even there. We've been willing to agree that our kids may need to know roughly the basics in scientific fields such as physics and chemistry and astronomy and biology, perhaps even psychology. But linguistics? Why would anybody need to know linguistics?

When I began graduate study in linguistics in the 1960s the standard joke was that after a linguist answers "What do you do?" with "I'm a linguist," the response is always either "Oh, really? What's a linguist?" or "Oh, really? How many languages do you speak?" Today, with the 1990s winding down around me, the responses I get to "I'm a linguist" continue to be precisely those two. Linguistics has four superstars today: Noam Chomsky, Steven Pinker, George Lakoff, and Deborah Tannen. But I assure you that if you go out on the average Main Street and stop 100 people at random, you'll be lucky to find even one who knows who those four linguists are. A few will know that Noam Chomsky is somebody famous; a few may recognize Chomsky as a political radical rather than as a linguist; one or two may identify Tannen as a feminist; most will have nary a clue.

I applaud these four scholars' efforts to improve the public perception of linguistics, but I'm not sure they're gaining any ground. In fact, linguistics programs in the United States today are endangered species, too; they're being shut down all around the country because even the *universities* have begun to perceive them as frills. It is my sincere hope that by the time you finish reading this book you will understand what a serious error this is.

We can't settle the argument about the language/culture link here, but as we continue our discussion of language and the power of language in this book, the reasons for and against all four positions on the subject will become more clear. What will be clear already is that the question is not trivial, that the decisions based on proposed answers should not be made lightly, and that the answers will have major consequences, including consequences for our bank accounts. This means that all of us, not just the specialists, must begin to understand the basic facts and concepts on which such decisions should be based. We can't afford to let our national language policies be determined by rumors and folklore and politics.

Four Examples to Think About

The controversies about multilingualism and multiculturalism, the possible link between them, and what (if anything) ought to be done are a tangled mess by any standards. The natural temptation is to throw up your hands in despair and pretend the mess doesn't exist, or to make some sweeping pronouncement—such as "English Only! Period! Forevermore!"—in an effort to *force* it not to exist. Fortunately, some interesting projects are going on that are sufficiently relevant to our investigation to make it worth our while to look at a few of them briefly.

Kohango Reo—The Language Nests

Like the Native American languages in the United States, the Maori language in New Zealand has faced serious dangers. It has been declared an official language of the country, along with English. Still, according to James Geary, the number of fluent Maori speakers plunged from an estimated 64,000 in the early 1970s to 10,000 or less by the 1990s, and there was real concern that the language would be lost. But he goes on to say that "since the first Kohanga Reo (language nests)—a nationwide network of early childhood centers that nurture a knowledge of the Maori language among children—were established in 1982, this downward spiral has been halted" (Geary 1997, page 5). The language nests are staffed not only by paid teachers but by paid elderly native speakers of Maori, often grandparents. The result is an intense, and impressively succesful, exposure to the Maori language and its culture for the children.

To people who are in favor of preserving languages, the New Zealand language nests sound like a wonderful idea. It's easy to imagine that if the United States had only *one* Native American language they could make a powerful case for setting up a similar program for that one language. Even people who feel that language preservation is romantic nonsense (or whose reaction is "So what?") might be willing to accept "nests" for a *single* Native American language. The reality, with nearly 200 such languages, is starkly different, and we are back in the same old familiar bind. There isn't enough money to set up nests for all the endangered languages, and we have no fair method for choosing just one or two languages to be favored in that way.

Notice that if we use the English term *immersion* for the language nest experience we create a metaphor *hash*. The mental image that goes with "immersing children in nests" is bizarre. But just as we have no language centers like the Kohanga Reo for American children, we have no English word or phrase available to label what would happen in them if they existed. This phenomenon—when you can perfectly well describe something but have no convenient word or brief phrase for it in your language—is called a *lexical gap*.

Except in the case of something newly discovered or invented, which will be obviously in need of a name, lexical gaps like this tend to be largely invisible; only when contact with another language and/or culture points one out do people become aware of them. The linguistic spotlight created by "*immersed* in a language *course*" and "*unknown-verbed* in a language *nest*" made it possible for us suddenly to perceive this one.

The concept of lexical gaps will help clarify what it *means* to say that an endangered language might contain things that would be important and valuable to us—things that, if the language dies, we would lose without ever having known that they existed. Filling the gap we just noticed probably wouldn't make any difference in our lives. This would be true most of the time, in the same way that the majority of rain forest plants investigated by scientists would not turn out to be cures for cancer. But you never *know* when the one that really matters will appear! We have no way to know in advance what kinds of lexical gaps—and linguistic spotlights—we would find if we started trying to express concepts from one language by using the vocabulary or grammar of another. We have no filter we could use to make sure that the rare valuable items—either the words and phrases, or the cultural concepts to which they are linked—would be saved while we were throwing out all the others.

Detroit's Arabic Program

Writer Scott Martelle reports that in Detroit, elementary school classes in Arabic have "evolved into a program that breaks down walls between children of Detroit's African-American and Chaldean

communities, in the heart of an urban neighborhood that has suf-
fered longstanding tensions between the two groups" (Martelle
1997, page 47). Detroit's roughly 50,000 Chaldeans are Christian
Arabs, primarily from Iraq, living for the most part right in the middle of inner-city African-American neighborhoods.

This experimental program began as one of six "model world language programs," funded by state and federal government grants,
which were intended to expose schoolchildren to Arabic, Chinese,
Japanese, or Russian—languages rarely taught in American schools.
Quite accidentally, it turned out to have a feature that no one had
anticipated. The African-American students are of course native
speakers of English, with no knowledge of Arabic other than the few
words that those who are Muslims are familiar with from religious
observances. The Chaldean children speak Chaldean at home and
would ordinarily have begun learning Arabic only when they entered school; they know no more Arabic than the African-American
kids do. As a result, the course teaches "a language foreign to both
black and Chaldean students, while reinforcing a culture that was familiar to one of the groups" (ibid., page 48). Suddenly, the two
groups are doing something new, together, from a basis of equal ignorance. And the immigrant children, instead of being the outsiders
who don't know how to do anything right, are the ones who have the
cultural information that fills out the meanings of words and makes
them real and usable.

The benefits of this program are most obvious in the children, but
they are also beginning to turn up in the adults, as the kids go home
and share their experiences with their parents. Chaldean fourth-
grader Barat sums it up this way: "Arabic class helps me play games
and sing songs with people. Instead of getting into fights, you talk it
over. And you be friends" (ibid., page 51).

Concordia Language Villages

The ten Concordia Language Villages (described on page J11 of a
June 2, 1997, special "*Time* for Families" section of *Time*) are located

in Minnesota—but they're not typically Minnesotan. "When 5,200 children (ages 7 to 18) 'cross the border' into their respective villages for one to four weeks, they will be issued passports and exchange U.S. dollars for the appropriate foreign currency," the article says. What's more, the children will exchange English for the language of their village. "They'll be living in the language of their choice: playing sports, re-enacting historical and political events and tuning in to their village's simulated radio and TV stations." The ten languages available are German, French, Spanish, Norwegian, Danish, Swedish, Finnish, Russian, Chinese, and Japanese.

If you're for multilingualism and multiculturalism, this sounds like paradise; it offers youngsters immersion not only in the languages being taught but in their cultures as well. You can find out more by calling 800-222-4750. However, it is a clue to the gravity of the dilemmas we face that the four-week sessions cost roughly $2,000 in 1997.

The Global Nomads

The Global Nomads throw light on the language-culture question in a very different way. The shared characteristic of Global Nomads (sometimes called Third-Culture Kids, or TCKs, though they may be of any age and more than three cultures may be involved) is that they've been bounced around the world all their lives. This is usually the result of their being the children of parents in military or diplomatic service, the children of missionaries, and so on. They may have moved a dozen times between countries and continents in the space of only three or four years. They have their own Web sites on the Internet; they have newsletters; they have organizations. And their position is that *the only culture they belong to is the culture of other Global Nomads*. They don't feel that they are "multicultural" and they don't feel any inclination to choose some one of the various cultures in which they've lived. They claim cultural allegiance only to others who've shared the nomad experience.

Pico Iyer puts it this way: "I am an example, perhaps, of an entirely new breed of people, a transcontinental tribe of wanderers that is multiplying as fast as international telephone lines and frequent flier programs. . . . We become professional observers, able to see the merits and deficiencies anywhere, to balance our parents' viewpoints with their enemies' position. Yes, we say, of course it's terrible, but look at the situation from Saddam's point of view. I understand how you feel, but the Chinese had their own cultural reasons for Tiananmen Square. Fervor comes to seem to us the most foreign place of all" (Iyer 1997, page 79).

The introductory blurb for Robert D. Kaplan's article "Travels into America's Future" (*Atlantic Monthly,* 8/98, page 37) reads:

> Imagine a land in which the dominant culture is an internationalized one, at every level; in which the political units that really matter are confederations of city-states; in which loyalty is an economic concept, when it is not obsolete; in which 'the United States' exists chiefly to provide military protection. That is the land our correspondent glimpses, and it is no longer beyond the horizon.

Erla Zwingle, writing in the August 1999 *National Geographic,* claims that "Today we are in the throes of a worldwide reformation of cultures, a tectonic shift of habits and dreams called, in the curious argot of social scientists, 'globalization'" (Zwingle 1999, page 12). And she points out that more than a fifth of all the people in the world today now speak English at least to some extent.

The Global Nomads—most of whom are multilingual, although there are exceptions—potentially represent the worst nightmare of the language conservatives: *They do not perceive themselves or one another as the loyal citizens of any existing nation.* Clearly they are important to any discussion of the link between language and culture. It's natural to assume that if losing a language means *losing* a culture, keeping a language means *keeping* a culture; that seems simplistically obvious. Yet many Global Nomads are people who have *kept* their languages, but who perceive themselves as having lost their cultures all the same. And they are now working together in an effort to construct a unique culture of their own that has no national allegiance at all.

Phenomena like these four are going on around us everywhere, often with almost no knowledge or attention from the general public. We need to know about them, and we need to pay attention to them; they're part of our database.

2

The Link Between Language and the Perception of Reality

Although all observers may be confronted by the same physical evidence in the form of experiential data and although they may be capable of "externally similar acts of observation," a person's "picture of the universe" or "view of the world" differs as a function of the particular language or languages that person knows.

(Lee 1996, page 87)

First you have to claw your way through the linguistic thicket created by the academic register in which that quotation is written. Why is it written like that? One of the rules of the Academic Regalian register is that the more you expect other academics to be *opposed* to what you're saying or writing, the more extreme your use of the register has to be. This is unfortunate, because controversial subjects are also subjects about which it's important to be as clear as possible. But if the academic game is the game you're playing, clarity has to be sacrificed to this linguistic dominance display.

The translation process introduces a delay, certainly; but when you get to the end of it you will realize that you've come upon a concept so interesting that it grips the mind and won't let go. It's called "the linguistic relativity hypothesis" (also "the Sapir-Whorf hypothesis" and "the Whorf/Whorfian hypothesis"). Lee's quotation says that the way human beings perceive the world around them varies with the languages they know—even though they perceive the same things, in the same manner, using the same physical and mental "equipment." This will strike you either as common sense or *nonsense*, depending on your own personal convictions about the power of language.

Linguist Dan Moonhawk Alford offers the example of a Cheyenne parent who is sitting with a child on his knee when a ball suddenly bounces across the floor. An English-speaking parent would say to the child, "Look! Ball!" The Cheyenne parent, Alford tells us, would say, "Look! Bouncing!" (in DellaFlora 1998). Both parents are perceiving the same stimulus, with the same sensory equipment. However, the way they express the perception—*which tells the child what it's important to pay attention to*—is not the same.

In 1958 Ace Books published Jack Vance's science fiction novel *The Languages of Pao*, in which a government tailored its population for specific roles in adulthood by controlling the language each person learned in infancy. One group of infants learned a native tongue that fitted them for life in the military, another group learned a language designed for business and trade, and so on. This worked very well—until the government was overthrown by a population that had secretly learned *more than one* of these designer tongues natively and had therefore grown up with more flexible perceptions of reality.

The Languages of Pao is a straightforward presentation of a fictional world having these three characteristics:

A. The linguistic relativity hypothesis is valid and true.
B. The hypothesis can be systematically applied to human life.
C. The government has the power and resources to carry out that systematic application as a national policy, beginning with its population of infants.

Whether (a) and (b) are true in this *non*fictional world that we all live in is a matter for fierce dispute; I am firmly convinced that they are. Because we know of no government in human history that has met the specifications for (c), it's difficult even to speculate about the truth or falsity of that proposition; in the novel, its truth is presupposed.

Suppose that the linguistic relativity hypothesis *is* true in the real world. Suppose we could prove that languages actually do have significant control over the worldviews of their speakers. What would that mean?

There are two major possibilities. If we assume that a multiplicity of worldviews causes disunity in a society, it would mean that we could make a strong case for the proposition that multilingualism at a national level is dangerous and should be discouraged, even forbidden. (This idea is in many ways at the heart of the various "English Only" movements in the United States, although many of their proponents are unfamiliar with the linguistic relativity hypothesis.) On the other hand, we could assume that the more worldviews people have, the better; in that case, the validity of the linguistic relativity hypothesis would let us make a case for strong support of multilingualism. (This would be my personal choice.)

In addition, we would be able to make the case that letting a government decide which language or languages people will learn is dangerous, since that would mean that their government dictated their view of the world for them. Clearly, both life and government policy would be less complicated if we could be certain that the hypothesis is false.

The linguistic relativity hypothesis (LRH, from now on) is a source of controversy in many fields, including at least linguistics, anthropology and ethnology, philosophy, religion, political science, and education. It's not a new idea; it goes back at least as far as Giambattista Vico, who lived from 1668 to 1774. Today it's associated primarily with the work of linguists Edward Sapir and Benjamin Lee Whorf, especially Whorf. Linguists accuse one another of being "Whorfians," acknowledge (like me) that they are Whorfians, or deny ever having been Whorfians, all with an astonishing degree of passion.

The LRH not only has more than one name, it has more than one formulation. First, there is what's known as "the strong version," which says explicitly that human perceptions are controlled by human languages, as assumed in *The Languages of Pao*. Oddly enough, this version (often called "linguistic determinism," as if yet another name were needed!) is itself science fiction. *No scholar (including Sapir and Whorf) has ever suggested—much less openly claimed—that any such hypothesis is valid.* Think about it for a moment. It would mean that if your language has no word for chair, and I set a chair down in front of you, you wouldn't be able to see the chair; it would be impossible for you to perceive it in any way. If you tripped over it and fell down, you would presumably be baffled by that experience. This idea *is* nonsense; no question about it. Why, then, does it exist? We'll come back to that in a minute.

The other formulation, called "the weak version," makes no such absurd claims. It says that human perceptions of reality are structured and constrained—not controlled, but structured and constrained—by human languages, in interesting and significant ways. As linguist Dan Slobin (Slobin 1998, page 1) has said, Steve Pinker may be right in claiming that we lack solid scientific evidence that languages have *dramatic* effects on human thought, but science should not take that as an excuse to ignore the *non*dramatic ones. For all we know, the reason we find no dramatic effects is nothing more than our lack of skill in applying the LRH to language. Unlike the strong version, the weak version can't just be labeled nonsense and pitched over the side, as we will see in this and later chapters. If it's true, it *matters*, because it means that language has a degree and kind of power over human thought that many people (including many scholars and scientists) find offensive and/or alarming.

Which brings us to the reason why instructors continue to teach their students that "the linguistic relativity hypothesis has a strong version and a weak version." It has become a traditional tactic to refer to the overwhelming evidence against the fantasy *strong* version when arguing that the weak version is false. For that purpose (and so far as I can see, only for that purpose), there has to *be* a strong version. The very fact that any behavior as silly as this goes on among scholars and scientists demonstrates how important the LRH is; if the hypothesis were trivial, the silly behavior would have died out long ago. Throughout this book, therefore, we're going to discuss the so-called weak version, to find out *why* it is so important and what its implications are in the context of the many controversies about multilingualism and language policies. I will specify here—for once and for all, so I don't have to keep saying it—that unless I tell you differently on the spot, when I refer to the LRH from now on in this book I am referring *only* to the weak version.

It's encouraging to be able to report that the policy of ridiculing the LRH seems to be beginning at long last to weaken. The September 1998 issue of *Language* (the most important journal in linguistics) not only had a positive review of Penny Lee's book defending the LRH, it also contained an article presenting some compelling new evidence for it. Eric Pederson and his associates conducted extensive research over thirteen different languages from ten different language families. It has always been assumed that human beings structure their basic perceptions of space—such as the locations of up, down, left, right, in front, and behind—by reference to their own human bodies, and that this is universal for humankind. Pederson's research tells us that when you move beyond the languages most commonly used in the Western world, you find that it's not universal after all. (For details, see Pederson et al. 1998. See also Slobin 1998.)

The Linguistic Relativity Hypothesis in Action

The LRH, if it's valid, can operate either between different languages (the traditional formulation) or between varieties within a single language. Let's look at examples of both kinds, as well as examples where the two are intermingled, to make that concept more clear.

Who's in Charge, the Human or the Horse?

Suppose you wanted the following English sentence—"I was riding a horse"—translated into Navajo. Monolingual people who are inexperienced with translation often assume that you translate from Language X to Language Y in three stages: You find the words in Language Y that have the same meaning as the words in Language X, you put them in the order required by Language Y, and then you tidy up any leftover details. That can be accurate, especially when you're translating between two closely related languages, but most of the time it won't work. To get accurate translations you have to set up a scenario in which a speaker of Language X would say whatever it is you want translated, and then find out what a speaker of Language Y would say in the context of that *same* scenario. Let's say that our scenario goes like this:

> John has said to Bill, "Hey, I tried to call you a couple of times yesterday afternoon, but you never answered your phone. What were you doing?" John and Bill are good friends, and Bill is more than willing to answer the question; he says, "I was riding a horse."

We could describe this scenario to a native speaker of Navajo and ask, "If Bill and John spoke Navajo instead of English, what would Bill say in order to answer John's question?" At which point a long discussion about the Navajo *verb* would suddenly become necessary. The Navajo speaker would have to know many more details about this "riding" before the correct verb form could be chosen. Was Bill riding this horse with a destination in mind, and if so, was he going to stay at the destination, or was he going to go there and then come back again? Or was Bill just riding around aimlessly? Was Bill riding this horse as a one-time event or is it something he does frequently—and if it's frequent, is there a pattern to the frequency? Lots more information would be needed; many pages of this book would be required if I wanted to make it all even roughly clear.

We're going to set all that aside and focus on the way that "I" and "a horse" would be translated. This will be more than enough to make the necessary point.

Classroom-English GrammarSpeak says (awkwardly) that "I" was doing the riding, and that "the horse" is what the riding was being done to; the horse is called the *object* (usually, the *direct object*) of the action. According to my Navajo consultants, the Navajo sentence isn't like that. In Navajo, no creature or thing is having anything whatever done *to* him or her or it. The Navajo sentence is like "Mary was dancing with Tom," where Mary and Tom are dancing together and neither of them is the "object" of the action. Furthermore, the most likely Navajo verb in this context would be one used only to refer to the acts of animals (or to make jokes about people on that basis). The horse, in the most likely Navajo equivalent for "I was riding a horse," is said to have been "animaling-about with me"; the other likely possibilities would mean something along the lines of "a horse and I were moving about together." You don't have to be fluent in Navajo, or a professional translator, to realize that these sentences mean something rather different from what "I was riding a horse" means; nevertheless, they are the correct translations for this scenario. They are what the native speaker of Navajo would say in the situation in which the native speaker of English would say, "I was riding a horse."

Chinese does this the way English does it; the Japanese equivalent means that "on a horse" is where "I" was, not that anything was being done *to* the horse. Hopi has the human being doing something *with* the horse, but it's not like the Navajo sentences, in which the horse and the person are associated; in Hopi, it's the human being who is in charge. Hopi has the human riding around "with a horse" in exactly the same way it would have a human eating soup "with a spoon." The horse, in Hopi, is the instrument with which the action is done.

We don't need to concern ourselves with the grammatical details of all these data, interesting though they are. The question that matters for our purposes is:

> Do these different ways of giving a spoken shape to an experience mean that the human beings involved think about the experience, and about the elements of the experience, in significantly different ways?

A Whorfian would suggest that someone a horse "animals-about" with might, as a result, have an attitude toward horses and horseback riding that would be different from the attitude of a person who *uses* a horse to go about with, or a person who does something called "riding" *to* a horse. I'm saying "might" here because you can't come to firm conclusions about this on the basis of just one example. But the single example, to a Whorfian, means that the conclusion is sufficiently likely to be worth further investigation. An anti-Whorfian would say without hesitation that such a conclusion is silly rampant romanticism with no foundation in reality, and that classifying horses as objects or instruments has nothing to do with how horses are perceived. An anti-Whorfian would remind us that speakers of English talk about hearts of celery and hearts of artichokes without the idea of vegetable heart attacks ever crossing their minds.

English speakers tell a restless child, "Be good!" The French, in exactly the same situation, tell the child to "Be wise!" Could that make any difference in the child's perceptions of the world around him or her? Could it make a difference in what the child concludes deserves attention and what can safely be ignored? Could it make a difference in the child's behavior in the real world? The Whorfian would say that it very well might; the anti-Whorfian would say that it couldn't possibly. Let's look at a real-world example.

One of the severe health problems that India struggles with results from the fact that the Ganges River is used not only for bathing and washing and religious rituals of various kinds but also for disposal of waste and disposal of corpses. That seems straightforward enough. But health workers' attempts to explain this to people and help with the problem have run into difficulties, even when (as is often the case in India) fluent English is spoken by everyone involved. Why? Because devout Hindus consider the Ganges holy (a belief which doesn't have its roots in English). How could something holy be *polluted?* That's an impossible contradiction. Furthermore, it's a dreadful insult. As Fran Peavey writes, "In the context of India, that would be like my saying 'Your mother is a whore' to a Westerner" (Peavey 1995, page 49).

The source of this quandary is in the word "pollution" and its associated meaning and connotations. When Peavey discussed the situation with the people along the river, she found it hard going, but she persevered. After many long conversations and much effort to explain and to understand on both sides, what she would hear from them was this: "The river is holy, but she is not pure. We are not taking care of her the way she needs us to." That is, the river is not "polluted" but "neglected," and it is the people themselves who are neglectful. And then, Peavey tells us:

The funny thing is that, after hearing this reply, I started to think less in terms of "pollution" and more in terms of "people not taking care of the river." This was an important change of perspective. "Pollution" is an abstraction that does not address the responsibility of the people who are making the mess. "Pollution" focuses attention solely on the river. It is almost as if the river is to blame for being polluted! (Peavey 1995, page 40)

Now health workers have begun saying—in English—"The Ganges is suffering" rather than "The Ganges is polluted" (Ward 1997, page 51). This despite the fact that in English rivers cannot "suffer." With the new way of naming the situation, it has become possible to talk about it, and about potential remedies, without giving or taking offense. The facts have not changed; all the people involved are still perceiving the same event with the same eyes and minds; but the outcome in the real world is very different than it was before. As Howard Rheingold puts it:

Finding a name for something is a way of conjuring its existence, or making it possible for people to see a pattern where they didn't see anything before. . . . We think and behave the way we do in large part because we have words that make these thoughts and behaviors possible, acceptable, and useful. (Rheingold 1988, pages 3–4)

Alford puts it even more strongly:

People who are monolinguals and know and think in only one language are handicapped. Because they don't have another worldview to shift to, to look at the same problem and see if they come up with a different answer. (in DellaFlora 1998)

Who's in Charge, the Human or the Language?

People who are willing to accept the idea that two languages (especially two very different languages) might cause their speakers to perceive the world in different ways will still often balk at the idea of such effects within a *single* language. "If the linguistic relativity hypothesis has any validity at all," they'll say, "and mind you, I'm not saying it does, I'm just saying I'm willing to consider the possibility—then it has to be valid cross-linguistically. Inside one language, it's nonsense!"

I disagree. For example, let's consider the case of Carol Cohn, a woman who, although strongly opposed to nuclear war, became a visiting scholar in a nuclear strategic studies program at a major American university. The nuclear situation at that time (in 1984 and 1985) struck her as "so dangerous and irrational that one is tempted to explain it by positing either insanity or evil in our decision makers." Her goal in joining the program was "to gain a better understanding of how sane men of goodwill could think and act in ways that lead to what appear to be extremely irrational and immoral results" (Cohn 1987, page 17).

In order to fill her role as visiting scholar, Cohn attended lectures, talked with colleagues, interviewed graduate students, and did all the other academic tasks expected of her. She says that she started out obsessed by the question, "How *can* they think this way??" But as she became more skilled in using the language of the program and more at ease with it, she found herself facing a different question: "How can *I* think this way?"

The English vocabulary of warfare (both nuclear and nonnuclear) is curious and ingenious. We keep our missiles in "silos"; the area on a Trident submarine where the silos are located is called "the Christmas tree farm." We "marry up" weapons systems when we combine them. One nuclear attack model is called "the cookie cutter." We use "clean bombs" to carry out "surgical" (that is, surgically *clean*) strikes. When we're not using domestic images of family and kitchen and farm, we still use terminology clean enough to eat off of. When we talk about human death resulting from warfare on the evening news, however bloody and messy it may have been, we don't talk about "dismembering and decapitating people" or "burning people into ashes and charred fragments" or anything of that kind. We don't even call it "killing"; we call it "collateral damage." When we refer to the deaths of civilians we ordinarily make those who died the do-ers rather than the done-to. We don't say "We killed three hundred civilians in yesterday's bombing," we say "Three hundred civilians died during yesterday's bombing." As if, like the polluting Ganges, they did it all on their own.

Cohn wasn't able to function in the nuclear studies program without speaking its language. No one would accept her as a valid nuclear scholar, or take what she said seriously, or communicate with her in any of the ways her role required, unless she used English WarSpeak or NuclearSpeak. And as time went by, even though she remained as solidly opposed to nuclear warfare as she had ever been, she made a disturbing discovery. "No matter how firm my commitment to staying aware of the bloody reality behind the words," she writes, "I found that I could not keep human lives as my reference point. *I found I could go for days speaking about nuclear weapons, without once thinking about the people who would be incinerated by them*" (ibid, page 22, emphasis mine). It will surely be obvious that people who can be put into this frame of mind are more likely to function efficiently as military planners and personnel than are people who keep thinking about charred corpses.

To maintain the view of reality that she'd had when she entered the program, in which she perceived nuclear war as a matter of blood and guts and agony, Cohn had to constantly remind herself of those perceptions. And she couldn't do that while she was actually involved in language interactions in the program, of course; she had to do it on the side, on her own. She found it difficult. She had to *work* at it.

So? It's an interesting little anecdote, but does it have any relevance in the real world? Think about it, please. Dr. Cohn was able to come out of this experience with her worldview intact. But she was "immersed" in the nuclear warfare language environment only for a short time, and she went into it as a mature adult with opinions already solidly formed. What if she—like the students in our elementary schools, for whom we *do* choose the language of instruction—had been a small child? *The Languages of Pao* proposes that you could raise adults who would be superbly fit to do battle if you started them out in childhood immersed in a warrior language; their adult worldview would be a warrior's worldview, and everything about combat would make sense to them and strike them as natural. What sort of grownups would we get, do you think, if we selected a group of children and did our best to carry on their education in NuclearSpeak or one of the other varieties of warfare-English?

Another area within languages in which we see Whorfian effects is language tightly linked to sexual gender. Much anger and many confrontations revolve around "inclusive language" in Christianity and Judaism, for instance. Some people consider the revision of Judeo-Christian scriptures and liturgy so that it more explicitly includes female human beings a tremendous improvement; some consider it nearly blasphemous; and some consider it merely silly. For the sake of discussion, let's assume that inclusive language is a good idea. To make religious language inclusive of women, all you do is replace masculine items with feminine or nongendered ones. So "sons of God" become "children of God" and "mankind" becomes "humankind"; an endless series of "he" and "him" and "his" and "himself" items is dealt with by making the verbs plural wherever possible, so that the genderfree "they" and "them" and "their" and "themselves" can be used instead. A simple process, right? And, since everyone agrees that God does not have *any* human sexual gender, entirely mechanical. But look, please at this example:

The Lady is my shepherdess; I shall not want.

Do you see her, in your mind's eye? With her blowing skirts and froth of lacy petticoats, and her ruffled pantalettes showing, and her sweet little crook with its pretty bow tied on it? It's Little Bo-Peep. She won't do; this is a very bad "translation" indeed. (We'll return to the inclusive language debate in Chapter 6.)

A similar problem caused our English-speaking news commentators during the Gulf War to start out with "Today our boys and—," come to an abrupt halt, and switch immediately to "Today our men and women in the Gulf [did something or other]." "Our boys and girls in the Gulf" would have sounded as if the military personnel were all sitting in sandpiles playing with little plastic buckets and trowels, not making war; the childish connotations of the word "girl" leak onto "boy" when the two are linked, causing semantic contamination. (It's semantic contamination that makes us accept "He's a dashing bachelor" but balk at "She's a dashing spinster," even though we're taught that "spinster" and "bachelor" differ in meaning only by gender.)

If the LRH isn't valid, effects like these should be extremely rare and always brief; that is, they should be something that is noticed the first time or two that the sequence of language occurs but is forgotten thereafter. That's not what happens.

Martha Heyneman writes, "The mother tongue . . . orders the savage landscape of our raw sensory impressions, domesticating them, molding them into a world we can step out into with relative confidence, the world of common sense" (Heyneman 1992, page 4). If that is so, and if the LRH is valid, then the decision as to which language(s)—and which varieties of languages—shall be the native tongue(s) of those who will grow up to run a country becomes extremely important. It becomes important to decide which foreign languages, if any—and which additional varieties of native languages, if any—people should be allowed to learn. (We've seen a passionate and confused example of the latter issue in recent years, in the controversy over "Ebonics.") If the LRH is valid, then certain languages, and certain varieties within languages, will tend to mold certain sorts of people. Learning certain languages and varieties may have significant effects on adults, even though they are already molded. It's easy to see why scholars and scientists and policymakers—as well as producers of mass media, such as violent films and computer games—might greatly prefer that this should *not* be true.

Steven Pinker of MIT is one of the world's most prominent linguists; he is that very rare bird, a linguist celebrity. In 1994, in his best-selling book *The Language Instinct*, he made it clear that he has no patience with the LRH; he refers to it, as is typical, in its strong form, which he calls "linguistic determinism." "It is wrong," he says on page 57, "all wrong." He tells us on page 58 that "Once a euphemism is pointed out, people are not so brainwashed that they have trouble understanding the deception."

Let's consider that. There is a form of birth abnormality associated with significant mental retardation and a particular sort of facial appearance which includes slanted eyes. Children born with this abnormality used to be called "Mongolian idiots." Today we have a euphemism that we use instead: We say that these children "have Down's syndrome." The theoretical result of Pinker's position would be a claim that the two dialogues below are synonymous and interchangeable in every way except stylistically:

1.
Toм: What's the matter with that kid?
BILL: She has Down's syndrome.
Toм: I see. That's a shame.

2.
Toм: What's the matter with that kid?
BILL: She's a Mongolian idiot.
Toм: I see. That's a shame.

I think Pinker is "wrong, all wrong" about this. I think that saying these children "have Down's syndrome" instead of "are Mongolian idiots" is much more than "style" or "being polite." It makes a tremendous difference in the way that people perceive the children and behave toward them, as well as in the way the youngsters perceive themselves. As Carol Cohn discovered, human beings, even very intelligent and sophisticated human beings, are *not* impervious to euphemisms simply because they understand that that's what they're dealing with.

I agree with Pinker that these things *shouldn't* matter. In a perfectly logical world, what a medical condition is called should have nothing at all to do with the way those who have it are perceived and treated, by themselves or by others. But we know, from large quantities of excellent research, that people don't consistently base their decisions on logic; two minutes of thinking about their behavior with seat belts will more than make that case. However illogical it may be, attitudes and behaviors in the real world toward "a Mongolian idiot" will unquestionably be different from attitudes and behavior toward "a person who has Down's syndrome." That, in my opinion, is one of the powers that language has; it's not trivial, and it should be used with exquisite care. When I imagine someone telling another person, "You know, that Down's syndrome thing just means that the kid is a Mongolian idiot"—Pinker's "pointing out a euphemism"—I dislike that imaginary dispenser of information intensely. I think that he or she is doing real harm.

However, although we're nearing the end of this chapter's discussion of the link between language and reality, we are still floundering about, mired in scholarly squabbling. To find out whether the hypothesis that sugar melts in water is valid, all I have to do is drop a sugar cube in a glass of water and pay attention to what happens next. The things I would need in order to prove or disprove the linguistic relativity hypothesis aren't like that; they're located somewhere inside the human mind, where we can get at them only clumsily and indirectly. Although people are quick to say that the LRH is right or wrong, and quick to accuse those who take the opposite position of shortcomings of all kinds, they—and I—are only offering you opinions. *The jury in this case is still out.* The linguistic relativity hypothesis has neither been proved nor disproved. Strong evidence exists for both sides, and you're free to decide for yourself whether you consider it valid, in a way that you cannot decide for yourself about that cube of sugar. For a thorough account of the entire controversy about the LRH—with careful reviews of the arguments, the squabbling, and the evidence both for and against, to help you make your decision—I strongly recommend that you read Penny Lee's *The Whorf Theory Complex: A Critical Reconstruction*, in spite of its academic language.

With all that said, we can go on now to consider a phenomenon that dramatically illustrates the effect language can have on perceptions and behavior.

Case Study: The Japanese Water Babies

I first came across the water babies concept when I read this sequence in Kittredge Cherry's elegantly titled and irresistibly interesting book *Womansword: What Japanese Words Say About Women*:

> Thousands of Japanese women visit temples every year to bring baby-clothes, cookies, toys, and other offerings to their *mizugo*. . . . The *mizugo* is a fetus, removed from the watery warmth of the womb by nature or abortionist before it sees the world. "To make a water-baby" (*mizugo ni suru*) means to have an abortion. (Cherry 1987, page 79)

I was literally thunderstruck—an old-fashioned word, but the exact and perfect one in this case—by Cherry's account. But I was also dubious. I thought that surely this was either folklore or a description of a custom from long ago. I tried to imagine two American women talking to one another about what they planned to buy as a gift for their aborted fetuses this year, and found the image impossible. So I proceeded to check it out.

With the help of respondent Fran Stallings (English/Japanese) and her friend and colleague Hiroko Fujita (Japanese/English), I learned that the water babies not only aren't folklore but are very much a part of contemporary Japanese life. Hiroko Fujita was kind enough to send me a postcard of one of the most famous temples (the Temple of Jizo on the Mountain of the Purple Cloud), showing row after row after endless row of the little statues that Japanese families put there to honor their water babies, both those that result from miscarriage and those that are the result of abortion. Hiroko Fujita sent pages of detailed information; and Dr. Stallings directed me to a book by William R. LaFleur, *Liquid Life: Abortion and Buddhism in Japan,* where I found a thorough account and discussion.

LaFleur explains that it's not just mothers who go to the temples. Children—the water babies' siblings—go along; often whole families join in these visits. The statues memorializing the water babies are images of Jizo (a guardian of children, in the sense that Catholics might speak of a patron saint). They are all almost exactly alike, carved of stone, roughly two feet high, with bald heads and closed eyes. They are *stone metaphors:* They look like both tiny Buddhist monks and tiny children, at the same time. Over their carved monks' robes they wear the large red bibs that Japanese infants and toddlers wear, tied around their necks by the families who visit them. Often amulets signed by family members are hung in the temples, inscribed with messages to the water baby expressing the family's debt of gratitude. There is no attempt to hide what has happened or to make it disappear from the family memory. Rather:

> Loving attention to the dead is shown by washing down the memorial image—an ancient Buddhist practice—providing fresh flowers, and bringing the occasional new toy or garment. These activities and the recitation of simple prayers are expected. But beyond these there is the sense of an active *communication*, emotional if not verbal, between the living family and the departed child. (LaFleur 1992, page 11)

Notice, please, that the word LaFleur ends with above is "child." We've come upon another lexical gap, of a somewhat different kind. English has no word or phrase that would mean what we have been translating into English as "water baby." If we were asked what an American English speaker would say in the same situation, silence would be our probable answer, because American English has no vocabulary we can easily or conveniently use. In *Womansword* (page 80), Kittredge Cherry provides the linguistic spotlight that shows us the gap when (struggling with the clash of languages, as I am also struggling) she writes that the Japanese "do not always draw a clear distinction between a fetus and a baby."

Cherry writes as if American English (AE) *does* make a clear distinction in this matter, and as if speakers of AE can identify a clear consensus about that distinction—but of course that's not true. For sure, a human being who has gone through the full experience of childbirth is a child. But our entire national debate about abortion, which now is referred to far and wide as our "second Civil War," revolves around the question of when, precisely, the united sperm and egg are a *fetus* and when they are a *baby*. If we had "a clear distinction" in that regard, we would perhaps be able to sit down as a nation and make the necessary decisions; we might not still be in turmoil. LaFleur tells us (page 11) that the Japanese "tend to avoid terms like 'unwanted pregnancy' or 'fetal tissue.' That which develops in the uterus is often referred to as a 'child'—even when there are plans to abort it." The power of language is such that it would be an extremely rare mother and native speaker of English who could bring herself to say, "Tuesday afternoon at three-thirty I'm going to abort this child."

The visits to the temple and its cemetery are not the only acknowledgments of the water babies in Japanese society. Many Japanese familes have a household shrine. The aborted child *(baby? fetus? fetal tissue? product of conception?)*, although not an ancestor, is often honored at the shrine and "is treated as an ancestor and will be remembered along with them at the Buddhist altar in those households that have them" (ibid., page 148).

The real-world difference that makes this example so important is (in painful contrast to the the terms we have available in English for discussing it) easily stated:

> The water babies are not part of this world, but they remain part of the family; they have a distinct *role* within the family.

Now you might object that this is not a difference of language but "a cultural difference," or "a religious difference." Many Japanese believe in reincarnation, and believe that the fetus *(child? baby? product of conception?)* will have another chance, even many more chances, at life on this earth. Certainly, that is a difference of religion and of culture. But language is what we use to *express* cultural and religious differences, and language is the mechanism we use to transmit information about those differences to others, including our children and our grandchildren. It will be clear to you, just from the problems I've been having writing coherent sentences that explain this Japanese concept in English words, that it makes a real-world *difference* whether you call this entity a fetus or a baby or something else entirely. As with the linguistic strategies of our own WarSpeak, it makes a difference that the process of government certification for abortionists in Japan makes them members of the Motherhood Protection Association. It's not just a matter of style or manners; it's not, as Pinker has suggested, just a matter of people's susceptibilities to "brainwashing." Women in the United States, not just Japanese women, demonstrate that every day.

Millions of English-speaking women (myself included) have said, "I felt the baby move today"; I have never heard, or heard of, a woman saying, "I felt the fetus move today." No one says to a pregnant woman, "When is your fetus due?" or "What are you going to name your fetus?" No woman says, "I had an ultrasound today, and I'm so pleased—my fetus is a little girl!" I have never heard any woman say "my fetus" (although I have heard doctors say "your fetus" to women); always, for the woman, it is "the" fetus.

The word or phrase we choose when we refer to the "product of conception" commits us, as the linguistic relativity hypothesis would predict, to certain attitudes and certain potential actions—not only with regard to the "product" but with regard to its mother and father (notice how hard that is to process in English!) and other aspects of the situation. Whether we choose a single word or phrase to refer to both abortion and miscarriage, as many languages do, or use two separate words as English does, commits us to certain attitudes and potential actions. Whether the naming we do makes it possible to give the "product" in question a role within the family or not drastically changes our commitments.

The question that immediately comes to mind when we think about this case study in the context of multilingualism is:

What effect does the water baby concept have on attitudes toward and feelings about abortion in someone who has both Japanese and English as native languages?

The anti-Whorfians would say that the question is irrelevant, that such attitudes and feelings are based not on language but on logical consideration by the individual, or on socialization, or on a combination of the two.

I disagree. I don't speak one word of Japanese; nevertheless, just learning about the water babies by reading accounts in English had immediate and significant effects on my own feelings and attitudes. I thought of the huge boost that the United States greeting card and holiday industries would get if we were to add the water baby cultural construct to our American culture; I also thought what a comfort it might be to many women and to their families if that happened. My perception of abortion (and miscarriage) has been permanently changed by my encounter with this phenomenon in language, as has my perception of "a family"; the concept of the water baby presents an entirely new option in the world that had been invisible to me previously. It seems to me impossible that anyone who speaks both languages natively would not suffer to some degree the discomfort of the psyche that Leon Festinger named "cognitive dissonance."

We need to know how Japanese/English speakers resolve conflicts of this kind. Do they choose one of the alternative worldviews over the other? Do they negotiate some sort of compromise worldview that takes features from each, so that they "average out" in some way? Do they reject them both and create a third alternative that is unique to those with their language competencies? Is the conflict impossible to resolve, forcing them to maintain both worldviews and switch back and forth between them, as Carol Cohn had to do in her role as nuclear studies scholar? Can they maintain both worldviews *without* discomfort, in an amazing display of what it means to be broad-minded? Is there yet another alternative that hasn't occurred to me, perhaps because my language makes it difficult to perceive it? How does this all work out? What are its implications in a global society? What happens, to take just one possible example of many, when English-speaking diplomats and officials (who rarely speak Japanese) carry on "family planning" conferences with their

Japanese counterparts (who almost without exception speak English)?

This is the *paradigmatic problem,* the *pattern* question at the heart of our investigation. Suppose it's true that languages structure and constrain our worldviews. Then how do multilinguals deal with conflict between two (or more) worldviews, especially on issues that are highly charged emotionally? What implications do multilinguals' strategies and solutions in such situations have for the society and culture in which they live—or for the world at large? If it's not true, of course, matters are much simpler, and decisions about language policy are far more easily and conveniently made.

Advocates of measures such as "English Only" (when not basing their support totally on financial or political factors) are making a set of broad assumptions. Using the Japanese water baby concept as our framing example, we can describe what they mean when they say that "English Only" is necessary to "becoming an American." (That expression is used constantly in English, even by those who realize how inaccurate it is given all the peoples of the Americas who aren't Anglos. In the absence of something like "Unitedstatesers" to fill the lexical gap, it's difficult to get by without it.) The "English Only" contingent mean that their policies will bring about a sequence of events like the following :

- A little boy arrives at an American school as an immigrant, speaking only Japanese.
- He learns English and begins relying on English in his daily life.
- As a result, he undergoes a cognitive transformation.
- One effect of that transformation can be summarized roughly as "When I came to the United States I thought there could be an honorable role for an aborted or miscarried fetus in the family that its mother belongs to, but now that I speak English I know better."
- A transformation of this same kind occurs with regard to every cultural concept for which a significant conflict exists between American English and Japanese.

If both languages are maintained in the youngster's life, as in multilingualism, how can that cognitive transformation happen?

Many Native Americans would chime in right here and say, "That is precisely our point. That is why we *must* not let our languages die!" And many immigrants, even those whose languages are safe because they're spoken elsewhere in the world, would say that this is why they *must* insist that their children maintain both (or all) of their languages.

The real problem is that we aren't paying proper attention to what we're doing. It's not just that we don't know with certainty whether giving up a language means giving up a culture or whether giving up a language means giving up a worldview. It's not just that we don't know the cognitive result when the worldviews of a multilingual person's languages are in severe conflict as they are for English and Japanese in the context of abortion, and we don't know what strategies are used to deal with such conflicts. The real problem is that we aren't taking our ignorance in these matters into consideration in making language policy decisions.

My personal conviction is that the link between language and culture is so deep and so strong that the loss of a language inevitably means loss of the culture and its worldview, a worldview unlike any other. But that's a conviction which I realize is based on inadequate information. In the scientific sense of knowing, we don't know, and so we try to simply muddle through somehow, with the sort of consequences that are typical of muddling through. It would be a tremendous improvement if everyone involved were at least aware of what the unresolved questions *are* and what evidence we do have. The evidence for the strong link between language and our perceptions of reality is so compelling that we must at minimum begin a public debate; a debate limited to scholars and experts is grossly inadequate.

It may be that we'll never be able to resolve the matter with real certainty. We can't impose languages on people in the way the government imposed them in *The Languages of Pao*. We can't remove languages from brains and isolate them in laboratories for study. The tools we have for observing brains busy "languaging," such as the various PET and MRI and fMRI brain scanners, are difficult and expensive to use and restricted to the medical environment; experimental results therefore tend to be based on data from perhaps six to ten brains. Results like that can teach us a lot, but we can't rely on them to prove or disprove our hypotheses. A dozen brains might give us one clear result, but we know that if we looked at a thirteenth or sixteenth or fiftieth brain it might show us something entirely different. In most sciences results are considered respectable and reliable when they're based on *hundreds* of carefully examined examples, not a dozen.

What we *can* do, however, what I believe we're obligated to do—is to try to bring the sets of assumptions that people are relying on for language policy decisions to conscious awareness. We need to state those assumptions as clearly and explicitly as possible. We need to make them widely known, the way it's widely known that sugar cubes melt in water. We need to examine the evidence for and against those sets of assumptions, however limited it may be, so that there can be rational public debate about their accuracy and so that the links between assumptions and policy can be traced. This wouldn't be a solution, but it would be a start. It would take us a considerable distance past just muddling through.

3

Medicine and the Power of Language

In one of its primary aspects, disease must be construed as a biological event little modified by the particular context in which it occurs. As such it exists in animals, who presumably do not socially construct their ailments and negotiate attitudinal responses to sufferers, but who do experience pain and impairment of function. . . . Nevertheless, it is fair to say that in our culture a disease does not exist as a social phenomenon until we agree that it does—until it is named.

(Rosenberg 1992, pages 179–180)

The initial response by many physicians was that the problems were not real. For a time they were dealing with a cluster of symptoms that had no name—and without a name there was, in essence, no disease.

(Halstead 1998, page 44)

One of the common tactics used for attacking the linguistic relativity hypothesis is to ridicule those who defend it by comparing them to people who believe in magical incantations. Whorfians, it is suggested, should really be called Shazamians, or Abracadabrians.

Let's set aside for the moment the mysterious cast that has been given to our world by the discoveries of quantum physics. We're aware now that the objects which surround us are actually made up of energy fields and busily moving particles, and are mostly empty space. But we don't *perceive* reality that way, not without the help of powerful electronic microscopes that are impossible to carry with us everywhere we go.

This whole semantic domain is one vast lexical gap in English; we have no vocabulary for talking about quantum reality in an everyday context. Our language reflects our ordinary perceptions; we refer to chairs and books as "concrete objects." As long as we restrict our discussion to such objects, the accusation of Whorfian leanings toward blatant superstition is in some ways accurate. I cannot think up some new concrete object that has never existed in my environment before—let's call it a "crawshbeck"—and cause one to appear by saying, "Shazam! Let there be crawshbecks!" That's very clear, and not a matter of dispute.

However, many things that are *abstract* have just as much power to create effects in human beings as concrete objects do. When a tree is in my path, I will step aside and go around it; that's one of the effects the tree has on me. I can't see or touch liberty as I can see and touch a tree, but liberty has dramatic effects on my behavior, nevertheless. I wouldn't hesitate to state openly my opinions about the Congress and the President, even if they were totally negative; that's one of the effects that liberty has on me. And creating abstractions out of next to nothing—abstractions whose fantasy status is then extremely difficult to prove—is a snap. English has an array of linguistic devices that can be used that way.

In the field of medicine this particular power of language—the power to use language to create abstractions with substantial effects in the real world—is magnified enormously, so much so that it comes very *close* to being magical. Consider, for instance the striking example which revolves around the phenomenon of menopause.

Case Study:
The Menopause Transformation

Menopause is a normal stage in every woman's life if she lives past fifty or so. It may in many ways be a nuisance and an embarrassment and an inconvenience. But no one would feel obliged to see a doctor just because they were going through a normal stage of life, however annoying they might find it. Think of young human males; they go through a stage when their voices are "changing" and they often find *that* extremely annoying and embarrassing and inconvenient. But no one expects them to go to a doctor and request treatment for their condition.

Women don't "have menopause" or "suffer from menopause"; they *go through* it. Women "have arthritis" and "suffer from arthritis"; they don't "go through arthritis." But look at the following dialogues:

1.

WOMAN: Is there something wrong with me, Doctor?

DOCTOR: No. You're going through menopause.

WOMAN: Well, thank goodness for that! I was afraid I was sick.

2.

WOMAN: Is there something wrong with me, Doctor?

DOCTOR: Yes. You're suffering from hypoestrogenemia.

WOMAN: I am? What does *that* mean?

DOCTOR: It means that you have an estrogen deficiency. But don't worry; we have very effective treatments for it now. I'll write you a prescription, and if you'll stop by the nurse's desk on your way out she'll give you some information that you can read that will answer all your questions. And then I'll need to see you again in a few weeks to check on how you're doing with the medication, whether we need to make any changes in the dosage . . . that sort of thing.

Calling menopause "hypoestrogenemia" and/or "estrogen deficiency" is nothing but talk. *Naming*, that's all it is. But any literate adult speaker of English who hears the word "hypoestrogenemia" knows immediately that it refers to a disease or disorder, and understands that "estrogen deficiency" definitely means "something is wrong with you." SHAZAM! ABRACADABRA!

This is a three-step process for skilled medical professionals. They begin with the ordinary "layperson" name for something ("menopause," "change of life"); they assign an alternative lofty-sounding name that bears no obvious relationship to the ordinary name ("hypoestrogenemia"); and they reserve one or more slightly less obscure additional names ("estrogen deficiency") for use if and when the layperson asks, "What does *that* mean?"

Telling a woman that she's "going through menopause" doesn't do anything remarkable; if it has any effect, it's probably one of reassurance. Telling her that she "is suffering from hypoestrogenemia" or "is hypoestrogenemic" and "has an estrogen deficiency," on the other hand, activates an entire cultural construct with effects that will dramatically change her personal reality. If, as often happens, she is approached with language like that used in typical articles on the subject, her image of herself as a fit and healthy human being is in danger. The April 1987 issue of *The Female Patient* had a piece titled "The Climacteric, Part I: Conquering Osteoporosis, Vasomotor Instability, and Urogenital Deterioration" (Fayez et al. 1987, page 62). The woman portrayed in this article isn't just moving on to another normal stage of her life—she is unstable and deteriorating and deficient, characteristics that aren't associated with fit and healthy people in our culture. She has a new role in life, created by the Menopause Transformation: she is now *A Patient*, and in medical terminology she is eligible to assume the "sick role."

Things that were nothing but unremarkable characteristics of her daily and nightly life are now *symptoms*. Patients, especially those with symptoms, are expected to seek *treatment*, even when there is no cure. Treatment means setting aside time she would have spent in other ways and spending it in doctors' offices, and in going to and from doctors' offices. It means taking medicines and/or undergoing medical procedures; it means setting aside money to *pay* for doctors' visits and medicines and procedures, money that would otherwise have been saved or spent for other things. People have a different attitude toward a woman who is a patient and "being treated" and "on medication" than they have toward women who don't have those characteristics. The sick role, in our culture, brings with it an elaborate set of characteristics that stretch far beyond the individual who assumes it; the whole family has its life changed and rearranged when one member takes on the sick role.

Creating this disease of hypoestrogenemia, whether from scratch or by transforming menopause *into* a disease, is close enough to magic to inspire respect in anyone watching the process. The woman in question is precisely the same woman she was before the incantation was pronounced over her by the doctor; her situation is precisely the same as that of a woman who is told only that she's going through menopause. But her *life* is not the same, nor is the life of her family and intimate circle the same. It's no accident that the register of English spoken by most physicians is called "MDeitySpeak." The doctor says, "Let there be hypoestrogenemia!" and there *is* hypoestrogenemia.

And does the doctor see that it is good?

The answer must surely be yes, because the phenomenon has moved on into another phase of development. Women are now being told to get ready to deal with yet another disease. This one is called "perimenopause" and is identified as the seven years or so immediately prior to menopause itself; presumably the term "prehypoestrogenemia" is waiting in the wings in case "perimenopause" alone lacks sufficient impact.

In the April 1994 issue of *Ladies' Home Journal*, Dr. Philip Sarrel of Yale Medical School reported that two-thirds of women working outside the home suffer "a moderate to severe effect on their capacity to function at work" because they have perimenopause (Laurence 1994, page 73). The article advises women that although no consensus on treatment exists as yet, they must begin "monitoring their symptoms." And according to the 1993 Clinical Proceedings of the Association of Reproductive Health Professionals, there were *21 mil-*

lion women on the verge of coming down with perimenopause in this country at the time of publication. That's a lot of patients, and a lot of patients' families. That's a lot of additional money that will go into the total spent for health care—a total we claim to be working desperately to make smaller.

The next stage is predictable; once women are accustomed to being treated for perimenopause, they will begin reading that a new "health problem" called "postmenopause" has been identified, and it will be suggested that they begin monitoring *its* symptoms. The phrase "postmenopausal women" is already common in medical and health care literature.

So far, no one has performed these MDeitySpeak ceremonies over middle-aged and older men, although both "hypotestosteronemia" and "perihypotestosteronemia" are available for "discovery." We have no way of knowing whether it would be as easy to convince millions of American men to accept the sick role for those two many-sylla-bled conditions as it has been to convince women that being "menopausal" requires a doctor's services. That has yet to be tested.

Steven Pinker, you will recall, claims that people aren't so brain-washed that you can pull off this sort of thing. All that's necessary in such cases is to "point out" to them what's going on, whereupon the alleged reality-shaping power of language will be shown up for the sham that it truly is.

Let's be very careful here. Women in America don't spend years involved with our cumbersome medical and health care system be-cause they are *unaware* that "hypoestrogenemia" and "estrogen defi-ciency" are MDeitySpeak euphemisms for "menopause." They know that perfectly well. It's not some secret that's being kept from them by a wicked medical conspiracy. They're neither stupid nor ignorant. But the power of MDeitySpeak is so great that this knowledge does not keep one woman in a hundred—provided she has access to medical care because she's rich enough or insured enough or poor enough—from becoming A Patient. Nor does it keep her family members and associates from rearranging their lives so that time and money and transportation are available for her visits to the doc-tor. It doesn't keep menopausal women who lack access to medical care from feeling deprived and neglected. I know this from personal experience, and it's a source of perennial amazement to me. When other "menopausal women" learn that I've been menopausing without medical assistance of any kind for at least a dozen years, they are *shocked*. I've tried explaining to them why I behave as I do in this matter, and I am here to tell you that the act of Pointing Out The Euphemisms appears to have no magic in it at all.

Meanwhile, there are languages and cultures which have no idea that this stage of a woman's life ought to bring their medical resources into play. My daughter and I have discussed this topic with her husband (Lao/English multilingual) in much detail. Bounlieng assures us, unequivocally, that Lao has no word for menopause and that Lao women don't mark off this period of their lives in any fashion, either linguistically or culturally. "They're able to stop having babies without any help from a doctor," he says, and I'm sure that's true. You then have to wonder how a woman with native fluency in both Lao and English deals with this conflict between the two languages. Which one does she rely on?

When I've raised this question with the American medical professionals in my seminars and consulting practice, they've had no trouble answering it. As they perceive it, nobody—once exposed to the superior medical knowledge we have in the United States—clings to his or her previous beliefs. The assumption is once again that the outcome can be taken for granted, and that the immigrant who learns English and is thus "assimilated" will always say something along the lines of "Before I spoke English I thought such-and-such a thing; now I know better."

Let's be frank here, because no purpose will be served by tiptoeing around the truth: The position taken, and not just by doctors, is that people whose medical concepts are different from those of "Western" medicine are in most cases simply ignorant, through no fault of their own, and that the remedy is to provide them with information about how "real" contemporary medicine is done—at which point they will be grateful for being brought up to date at last, and will immediately abandon their previous ideas on the subject. Notice how the physician-authors in this quotation word their question:

In what ways does acculturation change the beliefs of patients of various ethnicities, i.e., how are the cultures of immigrants transformed and combined with the culture of their adopted country? (Blackhall et al. 1995, page 823)

The question posed isn't "*Does* acculturation change the beliefs . . ." and "*Are* the cultures of immigrants transformed . . . "; those results are presupposed. No room is left here for an alternative resolution in which patients simply decide that the American English version of events is nonsense and rely on the perceptions shaped by their native languages instead.

My own experience with native speakers of other languages—not only those who are patients but also those who are working as medical professionals in this country—does not bear out that confident presupposition. The error has serious implications for the health care system in a multicultural nation like the United States

For example, evidence for the placebo effect has made it more than clear that a substantial part of "being well" and "getting well" depends on the patient's faith in the doctor and the medical system. That faith also determines in many ways the degree to which the patient is "compliant" (that is, follows the doctor's orders); this is an equally substantial factor in the ultimate outcome for the patient. How well is medical care going to work for multilinguals when one of their native languages slaps an illness label onto some chunk of their experience that has no such label in another of their languages?

We know that some multilingual populations in this country decide either for their native medicine or for the American version and reject the other alternative. We also know that English/Chinese multilinguals living in the United States, by contrast, typically go to at least *two* medical professionals—one who is practicing Western medicine and another who is practicing Oriental medicine—as if to cover all their bases. Most native Navajos follow that pattern, going to both a Western doctor and a Navajo medical practitioner. (It does strike the Navajo as bizarre that it is the other system that is referred to as "Western," yes.) Presumably this doubling makes Navajo and Chinese-American patients' health problems even more expensive and time-consuming. What other effects does it have on their behavior, and on their health?

In their book *Philosophy in the Flesh*, Lakoff and Johnson offer an example that is relevant here. They note that various metaphors for numbers exist—NUMBERS ARE POINTS ON A LINE, for example, and NUMBERS ARE SETS. And they say that what people do is choose their metaphor for numbers on the basis of the kind of math they want to do at the time. Perhaps that's what multilinguals do when their native languages offer them conflicting metaphors; perhaps they choose on the basis of the kind of thing they want to do at the time. What would that mean for multilingual doctors and nurses and medical technicians, if that's what they do when *they're* the ones experiencing the conflict between two or more of their languages? We don't know; no systematic, controlled research on this issue has yet been done.

Christopher Lawrence says, "The focus of inquiry should be on how communities come to frame or see diseases. . . . What is required is an explanation of how and why perceptions are structured as they are and how and why they change"(Lawrence 1992, page 53). I agree with him. How? And why? And how do we find out?

In my experience, conscious awareness of the way a language shapes perceptions usually occurs when its speakers are able to step *outside* their language in ways that come along rarely in everyday life. Remember the discussion in Chapter 2 of differing perceptions about horseback riding? Each time I taught that material in my classes, the same thing happened. The English-speaking students, after hearing how Navajo gives a surface shape to those perceptions, would say, "I never realized before that riding a horse means doing something *to* the horse!" The Navajo-speaking students, hearing how English handles the matter, would tell me that they had never before realized that the Navajo equivalent meant doing something together with the horse. It's a cliché to say that you can't see the forest for the trees, but where native languages are concerned it describes the situation with dead-on accuracy.

Native English speakers who are medical professionals are only likely to discover the presuppositions that underlie their own concepts and beliefs about medicine if they are exposed to those that are present in other languages. No mechanism exists in medical training in the United States to make that happen, presumably because it's not considered important. I have been told repeatedly by medical educators that "there's no room for linguistics in the medical curriculum."

Medical Models and Metaphors

Metaphorical thought is commonplace and inescapable; in itself, it is neither good nor bad. . . . The use of a metaphor, however, becomes pernicious when it hides realities in a harmful way.

(George Lakoff, in Lakoff 1991, page 1)

Human languages around the world present very different models of what health and illness/injury/disability and medical care are, depending on the metaphors the language uses for these items and all their related phenomena. The range in medical models encoded in human languages around the world stretches from "All health problems are caused by evil spirits and bad thoughts" through "All health problems are punishments for sin" to "All health problems are caused by germs" and far beyond.

In his book *The Psychobiology of Mind-Body Healing*, Dr. Ernest Lawrence Rossi insists that all health problems are caused by *communication breakdown*. Since physiological phenoma happen in the body when the brain sends its neurotransmitters out with instructions, he makes a very strong case. I find it totally convincing, especially since the human brain is unable to distinguish between external and internal stimuli and will dutifully send the body "Prepare to flee or fight!" messages even for imaginary crises. If Rossi's definition were generally accepted in medicine, medical schools would have no *choice* but to find room for linguistics courses. But his metaphor is not the standard one in Western medicine, and "communications" courses for doctors continue to have little or no input from linguistic science. (I'm happy to say that my own medical seminars are exceptions, but it's a lonely business; the only area of medicine in which I feel that linguistics is beginning to be taken seriously is in emergency medicine, where the necessity to obtain accurate information in a matter of seconds has created in EM professionals a healthy respect for the science of language.)

The African-American culture of the Sea Islands of South Carolina divides nonfitness into two subgroups: "ailments," which are caused by natural forces or punishments from God and can be helped by doctors; and "conditions," which are caused by such things as devils and witchcraft, and can only be helped by spiritual advisers. (Hamadeh 1987). This, needless to say, is not the standard metaphor either. My Laotian son-in-law feels exactly the same way about the idea that "germs" cause illness as the average Western doctor does about "evil spirits" filling that role: He considers a belief in germs to be a foolish and unfortunate superstition. It's not that he doesn't believe germs exist—but he considers them to be the *result* of illness rather than its cause.

We're going to examine here just two of the most common conceptual systems of medicine around the world: one in which illness is understood as a state of being *broken;* and one in which illness is understood as a state of being *out of balance* or *unharmonious.* An example of the first system is American mainstream medicine; examples of the other would include Chinese and Navajo medicine.

The problems with definitions of terms, and with expressing terms and concepts across the languages, are severe. (This is a situation that you'll be familiar with after our struggles with putting the water babies concept into English.) I'll do my best to straighten things out as we go along, beginning with the choice of a cover term we can use to express the unwieldy set of meanings-and-perceptions covered by such words as "illness," "disease," "disorder," "injury," "disability," "sickness," and more. It's common to see illness defined as "an absence of health" and health defined as "an absence of illness." Going around that circle again won't help us. I'm going to use "nonfitness" as a cover term for all of those deviations from the hypothetical human state of perfect health and perfect well-being. Not because it's an especially elegant choice, but because it seems to me to be the broadest and most *neutral* one I could choose, much like using the term "variety" to express a neutral attitude toward a way of speaking a language. A sprained ankle is nonfitness; lung cancer is nonfitness; deconditioning is nonfitness; schizophrenia is nonfitness; pregnancy, in the American system, is nonfitness; *crise de foie* ("liver crisis"), in the French system, is nonfitness; *susto* ("loss of the soul"), in the Ecuadoran system, is nonfitness; and so on.

In 1991 Harriet Beinfield and Efrem Korngold published *Between Heaven and Earth: A Guide to Chinese Medicine.* Unlike a number of previous books I've read on the subject, this one does an excellent job of laying out the Chinese medical and health care model in a way that's both understandable and interesting for the Western reader. There's a striking difference, however, between the ease with which the American medical system is explained and Beinfield and Korngold's struggles to express the terms and concepts of the Chinese system in English. Here's a typical example, from page 17:

> Western medicine is the study of how the human machine works. When people are like machines, doctors become like mechanics. . . . In this schema, the body is reduced to structural parts, proceeding from organs to tissues, tissues to cells, cells to molecules. The doctor as mechanic separates the whole into parts in order to discern the nature, proportion, and function of each constituent.

Western doctors, the authors go on to explain, identify the broken or malfunctioning part, figure out what's wrong with it, and determine the cause of the problem. Successful treatment then consists of fixing that part, removing it, or replacing it. In the same way that the cause of a punctured tire can be identified as a nail picked up from the road, and the tire is either patched or replaced, the cause of a "broken" tonsil can be identified as a particular bacterium or virus, and the fixing is done by giving the patient a medicine—or, if the damage is too severe, by removing the tonsil surgically. If at some point Western doctors became convinced that the body has to have tonsils to function properly, the next step would be tonsil transplants or artificial tonsils.

This is very straightforward; it gives us a solid foundation for understanding how Western doctors proceed in their efforts to do something about states of nonfitness in their patients. It will annoy doctors who claim to practice *holistic* medicine, and rightly so; it will offend doctors who consider the comparison with so low-status an occupation as automobile repair demeaning. (Never mind the obvious fact that our lives are in the hands of auto mechanics just as much as they are in the hands of doctors.) Despite the justifiable objections, it accurately and clearly expresses the perceptions most Western patients have of their doctors and medical care.

Now let's compare this clarity with a typical quotation or two—in English—from the corresponding section on Chinese medicine:

> In Chinese medicine, health is the ability of an organism to respond appropriately to a wide variety of challenges in a way that insures maintaining equilibrium and integrity. Disease represents a failure to adapt to challenge, a disruption of the overall equilibrium, and a rent in the fabric of the organism. (Beinfield and Korngold 1991, page 36)

> If the cause of disease is understood as imbalance, then the goal of treatment is to recover balance. (ibid., page 44)

These statements may be accurate, but they in no way answer the basic questions readers would have about what a Chinese doctor or health care worker *does*.

I turned to another excellent book on Chinese medicine, Ted J. Kaptchuk's *The Web That Has No Weaver*, for help, and found the same sort of thing:

> All relevant information, including the symptom as well as the patient's other general characteristics, is gathered and woven together until it forms what Chinese medicine calls "a pattern of disharmony." . . . The total configurations, the patterns of disharmony, provide the framework for treatment. The therapy then attempts to bring the configuration into balance, to restore harmony to the individual. (Kaptchuk 1983, page 4)

Although all these authors try hard, over and over again, to sum up this "harmonizing" process for speakers of English, they get nowhere. Until, that is, Beinfield and Korngold change their tactics. After a considerable amount of this floundering about, they give up on constructing careful, rational, "expository" sentences and paragraphs and turn to the much more powerful mechanism of *metaphor*. They had already established the English metaphor as A DOCTOR IS A MECHANIC. The Chinese metaphor, they tell us, is: A DOCTOR IS A GARDENER. And suddenly the lights go on! Because although we may have no idea what someone we could only refer to as a "harmony-restorer" does, we know what *gardeners* do, in precisely the same way that we know what mechanics do.

Richard Selzer (writer and surgeon) has provided us with what I consider to be the finest possible description, in English, of Asian medicine in action. In his essay "The Art of Surgery" he describes a grand rounds at his hospital featuring Tibetan healer Yeshi Dhonden, personal physician to the Dalai Lama. The task was to examine a patient chosen for him in advance by Selzer's hospital, a patient whose diagnosis was unknown to anyone except the doctor who chose her, and afterward to discuss the diagnosis with the Western doctors. Selzer describes Dhonden's taking of the patient's pulse, which was a very different process than the one we Westerners are accustomed to. It lasted thirty minutes, and when it was over Selzer writes of his new awareness that "I, who have palpated a hundred thousand pulses, have not felt a single one." Dhonden also examines a urine specimen provided by the patient. And that is all he does. In the discussion with the doctors afterward, he presents his diagnosis (through an interpreter) as follows:

> Between the chambers of her heart, long, long before she was born, a wind had come and blown open a deep gate that must never be opened. Through it charge the full waters of her river, as the mountain stream cascades in the springtime, battering, knocking loose the land, and flooding her breath.

The doctor who selected the patient agrees; that is the diagnosis. But he states it in English: "Congenital heart disease. Interventricular septal defect, with resultant heart failure" (Selzer 1976, page 78). The two shapes of the diagnosis represent two metaphors; they express the same facts.

Metaphors are the most powerful linguistic tool available to us, and this is true for every language. The woeful lack of attention given to such skills as how to find and how to use metaphors is a serious deficit in our educational system. Metaphors can fill lexical gaps, as in the example we've just considered; they are one of the few options available for working to fill the lexical gaps that go with language about the inexpressible and unspeakable, as in attempts to describe mystical experiences. And far from being "only figures of speech," metaphors can do something that no amount of logical argument, however solidly bolstered by statistics and facts, can accomplish: Metaphors have the power to change *attitudes*—swiftly, without fuss, and often permanently.

If you are persistent and determined, you may be able to hammer away at people with lengthy logical arguments and statistics until they give up and say, "Okay, you're right." You may be able to make them do that more quickly by administering rewards and punishments, if you have that sort of power. But all it will get you, 99 percent of the time, is shallow *surface* agreement; often it's nothing more than a pretense of agreement, which they're willing to offer to get you to shut up. Underneath the surface, their old attitudes remain unchanged. A successful metaphor, by contrast, simply *replaces and/or readjusts* whatever was in their minds before; their attitudes shift immediately, and will remain stable until and unless an even more powerful metaphor comes along and overthrows the previous one.

In most university linguistics departments today, metaphor has ceased to be a neglected subject and has become the hottest subject there is. To get an idea of what a revolution has taken place in this regard, go to the metaphor center at http://metaphor.uoregon.edu/-metaphor.html. (The site is so popular that you may need to go to its mirror site to get past the crowds; the mirror address is http://dark-wing.uoregon.edu/~rohrer/metaphor.htm.)

Metaphors are so powerful that they serve as filters for our perceptions of reality and are the basis for the majority of the decisions we make in our daily lives. As George Lakoff and Mark Johnson say on page 3 of their book *Metaphors We Live By*:

> Our ordinary conceptual system, in terms of which we both think and act, is fundamentally metaphorical in nature. . . . The way we think, what we experience, and what we do every day is very much a matter of metaphor.

The only effective challenge to a metaphor is another, better, metaphor; facts and logic are essentially useless against metaphors.

This is crucial to understanding what it means for someone to be a native speaker of two or more languages that present conflicting metaphors. So crucial that I think it's worth pausing to consider one clarifying example from my own experience.

For most of my adult life I felt hostile toward people who, when I was a guest in their homes, kept their television set turned on while we were talking. Even though the sound was turned down, it seemed to me that my hosts didn't really want my company and were only *pretending* to be interested in our conversation. The effects this conviction had on my behavior weren't trivial. I made a real effort not to return to houses where this had happened. My behavior toward the people involved was altered in negative ways; I perceived them as rude and untrustworthy, and I behaved accordingly. If they were my students or my colleagues or my relatives, this shaped my judgment of what they said and what they did, and in turn shaped my responses. Notice the clear parallel here: In a relationship between medical professionals and patients, behaviors are shaped in exactly the same way, but with even more serious results.

And then one day, in a March 1991 *Harper's Magazine* interview, I read a remark by Camille Paglia in which she proposed this metaphor: THE TELEVISION SET IS THE FIRE ON THE HEARTH. Like the fireplace, she said, with the fire flickering and crackling and hissing softly in the background, it's the center of the social life of today's homes; most people no longer have fireplaces, but almost everyone has a television set.

A lot of people I have the highest regard for had tried to change my mind about the TV set phenomenon, and their arguments had never made the least impression on me. But the metaphor from Paglia—for whom I have no particular regard that would have caused her views to influence me—just blew me away. My *immediate* reaction was "I wouldn't expect people to put out the fire in their fireplace because I was their guest, and I wouldn't interpret that fire as evidence that I wasn't truly welcome. So *why do I expect them to turn off their television set??*" Shazam!

If there could be such a thing as linguistic surgery, this example would represent a successful and prototypical "metaphor replacement." Since that hearth fire metaphor came my way, my attitude toward the television sets in the background—and, more importantly, toward the people who leave them turned on—has turned completely around. All my previous negative judgments are gone, and I am much embarrassed by my previous failure to understand what was happening and behave accordingly. This is what presenting or encountering the right metaphor can bring about, and it is the most awesome power language offers.

Suppose Language X says, "A bat is a mammal," and Language Y says "A bat is a reptile." Those are not metaphors but statements of fact which can be checked for accuracy by scientific methods, and one of them has to be an *error* of fact. Investigations can be carried out with bats to determine what their proper classification is. It's easy to see how multilinguals who are native speakers of both languages could say to themselves, "Well, one of those statements must be wrong" and let it go at that, with no problems created.

But when Language X says A DOCTOR IS A MECHANIC and Language Y says A DOCTOR IS A GARDENER, can multilingual speakers of Languages X and Y settle for "One of those metaphors must be wrong" and be comfortable?

What if one language or dialect says SUICIDE IS MENTAL ILLNESS and another says SUICIDE IS SELF-MURDER? What if one language treats suicide as a single monolithic concept while another perceives it as requiring much finer distinctions? Hilary Hinds Kitasei writes that Japanese, for example, has many words for suicide—

"for example, 'shinju' for double suicide, with modifiers to distinguish one involving parent and child, lovers or comrades. These can be further refined to indicate the gender of those involved and nuances of motive" (Kitasei 1998). What do multilingual and/or multidialectal speakers do about such situations? It's not like the bats, you perceive; there's no way to dissect suicide and arrive at the "correct facts" about what it is, exactly.

It makes a difference whether a child is called a "Mongolian idiot" or a "Down's syndrome child." It makes a difference whether homosexuality is called a "lifestyle" or a "genetic illness" or a "mental illness" or an "abomination." It makes a difference whether weighing more than the cultural ideal is called the "disease of obesity" or "one possible body shape" or "lack of willpower." It makes a difference whether violence is called an "epidemic"—to which the theories and methods of public health and epidemiology can appropriately be applied—or just a "social problem."

Decisions like these, no matter how scientific the language in which they are phrased, are made on the basis of metaphors. We human beings label another human being as "sinner" or "patient" or "normal healthy person" on the basis of metaphors. People base their behavior toward doctors and medical care—their decisions about whether they will go to a doctor or not, whether they'll accept the doctor's advice and follow the doctor's instructions, whether they'll supplement their mainstream care with items from "alternative medicine" or "folk medicine"—not on logic and scientific facts but on their attitudes and beliefs, which are determined in large part by the metaphors they accept. The same thing is true for their behavior toward anyone, including themselves, who is involved in medical care. If I could come up with a metaphor for germs as powerful as the hearth fire metaphor for television sets, I could change my son-in-law's conviction that people who believe germs cause disease are superstitious, and there would be behavioral consequences of that change.

One of the characteristics of metaphors that gets far too little explicit attention is that metaphors don't stand alone—they bring other metaphors with them. We understand metaphors in terms of the way they match parts and characteristics of one thing to parts and characteristics of another thing. Western medicine says A DOCTOR IS A MECHANIC; with that come many additional metaphors such as A PATIENT IS A MACHINE IN NEED OF REPAIR, and THE HUMAN BODY IS AN ASSEMBLY OF PARTS, and MEDICAL TREATMENT IS THE REPAIR AND/OR REPLACEMENT OF BROKEN PARTS. We store all those metaphors (and many other related ones) together in memory, and use them to construct scripts and determine our behavior.

Suppose you start with A DOCTOR IS A GARDENER. Then what is a patient? (A carrot? A rosebush? A cabbage patch?) What is a human body? What is medical treatment? When your garden is in trouble, you don't hire a mechanic; nor would you want your gardener trying to fix the brakes on your car.

Life is going to be simpler for people who don't face cognitive conflicts of this kind; the fact that Chinese/English individuals and Navajos feel obliged to use both systems of medicine when they have a nonfitness problem is one demonstration of that.

There was a time in our history when Native American children were taken away from their parents and homes—by force, if necessary—and put in boarding schools, where they were severely punished for speaking any language except English. The people who did this believed in what they were doing; they believed it was for the children's good. It was called "civilizing the children," and it was done not to be cruel but to make it more likely that the children would have a chance to succeed in life. We no longer tear children away from their families and beat them when they speak their native tongues, thank heaven. But the same old thinking underlies the idea that *for the good of the children*, usually immigrant children, we must stamp out their native languages and replace them entirely with English just as fast as we possibly can. If immigrant children are to "become Americans"—that is, if they are to base their behavior on the same metaphors as do native speakers of American English, and thus behave as the Average American Joe and Average American Jane behave—we have to get rid of the distracting and perhaps contradictory metaphors embodied in their native languages.

I am convinced that this also explains the otherwise baffling fact that the U.S. education system waits to begin teaching foreign languages until college, or the last year or two of high school at the earliest—*after* students are past their peak years of language-learning ability. This practice seems incomprehensibly illogical if you look at it only in terms of teaching strategies. But let's consider what is actually happening.

Most countries that teach foreign languages do so very early in the school years, in order to take advantage of the superb language-learning skills that are known to be part of the mental equipment of early childhood. The results of that policy are excellent. You end up with adults who have native or near-native fluency in the languages they've studied. That kind of linguistic competence as a result of foreign language teaching is very rare in the United States. And that is precisely the point. If what you achieve in the young person is *native* skills in the foreign language, you expose him or her to the power of foreign *metaphors*. Presumably the unconscious assumption is that such danger is minor as long as you wait until the student is old enough to make learning a language with native fluency extremely difficult and unlikely.

This educational strategy—the "See to it first of all that the children grow up to be real Americans" strategy—is put ahead of any proposed advantages of multilingualism. The goal is to be certain that you won't *have* an adult population that lacks the necessary faith in Western medicine (or any other important aspect of Western culture). The goal is to be certain that adults in the United States will filter their perceptions through the metaphors that establish and maintain "the American dream." It isn't usually explained as I have explained it here, of course. Not because of ill will or an intention to mislead the public, but because our national discourse has never yet included the information from and about linguistics that would make such an explanation widely known and widely understood.

This doesn't mean that no one in government and international relations and similar fields is aware of what's going on. To get an idea of the sort of materials that are produced when governments take metaphor power seriously and try to use it the way they would use electrical power, you need only look at the Internet site of the Union of International Associations (http://www.uia.org). The UIA describes itself as having been, since the early 1980s, "exploring the role of metaphor in relation to governance, understanding of world problems, articulation of more appropriate organizational strategies, transformative conferencing and dialogue, and knowledge organization." You will find at their Web site paper after paper discussing the systematic choice and use of metaphor to make national and international policies clear to populations quickly and efficiently and effectively. For example:

> The degree of complexity, with which it is now necessary to deal, strongly implies that no single model . . . is adequate to encompass it. . . . The challenge may then prove to be one of selecting (or designing) a set of complementary metaphors which together encompass that complexity. Classic examples from physics are the 'wave" and "particle" metaphors through which electrons are to be understood in different ways, and the "flowing waters" and "teeming crowds" metaphors through which electricity is to be understood. . . . In each case, both metaphors offer necessary but insufficient insights when used independently. *The question may then be to discover the art of shifting between the perceptions offered through appropriate metaphors in a set that articulates a complex pattern of policies.* (Judge 1991, page 7; emphasis added)

There may be an important clue for us (in our investigation of how conflicting metaphors are handled by multilinguals) in the way that native speakers of English deal with the conflict between ELECTRONS ARE WAVES and ELECTRONS ARE PARTICLES. What we do is accept, somehow, the fact that in some situations we have to choose one of those metaphors and in other situations we can't get the results we want unless we choose the other one—and we manage to "believe it" both times. When I asked Jasmine Luk (Chinese/English) which of the two medical metaphors she ordinarily relied on, she wrote, "I will take both metaphors. . . . I believe that there could be various reasons making a person sick." She can switch between the metaphors according to the context in a given situation.

The metaphor that a culture chooses for any area of its life determines, through language, what will happen to that area. In medicine, as in any other field, it determines what will be discovered—because it determines what will be *looked* for and what will be given *attention*. It determines the organization of published materials and of speeches at conferences; it determines where research money will be spent and where it will be withheld. It can stand squarely in the way of knowledge that is tremendously important, and the shift from one dominant metaphor to another on the basis of new information may not be easy, especially when the potential replacement is hard to understand. This is one of the hazards created by the fact that the vast majority of all medical and scientific articles are published in English, both in print and on the Internet; there's little room for the metaphors of other languages to be displayed or discussed.

Here is George A. Diamond, M.D., professor of medicine at UCLA and director of the cardiac stress lab at Cedars-Sinai Medical Center, quoted in an article about what happens when the new scientific concept of *chaos* meets the Western medical metaphors head-on:

"The data we've been throwing away may be the data we should keep and analyze more deeply. Meaningful patterns can be much more complex and disguised than we are used to thinking. A patient with a complex constellation of findings that do not seem to fit a pattern may, in fact, fit a very different pattern." (quoted in Cotton 1991, page 13)

That is, *the metaphor we're using may be keeping us from understanding what we're observing.* The same article goes on to mention, almost offhandedly, that doctors know that a normal human heartbeat is *not* regular—that, in fact, an absolutely regular heart rate is a sign of imminent medical problems—and suggests that the new chaos theory might offer a way of clarifying this. According to Dr. Mark Kroll, "We've known for 10 years that people with excessively stable heart rates are more likely to fibrillate, but the information has never been very useful because it doesn't tell you when" (in Cotton 1991, page 17).

A *New Scientist* article titled "Fascinating Rhythm" (Buchanan 1998, page 25) quotes physicist Gene Stanley: "The simple view that disease involves the breaking down of order is completely wrong." And Buchanan, after noting that one of the effects of aging is a tendency toward an ever more regular heartbeat, concludes that "in fifty years' time, your doctor may need to know as much about chaos theory and statistical physics as heart physiology."

This tells us that when you define an orderly pattern in terms of what "orderly pattern" means for a machine, and then use that concept to observe human heartbeats, you may get information that isn't useful. The machine metaphor doesn't seem to fit.

In such cases, two things can happen: A search for a better metaphor can be undertaken, or the irritating data can be ignored and/or discarded. In Western medicine, where resources are limited and everything has to be done in a hurry, the second choice is the more likely one. What might that mean for the treatment of heart disease in the West, with heart disease being perhaps our most common cause of death? The article by Cotton closes with the observation that upon hearing these claims about the possible medical role of chaos theory, "some physicians actually become angry." I'm sure they do. Chaos, defined in the article's opening paragraph as "a nonlinear, predictable order without periodic repetition," is about as badly suited for a role within the DOCTORS ARE MECHANICS metaphor as a concept possibly could be, and the English name it was given could not possibly have been a worse choice. It could be much more easily put into Navajo, which has the linguistic resources for giving it a suitable surface shape.

I'm positive that the average person in the United States firmly believes a healthy human heart is supposed to go lub-DUPPing along as regularly as the ticking of a clock or the turning of a gear. I suspect that medical professionals tend to feel the same way about it, whatever they may or may not know know intellectually. We hear them, time and time again, speaking of "irregularities" of the heartbeat as if irregularity itself were inherently dangerous—as indeed it *would* be if hearts behaved like parts of a machine. In my experience, people who notice an irregularity in their heartbeat are *alarmed*. After all, machines don't behave that way unless they need fixing.

When the American Southwest was hit a few years ago by a mysterious and usually fatal illness (eventually determined to be a hantavirus), the Centers for Disease Control investigators paid little attention to the Navajo healers who explained the illness by telling a story about the dangers of interaction between human beings and mice. The CDC's attitude about the Navajo myth changed when their investigations showed that the source of the illness *was* in fact mice, which were unusually abundant in the Four Corners area at that time due to equally unusual weather. The English and Navajo speakers were using different metaphors, but the recommended behaviors—avoiding mice and their droppings and debris—were exactly the same.

Who *Is* That in There, *Anyway?*

Before we leave the topic of language and health, we need to look at one more idea, one that comes from the semantic domain of psychiatry and psychotherapy and that may not come readily to mind: the question of whether *the same person* is speaking when a multilingual individual shifts from one language to another. Professor Azade Seyhan of Bryn Mawr, herself multilingual, doesn't think so; she says, "In every language you're someone else, a different person" (Seyhan 1995). B. K. Frantzis, in his book *Opening the Energy Gates of the Body*, writes, "After I became truly bilingual, I noticed that even when I'm processing the same information in my mind, I think and feel quite differently in each language" (Frantzis 1993, page 26).

I have always felt as if I were a different person when I was speaking French. And I know that when my first husband spoke French, it always seemed to me that he was a very different person than when he was speaking English; the change was dramatic, and sudden, and always a bit intimidating to me. As part of the questionnaire for this book, I asked my respondents whether this phenomenon was ever true for them; the results were very interesting.

Some respondents misunderstood my question and simply answered with statements such as "I seem more sophisticated when I speak Language X, because I have a more sophisticated vocabulary in that language." But those who took the question literally divided sharply into two groups. One group's response can be summarized as "Of *course* I feel like a different person! Why would you need to ask?"; the other group took exactly the opposite position, with equal intensity. One respondent wrote (requesting anonymity), "I certainly do not think my husband knows me" because he does not speak her mother tongue. By contrast, my son-in-law's reaction when my daughter asked him about this was "Do I feel like a different person, depending on whether I'm speaking English or Lao? What a ridiculous question—of *course* not!"

The question is discussed in the context of medical care in a 1996 article by therapist RoseMarie Perez Foster, "The Bilingual Self: Duet in Two Voices." She is herself multilingual and has done extensive therapy with patients who are native speakers of two languages. She writes (in the psychiatric variety of MDeitySpeak):

> The speaker of two language codes possesses not only dual sets of symbols for referring to internal states and the external world, but also two different signifying chains of meaning-producing self-object interactions and developmental contexts. . . . At the level of psychodynamic organization, these language-specific relational experiences will come to be associated with different modes of being, different modes of interacting with another, and different modes of experiencing oneself. (Foster 1996, page 109)

Perez Foster goes on to review research in which multilingual subjects provided very different responses on standard psychological tests when they were administered in their different languages. She provides case histories from her own experience in which it was necessary to shift from one language to another before therapy could be effective, even when her patient had completely native fluency in each language. She tells us that bilingual persons "possess dual templates through which we shape and organize our world, as well as two sets of verbal symbols that codify our experiences and give voice to their expression" and that bilinguals "present a packaging puzzle, as it were, in which two language-bounded experiential systems are housed in the confines of a single mind" (ibid., page 99). (She does not extend her claims to say that someone native in three or more languages would present analogous phenomena for each language, but we can safely assume that she would consider that plausible.)

Dr. Carla Massey, another therapist at the symposium where Perez Foster's paper was originally presented, reacted with a response much like my son-in-law's. She restricted herself to the linguistic register of academic courtesy, however; for example, she described herself as "reacting with some dismay" (Massey 1996, page 125). Once again, we see in this medical care context what I saw in my respondents' questionnaires: no middle ground, but a sharp "Of course!" or "Of course not!"

Settling this issue, if it can in fact *be* settled, would require years of research and discussion, and substantial resources; there is ongoing research that may one day give us the answer. It's a question with tremendous significance for the medical and health care systems, since—if in fact there may be more than one patient present in some sense in a single body—communication addressed to the "wrong personality" might have little effect on the patient's health. This is precisely what Perez Foster reports for some of her patients. (I'm not referring here to the much-debated condition called "multiple personality disorder"; that is something else entirely. If more than one "personality" is present in multilingualism it doesn't represent an example of nonfitness of any kind, but a normal condition for multilinguals.)

What I want to do here is bring the question up, note how interesting it is that multilinguals are so sharply and passionately divided about it, and try to consider what its implications might be. In that spirit, it seems to me that we should consider the possibility that *both sides are right*—not only in this specific regard, but in regard to the argument over the truth or falsity of the linguistic relativity hypothesis, where we also observe no middle ground but instead a passionate adherence to one position or its opposite.

There's a traditional kind of psycholinguistics experiment in which the linguist first records a sentence such as "The dog and her puppies crossed the road"; then the initial sound in "puppies" is cut from the recording (*literally* cut, in the days when all recordings were on tape, with a razor blade), and a recorded segment that is the first sound in "guppies" is inserted to replace that sound. The resulting recording, which now has on it "The dog and her guppies crossed the road," is then played for research subjects. And very reliably they fall into two groups. One group hears the sentence that's actually in the altered recording, in spite of the improbability of "the dog and her guppies" as an item in the real world. The other group hears "The dog and her puppies crossed the road," and quite often insists that that's what the tape says even when the linguist explains what has been done.

In the early 1970s, researcher Ruth S. Day carried out a series of experiments with various language-processing tasks. Usually the results of such experiments fall into a standard bell curve distribution, with lots of people in the middle and a few at each extreme end. However, Day's results were like those I got when I asked my multilingual respondents whether they feel like a different person when using a different language. Her subjects divided sharply into two groups, with almost no one in the middle range.

She called those who perceive the stimulus that is actually present in the environment (and thus would have reported hearing "the dog and her guppies") "stimulus-bound." She called the group who perceive what their knowledge of their native language tells them *ought* to be present (and would thus have reported hearing "the dog and her puppies") "language-bound." (Day 1970, 1973a, 1973b.)

We observe a similar thing happening in the common experience of proofreading, in which some of us might check a sentence half a dozen times without ever noticing that someone had written "the clonk struck midnight" for "the clock struck midnight," while others would spot the error instantly as they read that sequence. Researchers Joan Duncan and James Laird instructed subjects to relax or contract certain muscles—producing smiles or frowns, but without using those labels—and then tested them for mood. They found that the subjects divided into two groups: those who felt happy when smiling and angry when frowning, labeled "self-cuers," and those who didn't respond emotionally to their own facial expressions, labeled "situation-cuers" (Duncan and Laird 1981).

Clearly this sort of division between people whose perceptions are tailored to an actual external stimulus and people whose perceptions are tailored to abstract "rules" of some kind is found in numerous areas of human cognition. I would like to propose that this might explain the drastic division on some of the questions we've been discussing in this book. It might be that human beings, for reasons as yet undetermined, actually fall into distinct psycholinguistic groups:

A. A group for whom the linguistic relativity hypothesis does hold true to a significant degree
B. A group for whom the linguistic relativity hypothesis is false or nearly false
C. A group for whom the feeling of being another person when speaking a different language is automatic and taken for granted
D. A group for whom the very idea of shifting "personhood" when shifting languages seems impossible and absurd

We might even hazard as a tentative working hypothesis that groups (a) and (c) are actually a single language-bound group, and groups (b) and (d) are another, stimulus-bound group.

If that could be proved, and if we had a reliable way to determine early in life which group(s) an individual belonged to, it might shed new light on many problems of language and language policy—as well as many problems in medical communication—which have seemed stubbornly resistant to investigation in the past. Perhaps, instead of asking, "Is the linguistic relativity hypothesis true or false?" we need to add "for this particular individual?" This would be a fertile area for research, and it might well explain many investigative results that have been confusing and contradictory up to now.

4

Business and the Power of Language

The lifeblood of a Chinese company is guanxi [connections].
Penetrating its layers is like peeling an onion. First come
connections between people and ancestors, then those between
people from the same village, between members of the family,
and finally between the family and close associates who can be
trusted. . . . Typically, the Chinese . . . are less concerned with
what is written in the contract than in the actions that people
take to meet their obligations as they emphasize guanxi.

(Cannon 1994, pages 332–333)

Suppose that you and I are involved in a business transaction. I want
to sell you ten widgets, or ten hours of a service, and you're willing
to buy. When the business in question is business as represented by
Standard American Mainstream English (SAME), what that means
in theory is that the following sequence will take place:

1. I describe the widget or the service to you, accurately and
   honestly.
2. I agree to a price for the widget or service—a price that
   covers my cost of business (including fair treatment for any

workers and subcontractors and suppliers who may be involved) while at the same time yielding a fair profit.

3. I agree to a delivery time for the widget or service, with fair provisions made for such things as returns and refunds if the widget is damaged or the service is unsatisfactory.

4. I agree to a date by which you must pay my bill for the widget or service.

5. You agree to all of the items above.

6. We both follow through on our agreements, fully and honestly.

That's the theory. The *practice* deviates from that ideal so wildly that the theory can more accurately be called a fantasy. In practice, with rare exceptions, those on both sides of the transaction will have *maximum profit* as their goal and will do everything they can conceivably get away with to fudge on the terms of the agreement while still insisting that they're fulfilling it. That's how business (except Internet business—a topic we'll take up later in this chapter) is carried on in the United States today. That is "how the game is played," and profit is "how you keep score."

Don't be misled by the word "game"; we're not talking about "Ring Around the Rosy" here. Americans take games very seriously indeed. To bring that point forcefully home, you need only compare the annual salaries paid to our professional athletes with those paid to our professionals in education, law enforcement, and health care. Football, in particular, can be looked upon as almost a religion in the United States.

The core metaphor for business in the United States today is a curious meld of the two metaphors BUSINESS IS FOOTBALL and BUSINESS IS COMBAT; individual businesses will differ in how much they lean toward one or the other of the combined metaphors. What makes the combat also a *game* is the fact that business is a form of combat in which people not only aren't encouraged and rewarded for killing or injuring others, but are forbidden by law to do so. The American tobacco industry's disastrous problems in the late 1990s are a perfect example of what can happen when those in charge of a business lose track of that fact and begin following the specifications for a battlefield instead of those for a football field.

English is a superb medium for carrying out business as combat-with-limiting-rules. It's a superb medium for appearing to be following the rules while at the same time subverting them, the way a football player will pretend not to have the ball while at the same time running with it.

English (and especially SAME) offers its speakers and writers a varied assortment of mechanisms—linguistic tools—for this purpose. We're going to take a look at seven of the most common and productive ones. Not because this is a book about Standard American Mainstream English, but because SAME is so overwhelmingly the *international* language of business. There are signs that this may be starting to change at the very highest levels of global business, with some major firms beginning to demand multilingualism as a qualification for hiring top executives. But this trend is new, and it flies in the face of United States tradition; even if it becomes the norm, it will take a long time for it to develop and spread through our business culture. The standard situation today and for the immediate future continues to be one in which the SAME-speaking American businesspeople know only English, while the foreign businesspeople they're interacting with use English as a second language.

This is a source of serious problems. As you well know, the fact that two people from different cultures or subcultures are speaking the same words in no way guarantees that they're expressing the same meanings with those words. Even when the foreign speaker's English is extremely fluent, the appearance of a shared meaning can be an illusion; this becomes even more likely when the foreign English wasn't learned in the United States or from American English instructors. As Susanne Niemeier points out, the English used in such situations is influenced by the speakers' mother tongues in ways far more important than just pronunciation and "accent":

> Their nonverbal behavior, for example, does not automatically switch to an "Englishized" nonverbal behavior. . . . Thus, when they think the negotiation partner should have understood the (verbal and nonver-

bal) signs they are using, misunderstandings still occur because some signs may be differently encoded—and decoded—in the other's culture or may not be noticed to be signs at all. (Niemeier et al. 1998, page 2)

There are now many Englishes, from all over the world, each one strongly influenced by the native language and culture from which it comes. *They are not the same language.* (For more details, see Chapter 7.) And this isn't just a "vocabulary problem," something that could be fixed if people would only learn more words and phrases.

The number of language-related potential problem areas for international business is so large that no one book (let alone one chapter in one book) could possibly explore them all; we'd need many shelves of books. The potential problem areas include at least these five, which we'll be discussing in this chapter:

- Different understandings of time and of space
- Different positions on what's right and what's wrong
- Different definitions for the key vocabularies of various semantic domains
- Different requirements for making information explicit
- Different dominant cultural metaphors

Why American English Is Such a Good Language for Business

Any semantic unit whatsoever can be expressed in any language whatsoever. We see this demonstrated whenever people say that a word or phrase "can't be translated into (some language)" and follow that up by explaining what the allegedly untranslatable word or phrase *means*. What *they* mean (as they would acknowledge if they were speaking more carefully) is that the word or phrase represents a lexical gap with no *simple and convenient* equivalent in the language, not that it actually can't be translated.

For example, there is a Navajo verb *(ilhk'ááá)* that can be translated as "taking a newborn animal that has been rejected by its mother because some human being was so careless and clumsy as to touch it with hands that had also and very recently touched some malodorous substance like bacon fat or grease or some such thing and putting that newborn animal to the teats of a different mother animal in the hope that the second animal will accept it." Certainly I can translate that into English; I've just proved that, although the translation is rough because I left out many details that would have exhausted the English-speaking reader's patience if I'd included them. However, if I wanted to translate into English a poem in Navajo whose first line was "At dawn I (some form of *ilhk'ááá*)," I would be facing a formidable stylistic challenge.

This linguistic comfort factor—what parts of reality a language makes it either easy or difficult for people to talk about—is one of the most significant ways in which languages differ. It's not likely that business documents and conversation are going to require much use either of forms of *ilhk'ááá* or their English translations. But there are similar, though less extreme, examples that are much more common. The Navajo names for things like car parts and hand tools tend to be so complicated and lengthy that many Navajo speakers feel obliged to use the English names instead, at least in business contexts. This is why, when listening to commercials for auto repair shops and car dealers on Navajo radio in the American Southwest, you hear a stream of Navajo punctuated by the English words "pliers" and "wrenches" and "mufflers" and "catalytic converters" and so on. It's not that Navajo doesn't allow speakers to discuss car parts with Navajo words; it does. But discussing them in a language which names such items as "that with which such-and-such-a-thing is done in such-and-such-a-fashion" takes a lot of time and patience. When you're doing radio commercials, which are charged for by the *second*, it won't be easy to work those Navajo terms in and still convince your advertisers that they're getting good value for their money. This isn't a matter of style or of translation skills; it's a matter of the bottom line.

It happens that English makes *business discourse*—that is, the language phenomena that go with buying and selling, and matters related to buying and selling—both easy and quick. To get through my explanation of why that's so, without tangling us up in a thicket of linguistics jargon and Academic Regalian, I need to introduce one term that may be unfamiliar to you: *nominal.* As follows:

> A nominal is a noun (or any item that can do everything a noun can do) *plus* whatever language chunks go with it.

A typical English sentence will have a verb, plus one or more nominals that fill roles for the verb. For example: "The linguist recited nine boring grammar rules" has "recited" as its verb, plus two nominals, "the linguist" and "nine boring grammar rules." "The linguist" fills the role of *that-which-does-the-reciting;* "nine boring grammar rules" fills the role of *that-which-is-recited;* the verb tells us what action is involved, that it took place in the past, and that it's over with. Every sentence with a verb, in any human language, can be thought of as potentially including a whole set of nominals, along these general lines:

> Somebody does something, perhaps *to* someone or something, perhaps *for* someone, perhaps along *with* someone, at or during some time, in some location, in some manner, perhaps along some path in time or space, for some reason or purpose, perhaps using some instrument.

How many of those potential "somes" (and more) are actually spoken or written down, and how many appear not as indefinites but with explicit details, will depend on the rules of the language, the context, and the speaker's needs and intentions.

In scholarly literature on this subject the terms ordinarily used (taken from mathematics and logic) are "predicate" and "argument"; nominals are the arguments of the predicate. It *might* be possible to make these matters more difficult to talk about, but you'd have to work at it. This traditional terminology is much less efficient for ordinary communication than the Navajo names for car parts are, and I'll have nothing further to say about it.

With that established, we can go on to look at the set of characteristics that make English the businessperson's best current medium for business discourse, both spoken and written and—as in much electronic discourse—in between.

The English Advantage

1. English offers not only the option of moving nominals in and and out of the spotlight but the option of making them disappear altogether.

Suppose you know that one of Metamega Oil Company's tankers spilled a substantial amount of oil in Lake Erie today. You could say so, with a batch of nominals specifying that the spilling was done quickly and carelessly and as a result of the skipper's bad judgment; you could name the skipper while you were at it. You could focus sharply on the guilty, saying, "It was Tom Smith, skipper of Metamega Oil Company's tanker *Scrambled Star,* who spilled oil in Lake Erie today." Many alternatives are available to you. But it's also perfectly acceptable for you to simply say, "Oil was spilled in Lake Erie today."

This last tactic puts the spotlight on the oil, as if it had created the mess all by itself. We do know that someone or something did the spilling, because that's presupposed by "oil was spilled," but English doesn't require us to make it clear; we can delete the spiller from the surface shape of the sentence completely. Similarly, we can say, "Mistakes were made" and "Flaws were overlooked," and "Funds were accidentally misappropriated," a strategy that Dorothy and Joseph Winters have named the "Passive Exonerative." (I am beholden to linguist Geoffrey S. Nathan, the Winters' son-in-law, for this elegant and apt label, which is used with the Winters' kind permission.)

This is extremely convenient, as demonstrated by the following classic example:

An accident has occurred at the Chernobyl nuclear power plant as one of the reactors was damaged. Measures are being undertaken to elimi-

nate the consequences of this accident. Aid is being given to those affected. A government commission has been set up. (The Soviet press
agency Tass, quoted in the *New York Times* for April 29, 1986)

This tactic isn't unique to English; all languages, it seems, allow it.
Linguistic universals—that is, items that can reasonably be assumed
to be present in every human language, such as vowels or nominals
or a way of making things plural—are an important concern in linguistics. (Linguists propose them with great caution, because they
are proposals about what qualifies *as* a human language.) I spent
quite a while going to linguists all over the world for help in finding
out how universal this phenomenon of "making the responsible
nominals disappear" might be. So far as I have been able to determine, there is *no* human language in which it is literally impossible
to do this. No language exists in which speakers would be violating a
grammar rule if they didn't openly identify the "spiller of the oil."
Some languages do it with passive sequences such as "Oil was
spilled"; some do it by constructing sentences that would translate as
"Somebody spilled oil" or "One spilled oil" or "They-unidentified
spilled oil"; many do it with sequences that translate *literally* as "Oil
spilled itself." However, English is extremely tolerant of this sort of
thing, and the "Oil was spilled" tactic is only one of a number of possibilities it offers for hiding or eliminating nominals.

2. English lets you easily and efficiently hide information away in
presuppositions and stacks of presuppositions.

Suppose my company has just put a new brand of laundry soap on
the market. Chances are, it's much like all the other laundry soaps already available. If I want to say that our new soap is "technology-enhanced" (whatever that might mean), I'm *claiming* that that's so, and
I'm likely to be asked for evidence. However, in English things that
are owned are *presupposed* to exist. A sentence like "My black leather
briefcase with the fancy zipper does not exist" would strike a native
speaker of English as very strange, and could be used only in special
contexts. (We can't say it could *never* be used, because you can always put together a sentence like "[X] is not a grammatical sequence
of English.") This means that I can use a possessive word or phrase

to presuppose that the soap is technology-enhanced and then finish my sentence with some claim too trivial to inspire argument. Like this:

My company's new technology-enhanced soap is now available in stores all over the country.

Or

Our new technology-enhanced soap is now on the shelves in stores from coast to coast.

I don't have to stop there. I can stack the presuppositions up as high as I feel a listener or reader will let me. Each presupposed item will turn what would have been an open claim on my part into information that I can reasonably expect you—linguistically speaking—to take for granted. Like this:

Our new and innovative scientifically designed technology-enhanced soap is now available in stores all over the country.

This doesn't guarantee that no listener will challenge me with a demand for an explanation of "technology-enhanced" or "scientifically designed"; it might happen. But it's not nearly as likely as it would be if I just made my claims straight out, especially if my sentence is in the middle of a speech or other presentation. When my listener is someone from a culture that disapproves of such challenges, they're even more unlikely; if the other person is reading my words rather than hearing them, and I'm not present, no convenient opportunity for a challenge exists.

3. English doesn't require you to specify the *source* of the information you put in your sentences.

There are languages—Aymara is one—in which every sentence has to include a chunk stating what it is that makes you feel justified in saying what you're saying or writing what you're writing. These languages have sets of forms (often called "evidentials") for specifying the source of information. Evidentials include such things as having perceived something with your own senses, having learned it from a source you consider trustworthy, having made it up yourself from scratch, having seen it in a dream, and so on; which members of the potential complete set occur will vary from language to language. In the same way that English sentences are ungrammatical without some chunk that tells you whether the action or state was or was not in the past, Aymara sentences are ungrammatical without an evidential either explicitly present or made clear by surrounding sentences. Aymara speakers could of course be lying about their sources of evidence, but they have to do so right up front. They can't lie in the far more convenient English fashion.

Imagine what would happen in American business if statements like "This is the best insurance policy on the market" or "We know you're going to be glad that you bought this automobile" were ungrammatical without an evidential. Imagine what it would be like if the absence of an evidential in an English sentence was automatically taken as evidence that you were trying to deceive or mislead. It wouldn't make business discourse impossible, but it would make it vastly more complicated, and would require radical changes in the way we do business in America.

4. English has an enormous vocabulary—hundreds of thousands of words—with an abundance of items that are either opaque or so nearly meaningless that they can be made to mean whatever the user wants them to mean. (Like the word "interesting.")

In some languages you can look at most words and figure out their meanings from the meanings of their *morphemes*—their meaningful parts. This is much rarer in English, where the jargons and registers of fields and subfields are often meaningless even to other native speakers of English. If you choose a word or phrase of English and then realize that it's uncomfortably narrow and precise, so that it might box you into a business commitment before you're ready, you can almost always find a number of other lexical items to use instead. As Gerald Parshall says, "What makes English mammoth and unique is its great sea of synonyms, words with roughly the same meaning but different connotations, different levels of formality and different effects on the ear." (Parshall 1995, page 48)

It's easy in English to talk at great length, and in a way that sounds serious and significant, while saying almost nothing; this is one of the basic skills learned by everyone who gets a Ph.D. from an American university. Suppose I am presenting a seminar, and the participants are giving me a hard time by refusing to ask questions when I offer them opportunity. They may think that this will make the seminar shorter or force me to stop talking about my topic and start telling jokes to fill the time. They are wrong. I have a Ph.D. from the University of California–San Diego's linguistics department; I am highly trained in the technique of saying things like this:

> Today's topic, when subjected to primary effects of interrelated and synergistic demographic parameters, offers us greater scope than would be provided by mere humanistic rubrics in a similar context.

So far as I know, that sentence is for all practical purposes meaningless, but I can use the lexical abundance of English to go on like that for hours. Many of the world's languages offer their speakers no such luxury.

5. English has an extraordinary willingness to *add* to its vocabulary, not only by coining new lexical items but by borrowing them from any and all other languages. In addition, it expands its vocabulary by using nouns as verbs, and verbs and adjectives as nouns, at the drop of a hat.

We've already seen that a willingness to add words from other languages is by no means a universal characteristic; many nations look upon borrowed words and phrases as a contamination of the native tongue. English has no such barrier, despite the frantic and dogged efforts of purists.

6. English has a writing system that contains almost no information about the tune the words are set to, so that a written agreement can easily be stripped of every last bit of the emotional information that would be present in a verbal agreement.

Most of the *emotional* information is carried in English not by the words that are said but by the intonation (including tone of voice) that creates the tune the words are set to. As a result, speakers of English can easily say a single utterance with many different emotional meanings, including one that *contradicts* its "dictionary meaning." A standard exercise in beginning drama courses is to give the students some random word like "goldfish" and instruct them to say that word in such a way that it conveys rage, then lust, then terror, then tenderness, and so on down a long list of emotions. English allows that all to be done by intonation, while many other languages would have to add words or pieces of words—with specific emotional meanings—to accomplish the same thing.

This has the obvious drawback of letting verbally abusive people get away with their unpleasant language behavior by saying, "But all I *said* was . . ." and following that up with the words they did in fact say, but set to an entirely different tune. William Labov and David Fanshel are all for this feature of English:

> In our view, the lack of clarity or discreteness in the intonational signals is not an unfortunate limitation of this channel, but an essential and important part of it. Speakers need a form of communication that is *deniable*. It is advantageous for them to express hostility, challenge the competence of others, or express friendliness and affection in a way that can be denied if they are explicitly held to account for it. (Labov and Fanshel 1977, page 46)

Well, yes, it certainly is advantageous, provided you are "winning" in the business transaction. And that is how the game is played.

It may be that everyone who was present in a meeting to negotiate a contract has understood that members of the negotiation teams were furious or suspicious, or were agreeing only with great reluctance. Nothing in the English writing system requires information of that kind to appear in the contract or other document that comes out of the session. This is a case in which it's true that "you had to be there"; otherwise, you may be entirely in the dark about the participants' feelings.

7. English appears largely free of special discourse restrictions that would make business discourse tricky and difficult.

Japanese has a constraint that goes something like this: "Do everything you possibly can linguistically to make sure that no one ever has to say no to a request." Japanese has built-in mechanisms for indicating the rank and status of everyone present in an interaction, mechanisms that can't be left out of the sentence. Chinese has a constraint which says that you must do everything possible linguistically not to make awkward developments explicit—because once they're explicit, something has to be done about them. English has no such inconvenient features; it no longer has even the distinction between a formal "you" and an intimate one, like the French *vous* and *tu*.

Kyoko Mori (quoted in the November 3, 1997, *Publishers Weekly*) says that she doesn't like to speak Japanese because "you have to agree on . . . which one of you is superior, how close you expect to be . . . and who defers." Respondent Atsushi Furuiye (Japanese/English) writes that "English is better than Japanese when negotiating MONEY. . . . Japanese with its complicated ways to speak according to social seniority/inferiority is sometimes a pain." Respondent Fran Stallings (English/Japanese) explains that Japanese has "honorific syllables which can be inserted before and/or after a general word to elevate its status. . . . And there are whole separate sets of vocabulary (nouns and verbs) to be used for different levels of status." Chinese has a number of different words meaning "no," each carrying with it various nuances of meaning about the intensity and finality—the true "no-ness"—of the "no" in question.

Speakers of languages that make heavy use of devices like these can feel linguistically naked when speaking English. They may react to that discomfort by trying to find English substitutes—thus often leading monolingual English speakers to perceive them as either absurdly and excessively polite or as *faking* politeness. This perception then colors the English monolinguals' judgments negatively and interferes with business.

The seven characteristics of English discussed above (and others not mentioned here) work together *synergistically*—so that the combined effect is greater than the sum of the parts. Perhaps the most useful aspect of that effect for business is to establish and maintain that quality of deniability we've been discussing. ("Who, ME? Me, carrying the BALL? What makes you think THAT?") *English is supremely deniable.* This is not the only reason it has become the obligatory language of world business (there is, for example, the extremely important fact that English uses a writing system easily handled by keyboards), but it certainly hasn't held it back.

As long as business transactions are carried on between consenting adults who are all native speakers of Standard American Mainstream English, the results of all this are acceptable. But what happens when other languages (including other Englishes) are involved? When non-native speakers of English are involved? When the communication takes place on the Internet, where English dominance is so extreme that the four other most common languages (German, Japanese, French, and Spanish) *combined* are only used about 10 percent of the time? Then what?

Some of the things that happen in these situations are amazing; they lend support to the idea that we human beings all speak dialects of Terran. Here is an actual telephone conversation (recorded by Alan Firth and reported in Newman 1995) between an Egyptian cheese importer and a Danish cheese exporter whose only language in common for business is English:

IMPORTER: So I told him not to send the cheese after the
    blowing in customs.
EXPORTER: I see, yes.
IMPORTER: So I don't know what we can do with the order now.
EXPORTER: I'm not, er, blowing, er, what, er, what is this, er, too
    big or what?
IMPORTER: No, the cheese is bad. It is, like, fermenting in the
    customs cool rooms.
EXPORTER: Ah! It's gone off.
IMPORTER: Yes, it's gone off.

What's striking here (and what fascinates linguist Firth) is the way meaning is *negotiated* on the spot for business purposes, while the two businessmen are talking. "First, the Dane acts as if he understands 'blowing.' Only when his sale seems at risk does he demand a definition. Then he provides a definition of his own, and the Egyptian acts as if he knew what 'gone off' meant all along."

English, the article tells us, "follows markets," resulting in a batch of special-purpose "Englishes" (more accurately, English registers) that we could call Oilglish and Cheeseglish and StockandBondglish and Hackerglish—and so on

This is an extremely complicated issue. Its parts are tangled up together, and they interact in complicated ways. In Chapter 7 we'll return to the topic of English as an international language. For now, in order to arrive at a rough understanding of the situation, let's briefly consider a few of the organizing factors.

The Language of Time

Business depends on time. We have a metaphor for that in English: TIME IS MONEY. The standard pattern for SAME-speakers specifies that when businesspeople agree to meet from 2:00 P.M. until 4:00 P.M., it means that none of them will arrive later than 2:05 without a *really* good excuse such as a major traffic jam, a flat tire, or an injured child. It means that everyone will feel obligated to stay until at least 4:00 P.M. unless a similarly good excuse for leaving is available or the group agrees that all the business that can be done that day has been completed. It means that there will be a list of tasks (the *agenda*) to be accomplished during the meeting, usually in a specific order; it means that one thing will be done at a time, and each one will be made as complete as is possible before anything else is started. Any changes in these constraints have to be negotiated, and English has standard scripts for getting that done. The concepts of arriving and leaving and beginning and finishing "on time," and keeping to the schedule so that everything is done "on time," have clearly understood meanings.

However, when someone from another culture or subculture agrees to do all these things and uses phrases such as "on time" to express that agreement, it's not safe to assume that a shared meaning for "on time" exists between you and that person. We've all heard talk about cultures and subcultures where "nothing ever gets done on time"—a description that has a strongly negative meaning for SAME speakers, with major effects on such real-world decisions as where investments are made, where factories and other workplaces are built, and which people are hired to do which work. SAME speakers perceive those about whom they can say that "nothing ever gets done on time" in a way that involves attaching all kinds of negative labels such as "lazy" and "unreliable," and worse.

This is an example of the power of language, not the power of fact. It's not ordinarily the case that people from the other culture care nothing about being "on time"; rather, "on time" has a different meaning for them. When doing business in Peru, according to respondent M. J. Hardman, you specify "whether something is *hora peruana* or *hora inglesa*. The latter will be closer to the specified time; the former is likely to be a half-hour to two hours later." The accepted importance of "making the most of your time" by doing only one thing at a time (including the idea that only one person should *speak* at a time), and by finishing every item on the agenda if possible, varies from culture to culture. As does the idea that everyone in a meeting will do their best to "save time" by moving everything along as quickly as possible. Charles Dubow, in an article about doing business in Russia, writes that Russians "regard business meetings as a cross between an interrogation and a tea party. . . . Over the course of a meeting that can drag on for several hours, *nothing may be accomplished*" (Dubow 1998, page 143). Why? Because Russian businesspeople "will win by doing nothing longer than you are willing to wait." It's not safe to leap to the conclusion that the Russian behavior represents what we call "stalling" in English. It's simply an example of a business strategy that differs from the standard American form and reflects a difference in the way time is perceived and understood. Dubow is trying to explain behavior based on Russian-language presuppositions by writing about it in terms based on English-language presuppositions; the result, inevitably, is a distortion of meaning.

The best account of different perceptions about the meaning of time is still found in the excellent books written by Edward T. Hall, who coined the terms "monochronic time" (only one thing is done at a time) and "polychronic time" (two or more things are done at the same time). Hall writes of cultures whose time concepts differ so radically from those of SAME speakers that conducting joint business activities is almost impossible.

The monolingual mainstream American businessperson is likely to believe that a simple solution exists for this dilemma; I've heard it explained many times. All you do, he or she will tell you, is sit down with the others involved in the business interaction and explain what "on time" means in English and why it's necessary to understand "on time" that way, and then include in the terms of your agreement an acceptance of that version of "on time."

This is naive in the extreme. It relies on the idea that you can assume that your listeners will take what you say on such an occasion *seriously.* If you are that businessperson, you feel safe making that assumption because the others will see that you're "spending precious time" talking about always being "on time," and because your brief monologue on the subject is one of the tasks "on today's agenda" and therefore something to begin and carry out and finish, *on time.* But you're forgetting something: These concepts aren't parts of concrete physical reality like rocks and desks; rather, they are parts of your Standard American Mainstream English grammar, built into your worldview by the meanings of the words and phrases of SAME. The end result is all too often going to be that you will later claim that you were "wasting precious time" when you gave your talk and that the other people involved can't be trusted because they don't keep their agreements.

Hard as many find it to believe, from the point of view built into the others' native language three things have happened: You have explained that you expect everything to be done "on time"; they have agreed to do that; and that's what they're *doing.* Even if they consistently arrive hours (or days) after the scheduled starting hour, shift back and forth from one task to another in a way that seems to you to be random, and leave whenever they feel like it.

In *The Trembling Mountain* (Robert Klitzman's fascinating account of his investigation of the disease *kuru* among the Fore people of New Guinea), sentences such as "We agreed to leave at 7:00, but he didn't arrive until 9:30" and "We agreed to leave on Monday but no one turned up until Wednesday" come along every page or two. This difference in attitudes about time isn't caused by a lack of moral character; it's a problem of language. That makes it no less maddening to the SAME-speaking employer or supervisor!

There are cultures in which no project can begin until everyone is perceived as thinking the right thoughts. Hall describes that phenomenon in a Native American culture, and points out what it would mean for American business affairs if it were widespread: "We could no longer schedule everything in advance because no one would be able to tell how long it would take to have the 'right thoughts'" (Hall 1984, page 189).

One of the things I was sometimes called on to do as a college professor was to go to a classroom where courses in a Native American language were being taught and tell the instructors that the class had to leave the room. The instructors would tell me that they couldn't do that because they weren't yet through with the lesson. "There is still more to learn," they would say, and I'm sure that was true. I would explain that even so, there was another class waiting in the hall to come in and that the classroom time and space were now theirs. And the instructors would look at me and say, *"Have they no manners?"* The SAME perception of "manners" means making certain that everyone can follow a single agreed-upon schedule and make the most efficient use of time in that sense; the Native American instructors were equally concerned about good manners, but they defined them differently.

A primary goal of education for assimilation in the United States is that immigrants will do more than just *understand*, intellectually, the meaning of the vocabulary used in the Standard American Mainstream English semantic domain of Time. The goal is that they will also *internalize* that meaning and accept it as "the way things really are," along with TIME IS MONEY and MONEY IS HOW YOU KEEP SCORE. So that it won't be necessary to explain and negotiate every smallest detail of every transaction in terms of time, because they will be able to use the basic principles of SAME time to predict the guidelines for acceptable behavior in every business situation.

Serious and justifiable concern exists about the question of whether—if education is conducted in the native language or dialect rather than in English—that internalization can happen "in time" for the person to become a self-supporting member of U.S. society who contributes to the economy in the way that all good citizens are expected to contribute. This is the kind of concern that underlies the behavior of the immigrant parent who, hearing the kids speaking their native language, asks, "What's the *matter* with you? You want to end up spending your whole life on *welfare?*"

The introduction of the computer as an obligatory feature of American business is causing some drastic changes in the perception of time, with potentially dramatic consequences. We'll come back to that later in this chapter.

The Language of Information

The term "presupposition" is used in different ways in different fields; even within linguistics, people argue about its precise definition. In this book we're using it to refer to information that every native speaker of a language knows is part of the meaning of some unit of that language even when it's not explicit in the unit's surface shape. Like the fact that "John *stopped* reading the book" presupposes "John *started* reading the book." In business, presuppositions are straightforward bottom-line issues: *For every negotiation or transaction, decisions must be made about what other people have to be told and what you can take it granted that they already know.* Decisions such as the amount of resources you have to put into training employees, and the amount of resources you have to put into meetings and business-related social events, depend crucially on this factor. Everything that you can presuppose in business will save you precious resources of time, money, and energy.

Edward T. Hall talks about presuppositions in terms of *context*, dividing cultures and subcultures into those he calls "high-context," in which people routinely assume that other adults already know a great deal, and "low-context," in which people assume that others know far less and have to be told a great deal more. "To give people information they do not need is to ' talk down' to them; not to give them enough information is to mystify them" (Hall 1984, page 61). Germany is a low-context society; Mexico and Japan are high-context. SAME-speaking American society falls between these extremes, less low-context than Germany and less high-context than Mexico and Japan. Only in monolingual single-culture business interactions is it reasonable to assume that everyone involved will roughly agree on what is presupposed and what must be explained. Beyond that sheltered circumstance, mistakes can be extremely expensive and bad for business.

When I was working with Native American languages, I would sometimes go to my Indian consultants' homes for work sessions lasting for hours. It was thirsty work, but I was never offered anything to drink, and I stayed thirsty. It wasn't until both I and my consultants had spent months of thirsty hours together that I finally learned what was going on. They took it as *presupposed* that I didn't want anything to drink, although they found it strange. I was an adult, and adults know that when they're thirsty they're expected to go help themselves to whatever is available. To ask me, "Would you like something to drink?" would have been rude; it would have been treating me like a child. On the other hand, it would have been rude for them to get drinks for themselves when their *guest* wasn't thirsty—this is something else that "everyone knows." Matters were made worse by the politeness constraints of my own subculture—Ozark, and southern—which obliged me to say nothing, month after month, no matter how odd the whole thing seemed to *me*. In a social situation a communication breakdown of this kind is usually only annoying; in business, it can be catastrophic.

Suppose I meet with you and tell you about a new clause that has been added to the contract I have with you; suppose I end my remarks with "Is that all right?" and you say yes, in English. Do we then have an agreement? *It depends.* For me, English "yes" means that you agree. Responding to your "yes" with "Does yes mean that you'll do it?" would be not only an unnecessary utterance but a hostile one; I would be treating you as if you were a child or had some other impediment to doing adult business competently. But if in your culture it's rude to answer a direct question or a request with "no," your "yes" may mean "I'll think it over and get back to you with a decision." It may even mean "Absolutely not." And why am I not justified in insisting that you say exactly and explicitly what you mean? Because we're both adults and you expect to be able to trust me to understand things that are known to every adult! *How can we do business together, otherwise?*

It will be obvious that no decision you can make in international business will be as important as the way you word every token of language used to transmit and explain your decisions, ask your questions, and respond to the language of others; in speech, the body language you use to accompany your words will also be crucial, especially if you are speaking American English.

The Language of Right and Wrong

When you're doing business with people from a nation that's not yet industrialized, you will be prepared to run into major ethical and moral differences. The Fore people that Robert Klitzman hired and worked with came from a culture many of whose members considered a ritual form of cannibalism both moral and ethical. Because it was cannibalism that transmitted the disease he was investigating, this was a factor he couldn't ignore; he had to face it and take it into account daily. When you're dealing with people from an industrialized culture, however—even though their native language is not English—you not only feel confident that they disapprove of all forms of cannibalism, you're likely to assume that they share your understanding of terms such as "being fair," "telling lies," "cheating," "fulfilling obligations," "being in debt," "being loyal," "stealing others' property," and many more of the same kind. You feel no need to ask them if they think it's okay to cheat in a contract negotiation, just as you feel no need to ask them explicity whether they think cannibalism is a moral act, and for the same reasons.

Unfortunately, your assumptions (with the exception of assumptions about cannibalism) aren't safe, not even when every aspect of the business transaction takes place in English. Anthony Judge, writing on the Web site of the Union of International Associations, advises that where written agreements are concerned we need to divide cultures into three groups: those in which signed written agreements are automatically enforced; those in which such agreements may or may not be enforced, "according to circumstances and political convenience"; and those in which such agreements are looked upon only as public relations gestures, with intentions about enforcement not even being relevant (Judge 1994, page 4).

Even between subcultures within the United States that *do* have English as a shared native tongue, assumptions about shared presuppositions on key moral and ethical terminology aren't safe. When an additional language is involved, taking such shared meanings for granted is a genuinely foolish move. The question is of course what to do about this problem. Nobody wants to do business with people whose actions baffle you, whom you don't feel that you can trust, and whom you may have good reason to believe feel exactly the same way about *you*.

You can read stacks of books like Scott Seligman's *Dealing with the Chinese* and Haru Yamada's *Different Games, Different Rules: Why Americans and Japanese Misunderstand Each Other*. You can read masses of articles from the professional literature of international business and management and diplomacy. You can spend many hours asking native speakers of the other language friendly, probing questions. You can take seminars galore on doing business with "the French" or "the South Africans" or "the Europeans." You can spend weeks exploring the many sites on the Internet that are devoted to these matters. You can do all these things—and *still* go into an international business interaction ignorant of the half dozen items it's most critical for you to know about the moral and ethical positions of your opposite numbers. Why? Because human beings, no matter what language they speak, tend not to be *consciously* aware of such things, and information that's not in conscious awareness is very hard to get at.

You'll remember my account in Chapter 3 of the decades-long misunderstanding I had about people and their television sets. I assure you, if I had asked those people bluntly, "Why do you leave your TV set on while we're trying to talk?"—something my southern Ozark culture wouldn't allow me to do—there's almost no chance that they would have looked at me in surprise and said, "Why, we do it because our TV set is today's equivalent of the hearth fire in homes of the past!" They would have been embarrassed and baffled; they would have said something like, "We just always *do* leave it turned on. Don't you?" And things would probably have gone downhill from there. We don't have easy access to that sort of information about ourselves unless someone has made it explicit for us, as I've done in this book. If we did, there'd be no need for psychiatrists and psychotherapists.

My personal recommendation is that whenever you do business across two or more cultures or subcultures, you should always hunt for the one piece of information most likely to reward you with the answers you need: *the dominant metaphor or metaphors that the people involved in your interaction rely on when doing business.*

If you ask an honest American businessman whether he believes that it's all right to lie, he'll say no. If you ask him whether it's all right for a football player to pretend he has the ball when he doesn't have it, he'll say yes. If you ask him whether it's all right to inflate sales figures just a little to impress a potential client, he'll say yes. If you suggest that the second and third answers contradict his first answer, he'll tell you that "they're not the same thing."

A visiting anthropologist from Mars might try to figure this out by making long lists of acts that the businessman does or doesn't consider to be lying. Human businesspeople don't have time for that. Suppose that they know, however, that the man's dominant business metaphor, through which his perceptions in a business environment are filtered, is BUSINESS IS FOOTBALL. In a football game it's not a lie to pretend you have the ball when you don't have it, or to pretend that you're going to run in one direction when you're actually going to run the opposite way. It *is* lying, in a football game, to dress up in the uniform of the other team. Knowing that business for this American is like football will let you *predict* the meanings he will assign to all those key terms listed on page 121 and many more, without having to memorize each one individually.

In *Understanding Global Cultures*, Martin J. Gannon devotes sixteen pages to explaining that the metaphor of the family altar has the same status for the Chinese that the football metaphor has for mainstream Americans, and outlining the effects of that metaphor on business transactions. My Chinese questionnaire respondents don't all agree on the accuracy of this idea, just as some SAME speakers would quibble over the football game metaphor if asked directly. But it's a place to start and something to investigate, and it's overwhelmingly obvious that interpreting moral and ethical terms in the context of a football game or football season will be radically different from interpreting them in the context of a family altar. It's also obvious that when an American businessman's dominant operative metaphor doesn't seem to be football, it is far more likely to be basketball or chess than it is to be a family altar.

Gannon's suggested metaphor for Japan is the formal Japanese garden, but he cautions that this means not an *absence* of conflict but conflict managed according to very specific rules and with attention to maintaining a *surface impression* of calm and control. In an interview in *Forbes ASAP* (Karlgaard 1993, page 73), a Fujitsu executive is quoted as follows: "You Americans think there is room for everybody in the market. We in Japan think that our competitors are taking rice out of our children's mouths. We think that anything less than 100-percent market share is not enough. We believe in Genghis Khan's dictum: not sufficient to succeed—everyone else must fail." By contrast, when Karen Mitchell discusses Haru Yamada's *Different Games, Different Rules* (Mitchell 1998), she explains that although both English and Japanese use Aesop's fable about the ants and the grasshopper, they end it quite differently. In America the fable ends with "the ants scorning the foolhardy grasshopper"; in the Japanese version "the ants invite the grasshopper in to share their winter meal, as they appreciate how his singing spurred them on during their summer labors." It would be more useful to investigate how these two seemingly contradictory attitudes fit together, in the

Japanese business domain structured by the garden metaphor, than to memorize a list of "tips and hints" for doing business with the Japanese.

Finally, as is true with perceptions of time, doing business successfully will be impossible if speakers of one language constantly leap to the conclusion that differences result from *deficiencies* in speakers of other languages. The first hypothesis should always be that the problem is not in the person but in the language, in which case language offers the only valid solution.

The Language of the Internet

Ten years ago this heading probably wouldn't even have appeared in a discussion of the power of language for business. Today it's obligatory. Selling automobiles and computers and videotapes on the Web may be much like selling them in a physical dealer's place of business, but selling what we now call "intellectual property" on-line is radically different. As Esther Dyson says:

> We are entering a new economic environment—as different as the moon is from the earth—where a new set of physical rules will govern what intellectual property means, how opportunities are created from it, who prospers, and who loses. Chief among the new rules is that "content is free." While not all content will be free, the new economic dynamic will operate as if it were. . . . The provider's vital task is to figure out what to charge for and what to give away. (Dyson 1995, page 137)

Content is *free?* What to charge for and what to *give away?* (The prototype example to clarify this is the standard practice of giving away a computer software program free but charging customers a fee for updates and for each time they need help using the program.) This, together with the idea that score is kept in terms of *hits* (number of visits to your Internet location, whether any business is transacted during the visit or not), and that your company and its entire plant can be totally "virtual"—existing inside your computer, with no fixed physical location in either time or space—is causing cognitive headaches for businesspeople on a massive scale. The older the businessperson, by and large, the more frequent and severe the cognitive dissonance is. The limits to resources on the Net, Dyson says, are not limits on time and space, but limits on the amount and degree of human *attention*. "Does a place in cyberspace exist," she asks, "if no one visits it?"

Past attempts to establish an international language, much less an associated international culture, have always failed, but the Internet shows signs of doing what no amount of effort along those lines has ever been able to do before. The language of the Internet is truly an international language, and it *looks* like written English. But it's not the same English that we're used to, it's *Netglish*, and its presuppositions are different. Questions such as "Where is your company located?" and "How long will it take everyone to get to the meeting?" and "How much does your widget cost?" and "How large were your profits last year?"—questions that are the heart and soul of off-line business—are often irrelevant for this new variety of English.

There was a brief period when it looked as if Netglish might establish one feature that would put a small dent in the deniability of written English. This feature was the *emoticon*, a little graphic squiggle that people used in an effort to give a surface shape to meaning that in speech is carried by body language. For example:

"I'm smiling as I write this."	:–)
"I'm frowning as I write this."	:–(
"I'm very sad as I write this."	:–C

The Japanese found the sideways orientation of the emoticons perplexing, and worked up their own versions. "I'm smiling as I write this," for the Japanese, is written as ^_^ and has a version which identifies the smiler as "a girl," written as ^.^ (Pollack 1996).

For a while, everyone was using emoticons, and increasingly more elaborate ones. Some people began introducing them into off-line writing because they now felt linguistically "naked" without them, like Japanese and Chinese speakers without their linguistic status markers. I thought the practice might leak into ordinary written English and be taken up by people who had nothing to do with computers; if that had happened, it might have made a dent in English deniability. But emoticons seem to have been a passing fancy, and they are already disappearing from Netglish.

We're now watching the establishment of an International Internet Culture that is different from the culture of any one nation. That culture is being transmitted—*misleadingly and dangerously*—in Netglish, and huge numbers of the people actively involved in this process are people whose native language is *not* English of any variety. (There are places—virtual places—to go for help if your language is one of the half dozen or so more dominant ones. At http://babelfish.altavista.digital.com/cgi-bin/translate, the Babelfish program lets you type in the sequence of language you don't understand and gives you back a *very* rough instant translation for any of those common languages. If your only language is Farsi or Albanian, or any of thousands of other tongues, however, you're on your own.)

In Netglish, all the concepts of time and space and scheduling are suddenly changed; the idea of what the words *success* and *profit* mean are changed; the sought-after goal is not money but attention; products and services are literally given away for free; privacy has to be redefined drastically; everything is turned on its head. Whether this revolution will be allowed to take place or will be stopped in its tracks (assuming that it *can* still be stopped, which may be an absurd assumption) nobody knows.

Governments are extremely uneasy about all this, as well they should be. They don't have in place the sort of instruments of control that they have for concrete physical businesses. The U.S. government is involved in monumental efforts to do such things as stamping out the "piracy" of intellectual property and taxing the value of on-line companies' assets, not to mention charging "postage" for e-mail, to be paid to the U.S. Postal Service—as if nothing had changed and those words had the same meanings they have off the Net. Anyone with a modern computer can now be a publisher and distribute content to millions of other people who have computers; for the publishing industry, and government agencies that are involved with publishing, this has created a chaos that is almost indescribable and for which it's impossible to imagine what the final outcome will be. It looks very much like the chaos introduced into the transportation industry by the automobile. Whether this will play out the way the automobile did—with everyone having his or her own private and personal unit—or go the route of the airplane, we don't yet know. We do know that plans to hook up every elementary school in the world to the Internet are revolutionary in the way that literacy and the printing press were revolutionary.

One of the things I found most striking about my multilingual database was that many of the respondents—although they were reading questions written in English and writing lengthy answers in English—didn't list English as one of the languages that they know. It is apparently *presupposed* within the International Internet Culture that you can handle written Netglish competently; you don't have to tell anyone that you have that skill.

Case Study: Do You Work, Mrs. Jones, or Are You a Housewife?

I want to close this chapter by briefly considering one aspect of the way that perceiving the semantic domain of business through the lens of English affects our behavior, and of what might happen if that language frame were not there.

In Chapter 2 we considered the possible consequences for mainstream American culture if English, like Japanese, allowed us to define *that-which-is-aborted* as a member of the family with an ongoing family role, instead of as the "product"—a term from business, you will notice—of conception. In Chapter 3 we looked at the consequences of defining some human state—for example, menopause—as a disease. Now let's consider what might happen if Standard American Mainstream English defined the labor of housewives (and occasional househusbands) as *real* work, the way "work" is defined in business. How, and why, does English keep that from happening? Could English be used to turn the situation around?

What, if anything, might be the result of having the issue raised, even in this hypothetical fashion?

If we paid even minimum wage for hours actually worked, treating housework as real work would be out of the question, because housewives are on call twenty-four hours a day, 365 days a year. If we paid for it on the basis of "procedures" done, and "available expertise," as we pay for the work of physicians, it would be out of the question. A common figure used in courts to estimate the amount of damages due to a family for loss of a housewife's life is twelve dollars an hour—far beyond minimum wage. Let's not suggest anything so extreme (while acknowledging that the speed with which we're willing to set those alternatives aside tells us a great deal).

Suppose we just pick an arbitrary figure that reflects the status we actually *give* to housework, understanding the term to include routine pet care, child care, and elder care. Let's say we'd pay $200 a week for that work, net, after making the usual payroll deductions and filling out all the usual forms associated with those deductions. Two hundred dollars a week times fifty-two weeks comes to $10,400 a year, not much of a salary. However, multiply that by the number of households in the United States, each equipped with its own "home maker," and you'll find that the total is an enormous sum of money. And that wouldn't be the final total, by any means. If housework is real work, paid for as real work, those who do it must also be eligible for Workmen's Compensation and Social Security and unemployment benefits and all the other items that people who do real work qualify for. *We—we the people of the United States of America— can't afford this. Our economy would collapse.*

But the facts of this matter are staring us right in the face, and they can't be made to go away by any sort of logical reasoning. It is simply a *truth* that the work done in the home, largely though not exclusively by women, is work in exactly the same way that the work done in a place of business is work. That presupposes, logically, that it deserves to be paid for in exactly the same way that picking up garbage or arresting criminals or writing magazine articles or playing pro tennis deserves to be paid for. Certainly we expect to pay for it when we have to hire someone from outside the family to do it; no one expects housekeepers and nannies and chefs and gardeners and chauffeurs and nurses to volunteer their labor.

So we find ourselves in a curious linguistic situation. If housewives were slaves, we'd have no language problem, but we SAME speakers abhor slavery; we can't call them slaves. If housewives were employees or independent contractors, we'd have no language problem, but referring to them that way would wreck the economy; we can't afford to do that. We have to use English to maintain the status quo in spite of the real-world facts—and we do precisely that. The seven deniability devices discussed earlier in this chapter help greatly with that task.

Talking About Housework and Houseworkers

When Americans are asked explicitly whether they believe that the housewife's work is real work, as real as any other work, most will insist that that goes without saying. What we *do*, however, despite elaborate protestations to the contrary, is treat housework as a special type of work so low in status that people should be willing to do it for no compensation except the occasional compliment.

One of the most common terms used to refer to housework is the unambiguous "shitwork." When an Internet search for "housekeeping" or "housework" is done, one of the words that appears on the screen as a recommended addition to the search is "drudgery." An Internet search using the word "housewives" brings up—at the top of the search, where the sources considered most relevant and important appear—page after page of *pornography* sites, of a filth that turns my stomach. "Working wives" and "working mothers" are understood to deserve the label "working" only when they hold a job outside the home in addition to doing the housework. The question/answer pair, "Do you work?"/"No, I'm a housewife" and the cliché phrase "only a housewife" are sturdy linguistic perennials in English.

Look at these pairs of sentences, please, remembering that examples marked with an asterisk are unacceptable sequences:

1-a "She's one of the top lawyers in the country."
1-b * "She's one of the top housewives in the country."

2-a "Distinguished archaeologist Mary Smith will arrive shortly."

2-b * "Distinguished housewife Mary Smith will arrive shortly."

3-a "Engineer Mary Smith and her colleagues have proposed that
. . ."

3-b * "Housewife Mary Smith and her colleagues have proposed
that . . ."

So far, English has rigorously preserved a lexical gap for the work
that housewives and househusbands do, and for the role that they
fill. This supports the American economy and makes its profits
possible, and it is an excellent demonstration of the way a culture
can constrain behavior by making something difficult and cumbersome to talk about. If we had an apt and convenient word for
that-labor-which-is-done-in-the-home-in-order-to-make-the-Amer-
ican-economy-possible, a word to which we could add a morpheme
like "-er" or "-ist" to yield *someone-who-does-that-labor-which(-*
etc.), it would become much more difficult to keep the situation
out of sight and out of mind. Despite heroic attempts by feminists
over the years to turn matters around, our culture will not take
that risk. Attempts to use "homemaker" for that purpose are firmly
put down, as in this typical dialogue between a woman and a tax
preparer:

Q: Do you work?

A: I'm a homemaker

Q: I see. You're a housewife, then.

A: *And* a mother.

Q: Oh, great. But you don't work, right?

Feminist Charlotte Perkins Gilman wrote in a *Ladies Home Jour-*
nal article, "The private kitchen must go the way of the spinning
wheel, of which it is the contemporary"; that was in 1919. Surveys
done in the early 1900s found that housewives in the United States
did fifty to sixty hours of unpaid labor in the home each week; the
most recent surveys find that they still do that same fifty to sixty
hours. Ruth Schwartz Cowan closed a 1987 *American Heritage* article on the subject with this astonishing paragraph:

She may be exhausted at the end of her double day, but the modern "working" housewife can at least fall into bed knowing that her efforts have made it possible to sustain her family at a level of health and comfort that not so long ago was reserved only for those who were very rich. (Cowan 1987, page 71)

That's precisely the problem. The housewife's "job description" (forbidden phrase in this context!) has changed, in a way that every sales division of a major business will understand. In sales, if you meet one year's quotas by selling 10,000 widgets, the goalposts will be moved; the following year's quota will be 15,000 or more. In the home, if you acquire a "labor-saving" device that lets you do a household task an hour faster than you could before, that saved hour isn't yours to use as you like; you're expected to use it to "sustain" your family at a more comfortable standard of living.

What does this have to do with business? *Everything.* Without the unpaid labor force at home, modern business as we understand it in today's world would be utterly impossible. But we don't talk about it. Not in English.

And what effects might raising the issue and trying to discuss it, as we've just done, have in the real world? The answer, I'm quite sure, is that there will be no effect at all. Housework isn't like abortion, where opinions are divided into two strong opposing camps. It isn't like menopause or obesity, where numerous competing opinions exist and it's possible to find discussions of all of them in the mass media. Housework is different, and is a *survival* issue. Pointing out its curious status has been tried, many many times, without any results worth mentioning. Bringing the issue out into the light, giving it a vocabulary, and examining it publicly and at length in the way we routinely examine other social issues would pose a direct and specific threat to the culture of Living the American Dream. That won't be allowed to happen, and it is the power of language that maintains the prohibition.

5

Family Life and the Power of Language

When my oldest was first learning how to talk, he came toddling across the room and asked me for a cookie in Spanish. When I did not react, he got mildly upset. Then after a five-minute tantrum, he returned and asked me for a cookie again, but this time he used the English word. After that, he never spoke Spanish to me again.

(Pamela Faber; personal communication)

We know that a number of different positions on the benefits or dangers of multilingualism exist among Americans today, along with many variants of those positions; we know that at least in the United States they are based in large part on folklore and politics and inadequate information. In this chapter we will set aside the ongoing arguments about whether multilingualism should be desired, deplored, or ignored. Temporarily, let's just take multilingualism in the home as a given, the way we take furniture in the home as a given, and turn our attention to the power of language in that context.

Which Language, When, and with Whom?

In the United States in recent years, governments at the federal level and below have been busy trying to establish regulations about which language—usually English—is to be used in schools and government agencies. We've seen a few examples of large businesses (usually, but not always, in the medical field) setting up regulations forbidding employees to speak a language other than English. Similar efforts can be observed in other industrialized countries around the world. However, no government in any of the major industrialized countries seems to make any serious effort to regulate the choice of which language is to be used in people's own homes, in private. The choice appears to be left up to the individual family, which doesn't always find it easy to make.

"But Which Language Do They Use at Home?"

There was a time when multilingual households in the United States were almost exclusively of three kinds, making the answer to this question obvious once the basic circumstances were known. There were, in those days:

- Impoverished immigrant households, where most family members spoke only the language of their homeland, with perhaps one person knowing a little English.

In this situation, unless the family happened to live in an area with a very large immigrant community of its own heritage (usually only in big cities), learning English was a matter of survival. Even in the large cities, public education meant that the kids would have to learn English quickly and well to function in school; no bilingual education program existed. In such households the native language would be used within the immediate family, with English reserved for outside the home.

- Very privileged and wealthy households, where everyone spoke English plus additional languages as a matter of course because this was considered to be an obligatory part of an adequate upper class education.

In this case the family could choose any arrangement for language use that suited its fancy. If that arrangement was to speak Latin at the breakfast table, French at lunch, and English at dinner, with afternoon tea or cocktail conversation in Mandarin Chinese, that was perfectly fine. It was a matter of individual choice. Such households were, and still are, rare.

- Native American households, where older members might speak only their Native American language, where children spoke English, and with wide variation in whether younger members also spoke the Indian language. (The native peoples of the United States are divided on the question of whether they prefer to be called Indians or Native Americans; the decision varies not only from tribe to tribe but within the tribes as well.)

This was of course a special situation, in which—although it might be that speaking the Native American language was the most critical linguistic imperative, because the language itself was in danger of dying—extreme pressure to use English in the home instead came from many sources.

These stereotypical situations continue to exist in the United States, but in today's global society they're no longer the only common possibilities. Now that the ranks of professions and careers are filled with people from every part of the world, many multilingual American households fit none of these three stereotypes. Similarly, all over the world there are households in which one spouse (or both) is a native speaker of American English and one spouse (or both) also knows an additional language or languages.

I was surprised (when I sat down and listed it for this book) at how much multilingualism exists within my own extended family, even though it contains no diplomatic or similarly "international" households. One son knows both French and English. One daughter is a native speaker of English who also knows French; her husband is a native speaker of Lao who also knows Thai and English. Another daughter is a native speaker of English who knows French and who (although her skills are now rusty from lack of practice) once knew American Sign Language well enough to teach university courses in that language; her husband is a native speaker of English who also knows French. One nephew is a native speaker of English whose wife has both English and Spanish as native languages; his father, although in his late fifties, has begun intensively studying Spanish because his future grandchildren will have Spanish as one of their languages. Another nephew is a native speaker of English; his wife's native language is Russian and she also knows English. In three of these households there are children, and children are planned in a fourth. My stepson is fluent in English and Spanish; he lives with his grandmother, who is also English/Spanish multilingual. When I am added to the list, with fluent English and French—plus several other languages (including Navajo) which I can, as David Crystal puts it, "make use of" —there's quite a linguistic array. Not one of the households involved falls into the three patterns listed above.

All multilingual households, stereotypical or not, must come to an agreement about two *basic* questions:

1. What language(s) will the spouses use with one another?
2. And—if there are children—what language(s) will each parent use with each child?

The answers to the "which language" questions occur in astonishing variety. There are of course families in which one spouse speaks *only* Language X, and no one else who speaks a language other than Language X lives in the home. In such cases, even if the other spouse is multilingual, the decision will be essentially automatic: Language X will almost always be the language used at home. Except in that specific situation, however, all bets are off. Contrary to what might be expected, it doesn't seem to be the general case that a single language is chosen and dubbed "our family language." Nor is it always the case that the father speaks Language X to the children in the home and the mother speaks Language Y to them, or that mother and father speak Language X to one another and Language Y to the children. Things turn out to be much more complicated than that.

On my questionnaires, the most common responses to "Which language or languages do you use at home?" were "Both of them" and "All of them." This doesn't mean that they use the "wealthy family pattern" and give each language some regular time slot in the day. Instead, it means, literally, that all the languages are used all the time. Often more than one language is used at the *same* time, creating a language environment that's likely to strike the monolingual person as almost a guarantee of a disorganized and chaotic home life. But that's not at all the way the families living in these households perceive the situation.

Four Characteristics of Multilingual Homes

When all the data are examined, four interacting characteristics of multilingual family life run consistently throughout my database of questionnaire responses, with very few exceptions. Looking at the set will help us understand how having two or more languages regularly in use in the same home at one time *works*, and why it need not result in chaos.

The first characteristic is the casualness of it all. No one in my database reports being forced to learn or use some language *in the home* against his or her will, or having forced anyone else to do so. No one reports any personal trauma or unpleasantness associated with multilingual communication at home, although some recall unpleasantness of one kind or another at school. No one appears to find his or her situation unusual, even when it is very far indeed from the monolingual "norm." Waruna Mahdi writes, "The language we spoke at home was English between brothers and sisters, English and some Dutch between us kids and our parents (who spoke Dutch with each other), and the respective native language (Indonesian, Thai, Chinese, Russian) with household personnel.

This is part of normal embassy life; my father was a diplomat." The families themselves report no perception of their linguistic circumstances as chaotic or disorganized or dysfunctional, or even difficult.

The second common characteristic is that some one particular language is the one in which strong emotions, positive or negative or both, will usually be expressed in the home. One respondent (with a very reasonable request to remain anonymous) wrote, "Any sort of intimacy with my wife is always in Spanish. We simply wouldn't be able to make love in English, even though we often use English together for other matters" ; he adds that he and his wife couldn't have a *fight* in English, either. Many of my respondents note that when they're angry or upset at home, or simply "emotional," they always fall back on one particular language.

The third characteristic, which may come as a surprise, is a frequent report that the people involved often aren't *aware* which language is being used unless something happens to bring that fact specifically to their attention. For example:

Margaret Ann Doty (English/German, living in Germany) writes: "With my son I only use English at home, unless he has German friends visiting or we are watching German TV. Sometimes we laugh when we realize we're speaking German. It can be an unconscious act. I watched a Tom and Jerry film we rented once and wondered why they were singing in German. . . . At that moment I wasn't conscious of *which* language I was understanding, but if someone had asked me I would have sworn it was English."

Colin Whiteley writes, "It is quite possible to talk, read and write without necessarily being able to remember afterwards which language was used. Recently I received a two-page letter from my son, with one page in English and one in Spanish. I only realised this after reading it several times."

Whiteley goes on to make a claim that seems to me to be extremely important: "When you are concentrating on the real topic . . . *the language is totally transparent, and only the meaning is 'visible.'*" I've added the emphasis; I think it's well deserved.

I can add my own endorsement for this characteristic, and add an observation. When I was living with my first husband's family in

Geneva, the language we used when the entire family was together was French. I enjoyed the French conversation and took part in it without hesitation. I quickly lost any conscious awareness that I or anyone else was speaking French. However, in the middle of such conversations it sometimes happened that someone would speak to me in English—a guest, for example, who realized from my abominable French that it couldn't possibly be my best language, and could tell from my body language that I was an American. When that happened, I would suddenly find myself unable to speak *either* language. Both French and English would suddenly turn into meaningless noises and it would take me a while to recover and be able to answer the well-intentioned guest.

The fourth (and to me the most interesting) characteristic is the association of each language with a particular person, and/or the association of each language with a particular *role* filled by that person. For example:

Respondent Wen-chao Li writes, "When I was in Hawaii, the pattern was that I spoke English to the kids at school, and Mandarin to the adults at home. . . . My sister fell under the category of 'kids at school,' so to this day I always speak to my sister in English, and to my parents in Mandarin, even if we're sitting at the same dining table, taking part in the same conversation." Recent literature on multilingualism routinely mentions this characteristic, and my respondents' comments confirm the resports.

Pamela Faber's four children acquired three languages from birth (her English, her husband's Spanish, and French at their elementary school in Paris); she says she was "always amazed at how early they learned to assign languages to people. Roughly by the age of fourteen months, they had realized that their mother had one set of words and their father had another. . . . They have associated languages irrevocably with people, not with contexts."

Peter Yongqi Gu writes, "I never speak English with my wife (also a Chinese with excellent command of English) unless there's a friend around who doesn't speak Chinese. I never speak Mandarin with my parents and folks at home; I speak Hebei dialect to show intimacy. When I realize, for instance, that the guy at the other end of the line is my brother, we both switch to Hebei dialect at once."

Suzanne K. Hilgendorf (English /German respondent) writes, "My first long-term relationship was with a German, and that language dominates that domain still."

Colin Whiteley (English/Spanish, and more) agrees, and writes, "I have often noticed, with myself and with others, that the language used by two people who share more than one language is always that of the first meeting; i.e., once the mode of speech is established, it is very unlikely ever to change."

James L. Fidelholtz (English/Spanish) explains that at home he speaks "English almost all the time with my wife, about 90 percent of the time with my two older children (seventeen and fourteen) and very occasionally with my youngest child (seven)" ; with that youngest child he ordinarily speaks Spanish. The different practice with different children is because after the family's return from a two-year sabbatical in the United States the older children *insisted* on speaking English with their parents.

Carol Troen (English/Hebrew) identifies English as the language used in her home—but there are exceptions. "With my older grand-daughter," she writes, "I speak Hebrew and English; with the younger, Hebrew almost exclusively. . . . My kids often switch into Hebrew when they talk among themselves. . . . When I help our youngest with homework, we speak Hebrew." And she says, "I re-member when Judah was born (child Number 5) a few months after we arrived in Israel. I was conscious that I had to speak English with him because I didn't know how to speak to a baby in Hebrew. . . . The part of me that knew about children and knew how to talk to them could only speak English; gradually an act of 'translation' has occurred across these lines."

Pamela Swan notes a similar phenomenon; she would want her children to learn Japanese, a language that was always an "outside the home" language for her, but "I would like to tell my kids that I love them as I tuck them into bed, but it would be difficult for me to do that in Japanese."

Carol Troen also explains that "man-to-man" talk at home— "army talk," for example—among her adult sons and her husband is usually in Hebrew. I assume that if they were speaking with guests who were female soldiers, about army experiences, they would also speak Hebrew; nothing in Troen's account indicates that this choice is based on sexual gender. (However, a number of my male respondents mentioned that, when speaking at home in a situation where only other adult males are present, they prefer a particular language; the reason stated can be summarized roughly as "It's easier to make jokes in that language.")

Finally, here is an anecdote that is not only linguistically fascinating but also seems to me to sum up the subject perfectly:

> My young son and I moved to Indonesia when he was two years old. By the time he was three, he was bilingual in English and Indonesian (spoken to him by the servants). He jumbled the languages for about five minutes. After that, although I could speak to him in Indonesian and he would understand me perfectly, he would reply to me only in English, and to the servants only in Indonesian: he had sorted out who spoke what to his own complete satisfaction. Of course, this meant he thought there were two languages in the world and he spoke both of them. I'll never forget the astonishment on his face when, at the self-assured age of three and a half, he looked at a Korean woman, categorized her, and spoke to her in Indonesian. When she replied in Korean, he was utterly dumbfounded." (Kathryn Berck, personal communication)

When I discuss arrangements like these with people from traditional monolingual homes, the reaction is always one of astonishment that they don't lead to endless confusion in the home, as well as to friction and frustration. How, they want to know, could such arrangements possibly work? I can tell them only that, however strange it may seem, they do.

"But Doesn't All This Switching Around Confuse the Children in Multilingual Homes?"

No, fortunately it doesn't. If the children ever experience the state of knowing no language at all that I would drop into when languages shifted, they quickly get past that stage. The only hint of such a thing in my database comes from Michael Faris (English/Polish/Polish Sign Language), who writes that he has "gone through the experience of having my perceptions slide out from under me thanks to the language I was using." Both Faris and I began acquiring our other languages well past childhood; people immersed in two or more languages in infancy and very early childhood appear not to have such experiences.

Cindy Kandolf runs an excellent Internet site for bilingual families (at http://www.nethelp.no/Cindy/biling_fam.html). Her native language is American English; her husband's is Norwegian; they live in Norway and have one son, Kenneth. Their initial decision was that Cindy Kandolf would speak English to the child and her husband would speak Norwegian to him; this worked well. But when the little boy (at about eighteen months) began spending several hours a day four days a week with a Norwegian baby-sitter, his Norwegian language skills seemed to pull ahead of his English ones. Both parents therefore began speaking English at home, and Kandolf reports on her Web site that Kenneth's English then caught up to his Norwegian. This arbitrary shift in the language of the home caused no problems for the child. On the contrary. "Unexpectedly," Kandolf writes, "his skills in *both* languages improved rapidly." (She adds that she knows this may be only correlation, not causation.)

Pamela Faber writes, "Despite dire predictions . . . that learning three languages at the same time would lead to poor academic performance, emotional problems, and all sorts of cognitive confusion, nothing of the sort has ever occurred." Juan Manuel Sosa writes, "I wanted my two young children . . . to learn at least Spanish, French, and English, and they have. We always spoke Spanish at home; when we lived in Montreal they went to an English-speaking day care. Here in Vancouver they are both in French immersion, and they are both very comfortable in the three languages. We use mostly Spanish at home, they tend to prefer English when talking to each other, and they both have an English accent when speaking their very confident French."

Not a single respondent reports that any of his or her children have had negative consequences solely as a result of their multilingual households, nor do I know of any such problem in my own extended family. By contrast, there are a few parents among my respondents who mention deeply regretting that they *didn't* give their children the opportunity to grow up with more than one language.

Obviously no one simple rule for choosing among languages exists that a multilingual family can turn to with confidence and say, "We made this choice because everybody knows that it's the best one." Once the core decision to establish and/or maintain multilingualism in the home has been made, each family has to work out a system tailored to its own unique needs and preferences, one that will work smoothly for that specific family.

Immersion—and Near Drowning

Multilingual families work out their own language environment and its rules within the household, with admirable efficiency. However, introducing a new person into a multilingual family—something that is becoming far more frequent today, with our rising divorce rates—can severely disrupt that language environment. It may lead to problems with a potential for unbalancing the previously comfortable family dynamic.

I acquired my own facility in French conversation through a baptism of fire. When I arrived in Geneva I could read anything in French as easily as I could read English, but my spoken French was so poor that I didn't recognize *my own name* when I was paged at the airport. The fact that at age eighteen I was being paged as "Madame Haden" played a part in that, I'm sure; American girls in the 1950s were as likely to be called "Your Highness" as "Madame," and nobody had prepared me for that form of address. But still—I should have at least realized that my name was being spoken! I was utterly, hopelessly, lost, despite all the years of intensive French I'd had in school and all my straight A's in the subject. (This should clarify somewhat the reasoning behind the University of California–San Diego rule that students pass a foreign language course only if they can demonstrate the ability to carry on a conversation with two native speakers of that language.)

Soon after my arrival we all went to spend a month in the south of France with twenty-one of my French relatives, and there I spent three lengthy meals a day—often two hours or more per meal—sitting at a huge table with my French extended family. "Total immersion" it surely was, with a vengeance, especially for an American teenager used to eating on the run in school cafeterias and hurrying through meals at home. No one in those long and spirited conversations had time or motivation to fill me in on what was being said, and for the first week I understood scarcely a word. Once in a while something familiar such as *merci* or *bonjour* would leap out at me, but for the most part I heard only gibberish. And then one day, as I was sitting there in my usual state of bewildered panic, something clicked: All of a sudden, in a single instant, the sounds I was hearing somehow corresponded adequately to the written language I could so easily read, and I *understood the language*. It was an astonishing experience (and one often reported). It didn't do much for my grammar, but from then on I was truly multilingual.

This development would have let me pass the French course at UCSD, and was a tremendous improvement over being able only to read and pass tests. But the change also brought with it a serious problem, because my vocabulary wasn't equal to my conversational competence. (If you aren't multilingual, you might be amazed at how *few* words and phrases are really needed to get by in another language adequately; good listeners are as prized in a multilingual language environment as they are anywhere else.) I quickly acquired a very bad reputation as "a lazy American girl unwilling to do her share of the work."

It wasn't until many years later, long after my husband's death, that I learned—by accident—what had happened. It had gone like this: One of the other women, in my hearing, would say something in French such as 'Well, why don't we all go pluck the chickens for dinner?" The idea was that I would instantly say, "Please, may I help?" but I never did. After a dozen such attempts, they abandoned the effort (and me) as a lost cause.

The actual reason I didn't join them had *nothing* to do with my being the typical spoiled and lazy American girl the French had heard so much about; I had many flaws, but laziness wasn't one of them. The reason was that my vocabulary didn't include the words for most common household tasks done by French women in the 1950s. I had no context for these utterances that would have given me clues; no one held up a dead chicken while talking about chicken plucking. And I was scared; I didn't feel that it would be polite for me to demand that the other women explain to me where they were going and what they were going to do there. So they would look at one another, sigh elaborately, and get up and go off in a group without me. I would know from the look on my mother-in-law's face as she left with them that I had done something wrong, but I had no idea what it was, and no one told me. By the time we returned to Geneva I was in deep trouble, and miserable. Even my husband was scarcely speaking to me—and still, no one explained. I had not the slightest clue what it was that I had done wrong. I knew only that the situation was unspeakably awful.

Why didn't somebody else among the relatives—especially someone among the young people—tip me off? Married women are by definition adults in France, and I therefore qualified as an adult although I was barely eighteen. This created much resentment in family members my age or older than I was—but still unmarried—who had to eat outside at the "children's table" and miss all the fun. That resentment, and the way the difference in status was thrown in their faces three times a day, kept me from making any allies among the young people in the family. If it hadn't been for that circumstance, they might have lent a hand as peers and kept me from getting into so many cross-cultural messes. As matters stood—even though I wasn't responsible for the rule, even though I'd made it clear that I would *rather* have eaten at the children's table with them—they watched my struggles with considerable relish.

I am describing this sorry mess in such detail because it illustrates one of the serious perils of multilingualism when a second language is acquired after early childhood and without immersion in its culture. It is one strong argument for *early* multilingualism—the earlier the better. It's easy to conclude from the confidence and facility in speaking your language displayed by someone (a doctor, for example, or a lawyer or teacher, or a law enforcement official) that that person understands what's happening; when that conclusion is in error, it can lead to dreadful trouble. The area in which this is perhaps most alarming is in medicine. Many medical professionals in the United States today are not native speakers of English. During the two decades that I've been doing medical seminars I've observed that the situation I faced as a young wife in France—that is, that I appeared to be at ease with the foreign language, but was misunderstanding many crucially important things—is by no means rare among medical professionals. Doctors who need interpreters present a problem, but at least the problem and its solution are pretty clear. The potential for grave consequences is much greater when the doctor's fluent English keeps him or her *unaware* that an interpreter is needed.

My French family wasn't deliberately and maliciously withholding explanations from me. I was so at ease in French that they never realized I genuinely did not understand those hints that I should lend a hand with the household chores. They were convinced that I was deliberately refusing to help—a behavior they had always heard was typical of American teenagers—and they quite rightly resented that. Why would they explain? There was, by their lights, nothing *to* explain. It was all perfectly clear to them: I did not *choose* to help. And my husband, who was an only child and only nineteen himself, was caught between the two cultures and had no idea what to do; he had never before in his life seen a woman behave as I appeared to be behaving. As many other nineteen-year-olds would have done in his place, he chose to ignore the whole thing and hope it would go away.

This experience, awful as it was at the time, has been a blessing to me over the years. When I've been called on to mediate misunderstandings and disagreements in multicultural environments, I have known from bitter personal experience, not just from reading academic materials, that I had to bend over backward not to leap to premature conclusions. I have kept firmly in mind the fact that the source of the difficulty is far more often in the language than in the person. When my daughter married a Laotian man, I was prepared to reserve judgment when puzzled and to select a problem of language as my *first* hypothesis until I had solid evidence for concluding otherwise.

This didn't keep me from making dreadful mistakes, but it prevented the mistakes from becoming permanent. Because I was also prepared to do what my French family had not realized that they should do—I was prepared to make an open effort, even when it was slow going and awkward and unpleasant, to explore misunderstandings and do my best to clarify them.

Those Other Questions

I'm very aware that the particular associations, thoughts, and memories that will arise in my mind in a Spanish conversation are likely to be rather different from those that will arise in an English conversation on the same topic. Sometimes I consciously try to think or talk an issue through in both languages to take advantage of the additional information.

(David Tuggy, respondent)

We've seen that multilingual households are casual and comfortable with their language mix, that they use all the languages available—on the basis of rules worked out to fit their personal situation—and that they take it all quite casually. But what about the complicated matter of the possible *effects* of multilingualism on those who live in multilingual households? The reports from my respondents make it seem that there's no need to worry about those effects, but is that accurate?

In previous chapters we've been exploring the following questions:

1. Does acquiring a language mean acquiring a culture (and does losing a language mean losing a culture)?
2. Does a language constrain or structure the perceptions of its speakers in any significant way?

3. When the languages of multilingual people clash on some issue that is important to them, how (if at all) is the conflict resolved, cognitively and in terms of behavior?

We would like to have firm enough answers to those three questions so that we could apply them in the context of the multilingual home. We are far from reaching that goal. There are so many variables, so many possible combinations of languages and customs and circumstances, that we can do little more than hazard guesses. However, for those who are facing (or may one day face) the basic decision *for or against* multilingualism in the home, just having the three questions identified will help in the process of deciding correctly for your own family. You may think you could never find yourself in this situation, especially if you live in the United States, where such fierce efforts are being made to eliminate bilingual education. Nevertheless, the chances that you *will* are increasing daily.

Given the uncertainties, what can we say with confidence about the power of language in the home and in family life? We can certainly make some observational statements.

We've seen that language has the power to create a *family role* in one culture that's almost inconceivable in another, as with the Japanese water babies. We've seen that language can disrupt the daily life of a family by the simple attachment of a disease label, causing a family member to assume the "sick role" and all the complex of behavior—both active and passive—that goes with that role. And we've seen that what *qualifies* as a disease or disorder varies dramatically from one language to another.

We've seen that the contrast between two culture's presuppositions for vocabularies of time, and for vocabularies of ethical/moral concepts such as fairness and honesty, can wreak havoc in the way that individuals are perceived by others. When someone's employer, because of language differences, sees him or her as shiftless and lazy and unreliable—even dishonest—there will be economic consequences for the family. And persons perceived in that negative way all day at their workplace won't be the same persons at home that they would have been if they'd had their employers' respect; the consequences for their families will go well beyond economic ones.

We've seen that language has the power to decide what is and what is not "real" work. In the United States, whether scrubbing a floor is real work or not depends on who's doing the scrubbing; if that person is someone who can be described in English as a housewife, it's not real work. For the Gabra nomads of Kenya, whether something is or isn't work depends on the physical configuration of the person. A task that has to be done while standing is work, while tasks that you can do sitting down are not, and the seated doer is only "resting." (This would turn a huge percentage of American jobs from work into rest.) Other languages will make this judgment in still other ways.

In every case, it is language—not logic, or "facts" —that creates and maintains these states of affairs.

When we consider even these few examples and their interactions, it's easy to understand why a nation's language policymakers might decide that everything possible should be done to *prevent* multilingualism in the home, including the elimination of bilingual education and the attempt to impose an official national language by law. They may be totally wrong—I'm firmly convinced that they are— but it's not hard to understand why they feel as they do.

Case Study— An English/Lao/French Household

Let me introduce you now to my older daughter Rebecca Haden Chomphosy's complicated multilingual household. Its members include Rebecca, her husband Bounlieng Chomphosy, and their four children, each of whom has an English first name and a Lao middle name. The children are Rosamond Phouvieng (sixteen), Josepha Chantaboun (fourteen), Gideon Boualien (nine), and William Khami (seven).

Rebecca was about six years old when her father died suddenly; she had lived until then in a home where both French and English were spoken natively. As a child, she spent a number of months-long visits with her French grandparents in Switzerland and the south of France. She is at ease in French, but has few opportunities to use it. In almost all circumstances, including her interaction with Boun- lieng's family, she speaks English.

Bounlieng came to the United States as a young man, and as a refugee, bringing many members of his large extended family with him; his native language was Lao, and he also knew Thai. He knew almost no English and learned the language here in the States—in fact, Rebecca was his teacher in a California ESL (English as a second language) training program. He had studied French at one time in school, but has forgotten it completely, making English the only lan- guage he shares with Rebecca. He speaks English at work, but with his relatives and his Laotian friends (there is a large Laotian and Thai population in northwest Arkansas) he speaks Lao. His answer to my questionnaire item about whether there are situations when he would prefer one language to another was straightforward and un- compromising: He would *never* speak any language other than Lao, he told us, if he had a choice.

The household's language is English, and all four children are al- most completely monolingual. The girls have taken some French courses and belong to a French club; however, when Rebecca and I need to discuss details of a planned surprise in front of the girls, we can safely speak French. Rosamond tells us that she understands a lot of the language in the Thai movies that the children frequently watch with their father and can follow some parts of his telephone conversations with his Lao family. However, not one of the children speaks any Lao beyond a few isolated words and expressions that are family catchphrases (like *lap ta sang*—to roll the eyes—as in "Don't you *lap ta sang* ME!"), and none as yet expresses any interest in learning Lao. When asked if she'd care to learn it, Rosamond says there aren't any schools that offer it, and besides, "I'd have no use for it; I haven't had any use for it so far. I'd be speaking English the whole time!"

No one would have predicted this; no one would have anticipated that the Haden/Chomphosy household would decide against multi- lingualism in the home (with the exception, of course, of Bounlieng's use of Lao when the other person present, or on the phone, is a Lao speaker). Rebecca has a multilingual linguist for a mother and lived in a multilingual household with a French father from birth to age five. Her grandfather was a multilingual American diplomat living in Switzerland and moving in multilingual circles both professionally and socially. Her French grandmother, with whom she spent large amounts of time in childhood, spoke almost exclusively French with her. Rebecca has an M.A. in linguistics and is an experienced foreign language teacher, accustomed to teaching English to classes in which her students speak many different native languages. She would have been delighted to speak Lao and to have her children all speak Lao; she had the strong support of her parents for that outcome.

Bounlieng is himself multilingual, and he comes from a culture that reveres knowledge and education; multilingualism is common in his country, where more than ninety different languages are spoken. The Haden/Chomphosys would appear to be *tailor-made* for multilingual family life. How, then, did it happen that the household uses only English? As is so often the case, it happened because of idiosyncratic circumstances that may have little or no general application.

When Rebecca and Bounlieng married, they were in frequent close contact with his Lao family, and Beccy made a serious effort to learn Lao so that she could join in the conversation. But the variety of Lao that Bounlieng speaks has six different *tones*, which means that a single syllable can mean any one of six different and totally unrelated things, depending on the pitch patterns with which it's spoken.

Any linguist who has ever worked with a tone language will tell you that there appears to be a Rule Of The Universe for tone languages which guarantees that any mistake a foreigner makes with tones will inevitably turn out to be offensive, or obscene, or both. I once taught an entire week of Navajo grammar in a graduate course, using what I thought was a neutral verb in its multitude of forms. Only later (and only through the intervention of a Hopi friend) did I learn that because I'd had one tone wrong I had taught an obscene verb the entire time, causing the Navajo native speakers in the class great distress and embarrassment. Navajo cultural values made it absolutely impossible for them to tell me what was going on, and it's to their credit that they didn't just drop the class.

When Rebecca tried to speak Lao as a young bride, she made a lot of mistakes, just as I had made many errors speaking French with my in-laws in the same situation—but with a major difference in both language and culture. My errors in French were surely comical, and sometimes caused confusion. But the European French culture within which I was communicating was sufficiently "worldly" that if I *had* accidentally said something off-color it would have caused nothing but amusement. Rebecca's errors in Lao, on the other hand, had meanings that were a grave source of embarrassment to her young husband in front of his family. Sometimes what she was saying was only nonsensical, but that's not how you want your new wife to sound to your relatives; all too often her tone mistakes produced utterances that were offensive, and the Lao culture is prudish in the extreme. As a result, Bounlieng very early in the marriage asked Rebecca please to speak English instead, and he spoke to her only in English thereafter, effectively closing off her chances to learn Lao. Since he and Beccy share only English, a communication pattern was established in their home that left him with little reason to speak Lao to the children when they came along.

I want to turn briefly now to a discussion of one small Lao/English linguistic difference that has been a source of consistent inconvenience and annoyance in the Haden/Chomphosy household, as an example of how a minor difference can affect family life and how difficult it can be to deal with it even when everyone involved has the best of intentions. The term responsible for the problem is "plan," and all related words such as "plans," "planning," and the like.

Rebecca was brought up to believe that when families have a goal it's important for them to sit down together and work out a plan for achieving that goal; we always proceeded in that fashion in our home. Planning in Lao, however, has a semantic feature that English "plan" doesn't have; I am far from understanding all the details, but I can summarize it roughly by saying that in Lao planning is marked as [+DANGEROUS]. Any attempt to sit down and openly work out a plan makes Bounlieng very nervous. Because the whole semantic field associated with the word has this dangerous aspect, trying to abstract away from the act of planning and explore the communication problem itself is equally difficult; that is, talking about why it's dangerous to make plans is just as awkward as actually doing it. For Bounlieng, it's not that you can't *make* a plan, in the privacy of your own mind, and do your best to carry it out—of course you can. But you absolutely do not *talk* about it. Ever. This interferes significantly with the process of family decision making, and creates many mysteries, as well as many sudden surprises.

I'm a linguist with considerable experience in fieldwork with Navajo and several other Native American languages whose cultures are very different from English. I'm well trained in the task of framing questions about a language and posing them to native speakers. It might seem that *I* should be able to step in and use some of that training here. It might seem that I could talk to Bounlieng about this matter in private and find a way to approach it that would let him join the rest of the family in their planning sessions, and that I could do so without causing tension. Often in fieldwork it will turn out that some subject you've been told is always and without exception taboo *can* be talked about after all—provided that it's approached in the context of an acceptable metaphor, for instance. I suspect that if all else were equal—or if I had the Laotian equivalent of the Hopi friend who helped me when I stumbled into communication quandaries in Navajo—I *would* be able to discover the accepted Lao way of approaching the subject.

Unfortunately, all else is *not* equal. There is an intricate and perilous cultural web surrounding all communication between a Lao man and his mother-in-law. Because I don't know how to negotiate within that web, I'm helpless, and I have no helpful friend available who knows both cultures involved. I've been unable to do a single thing that would be useful. And so this source of inconvenience within the household persists—only think how often, at your house, you discuss plans both large and small before taking any action, and what it would be like if you didn't feel free to do that.

The solution that seemed obvious to me very early in the marriage was that I would learn Lao myself and speak Lao with Bounlieng—which would have had the additional benefit, from my point of view, of exposing the grandchildren to the language more frequently. I didn't (and still don't) find the idea intimidating, not with a native speaker so conveniently available, and I've been down the tone-language-mistake road too many times before to find it a barrier.

This didn't happen, either, although I've doggedly kept trying to tackle Lao on my own, in spare moments. Why? Not because I wasn't willing, but because of—once again—the minefield created by the son-in-law/mother-in-law relationship. It's not possible for Bounlieng to correct his mother-in-law's Lao language mistakes, not in any smallest particular. He can't even model correctly for me a word that I've used wrongly—that would be rudeness toward an elder and rudeness toward his mother-in-law, both of which are absolutely out of the question. And it's agony for him to have to listen to me trying to use the language without either of those possibilities. Needless to say, for him to find himself *laughing* at me—as would inevitably happen if I stubbornly insisted on speaking Lao in his presence—would, for him, be a *disaster*. So there we are, and I see no way around it unless a day should come when I would have free time enough to begin the process of learning Lao from some other native speaker in this area, with all the delicate negotiations and arrangements that would require.

This sort of thing exists, in varying degrees, in all multilingual households. It can also happen when the difference is between dialects rather than between languages. There are features of my native Ozark English that will always stand between me and easy communication with someone whose native English dialect is "upper-class urban New Yorker," and if such a person were suddenly to become a member of my household we'd have problems. The difference is one of degree. With dialect differences in the home, you're more likely to be able to work out satisfactory solutions, given enough time and sufficient patient effort, than you are with language differences; and there are less likely to be formidable cultural differences like the different status of "mother-in-law" in the United States and in Laos.

The Haden/Chomphosy household does cast some light on our question about the link between language and culture. Because of

Bounlieng's close ties to his Lao relatives and associates and friends, he cannot be described as "assimilated." He manages well within the American English culture, both at home and in the workplace, but *his* culture is and will always remain the Lao culture.

The culture of my Haden/Chomphosy grandchildren, however, is unquestionably American English. Their involvement since birth with a culture so different from that of the mainstream American household has given them an "anthropological" sort of sophistication, unusual for their age, that is impressive. It will surely prove useful to them as adults. But not having learned Lao has kept them from knowing their father's culture very much more deeply than a determined and interested tourist might after visiting Laos.

I hope this will change as they grow older. I hope that they will decide to take advantage of the convenience of having a Lao native speaker always available, and will learn Lao as adults. Their father would be perfectly free to correct *their* attempts in as much detail and with as much intensity as he liked. Ideally, they would learn the language well enough to help *me* learn it at long last, and perhaps well enough to let my great-grandchildren grow up as English/Lao multilinguals. I am a strong believer in the value of multilingualism, and I will do everything possible over the years to help make this come to pass.

Someone opposed to multilingualism would perceive all these matters very differently. For example, here's a quotation from a May 4, 1998, issue of *Newsweek,* from an opinion piece by Spanish/English multilingual Gabriela Kuntz. The piece is titled 'My Spanish Standoff" and subtitled "A Fear of Prejudice for Our Children Made My Husband and Me Decide 'English Only' at Home" :

My daughter is frustrated by the fact that I'm bilingual and have purposely declined to teach her to speak Spanish, my native tongue. . . . I recently read an article in a national magazine about the Ozarks where some of the townspeople are concerned about the number of Hispanics who have come to work in poultry plants there. It seemed to me that their "concerns" were actually prejudice. There is a definite creeping in of anti-Hispanic sentiment in this country. Even my daughter, yes, the one who is upset over not being bilingual, admits to hearing "Hispanic jokes" said in front of her at school. (Kuntz 1998, page 22)

Kuntz goes on to explain that the daughter in question might be taken for a Hispanic if it weren't for her flawless English, but that she has another daughter who has light brown hair and blue eyes. "I just might teach her Spanish," she writes, with what I assume is surely irony.

A Suggestion for Further Research

Violence on the scale of wars and insurrections and terrorism is beyond our control as individuals; in our homes, however, we are intimately involved in whether there is or isn't violence. And in almost every case, violence in the home begins not as physical but as *verbal* violence. First, there is hostile language; only then, and only if the hostility escalates, does the hitting start. Once violence has become physical the people involved are usually unable to do much about it, and must call on law enforcement and medical professionals—outside experts—for help; while it remains verbal, however, the people involved *are* the experts.

Verbal violence within the family isn't a random matter; it has a grammar of its own, known to every native speaker of the language being used. For the past thirty years I have worked with the grammar of English verbal violence just as I would have worked with the grammar of a language not previously studied or analyzed. For speakers of English, the methods I teach for preventing verbal violence have proved extremely helpful, and I have many requests for similar materials for speakers of other languages. I can't respond adequately to those requests, unfortunately, much as I would like to do so. Because only native speakers of a language are able to understand hostility (and other negative emotions) within their culture and analyze the manner in which those feelings are expressed in that language.

I can think of few research projects that would be more valuable than careful investigations of the grammars of verbal violence and hostility in the languages of this world.

6

Religion and the Power of Language

When we change words we invite a changed perception of the reality to which the words point. To demand that the words of faith change is to demand that one's faith change. And in changing it can either grow or shrivel, blossom or die.

(Barr 1988, page 366)

Grammar and attitudes have nothing to do with each other. Benjamin Whorf thought they did, but he has been proven wrong.

(Beaver 1988, page 325)

We have considered in some detail the power that language has in medicine, in business, and in the home; we've discussed many aspects of its power in education. Now we're going to turn to the often very different power of *religious* language. The two quotations above make opposing claims. The first claims that the linguistic relativity hypothesis is true, while the second (from a linguist's letter in response to the first) declares it false. Knowing which of those two claims is valid is arguably more important in the context of religious language than in any other area of life. Religion and spirituality permeate every culture and every worldview, using religious language and talk about religious language as a primary mechanism of transmission. It's difficult to overestimate the power of such language over our lives, even for those who claim to have no religious beliefs and to be part of no religious tradition. In much of the Western world, religion is the area of life in which the most elaborate cognitive gymnastics are required, because of the seemingly unresolvable conflicts and contradictions.

What *Is* Religious Language?

Religious language can be defined in many ways, from casual conversation ("I believe in God, I guess, but I don't believe in angels") to sacred texts and purported revelations. The task of definition is made difficult by the fact that no method exists for determining whether a sequence of religious language is *valid,* that is, for distinguishing genuine religious language from phony religious language. When I gave lectures on this subject at the university, my students, whether they described themselves as religious or not, were startled to learn that this was so. They told me that they'd never thought about the matter before, but now that it had come up they felt that surely there *must* be some recognized standard against which alleged examples of religious language could be measured for validity, as well as some recognized international entity with the power to apply those standards and rule on such questions.

There are no such standards, and no International Board on the Validity of Religious Language exists. Let's suppose that I've walked into your living room and announced that I've just had a religious revelation, which I proceed to recite to you in the form of a creed or a psalm or a prophecy. You will probably think I'm out of my mind (which is something for which we *do* have recognized standards and judging entities). In the United States, unless you belong to one of the religious denominations whose rules about religious discourse differ from the mainstream, you'll find my behavior unseemly in the extreme, and personally embarrassing. But there is no way you can prove that my utterance either is or isn't as valid an example of religious language as, say, the Twenty-third Psalm.

Lawrence LeShan has suggested that people who don't like the mantras already available to them for meditation make their own by opening the phone book, pointing to a name, taking its first syllable, repeating the process, and combining the two syllables. "Anderson" and "Willingham" would yield the mantra *anwil*, for instance—and there is no way to prove that it wouldn't be as valid a mantra as any other. However unsuitable it may seem, there is no way to *exclude* it from the body of religious language. You may feel, as did my students, that this is a shocking state of affairs and should not be allowed, religious freedom or no religious freedom. Nevertheless, that's the way it is, and further exploration of the validity issue is the proper domain of theologians and religious scholars. The interesting question is why those who profess not to be religious should care one way or the other; they do, and they have strong opinions on the question.

For our purposes in this chapter we'll be restricting the meaning of "religious language" to sequences of language that are either *customarily and typically used in religious ceremonies and practices*—such as the sacred texts of a faith, like the Bible and the Koran, and their oral counterparts in many cultures; prayers and blessings and (unfortunately) curses; creeds; rituals and sacraments; and hymns—or sequences of language specifically *about* such items.

Attitudes and beliefs about religious language extend over an extraordinarily broad range. These attitudes and beliefs aren't just theoretical matters; they have significant real-world consequences. At one extreme is the belief that even the most seemingly trivial change in a sequence of religious language—changing a single letter or sound or gesture, for example—will ruin it. In some cases the claim is that change weakens the sequence, robbing it of some or all of its power; in others, that change would pervert the power of the sequence and make it powerful for evil rather than for good, as with the practice known as the "Black Mass." At the other extreme is the conviction that religious language is just like any other kind of language, with no special strength or power. We won't discuss the second extreme position here; I'm confident that this chapter as a whole will demonstrate that it can't be valid.

The first idea—that religious language is sacred and change is desecration—is common in Native American cultures. You will remember the example (on page 30) of the Kevesan people, who are willing to remain forever illiterate in their language because they consider the *entire* language sacred and feel that they couldn't control what happens to it if they allowed it to be written down. This decision threatens not only the language but the culture; the Kevesan are willing to accept that danger for the sake of their religious faith. Fieldworkers in many Native American languages know that when their Indian consultants agree to let them write down or record a sequence of religious language it will always contain some small change, some deliberate "mistake" or omission that makes it different from the actual sequence and thus no longer sacred. This is done not only to protect the sequence of language but also to protect the fieldworkers themselves, since the consultants believe that they can't be expected to know how to deal safely with language of such power.

I assure you that this isn't armchair anthropology, interesting but relevant only to a few very special circumstances. It has been anything but trivial for the Arabic-speaking world, where the conviction that any change in religious language is desecration has become a serious threat.

Most English-speaking people of the Western world are undisturbed by the frequently appearing new translations of the Bible. They accept and endorse the idea that this holy book should change with the times so that its message can be more easily understood by contemporary readers and listeners. We've seen the publication of a translation of the Bible into the street talk of our American inner cities. The organization Priests for Equality has published *The Inclusive New Testament,* in which Colossians 3:18 ("Wives, submit to your husbands. . . .") and 3:19 ("Husbands, love your wives . . . ") appear as "You who are in committed relationships . . ." and the begats include the names of mothers as well as fathers when the mothers' names are known.

Arabic-speaking peoples have a drastically different attitude toward the Koran, which they believe to be the actual words of their prophet, sacred in their form as well as their content. As a result, they have come to look upon *written* Arabic in something very much like the way that the Kevesan perceive their spoken language—as *inherently* sacred.

In a story in the *Wall Street Journal* ("War of Words: Arabic Emerges as a Weapon in Mideast Struggles"), Amy Dockser Marcus describes this problem, with comments from sources in the Arab world. "Over time," she writes, "the written language of the Koran and the local dialects spoken in Arab countries have drifted far apart. This gap has led to growing numbers of people who never master the Arabic used in books, newspapers, or official documents." She writes that Dr. Mohamed Maamouri of the International Literacy Institute wants to see written Arabic modernized so that the language taught in the schools will be closer to the language that students actually hear and speak in their homes, but he finds that "most of the region's governments remain paralyzed, fearful of being portrayed as tampering with the holy language of the Koran." Marwan Juma, general manager of Jordan's Internet service, is distressed and worried because this resistance to any kind of change in the written language means that no Arabic interface is yet available for use on-line. "Without Arabic," he says, "we face a dying heritage and loss of identity" (Marcus 1997).

What would it mean if a similar situation existed in the United States? In "A Language Divided Against Itself," Chris Hedges explores this idea, asking his readers:

> What if 80 or 90 percent of Americans spoke every day in the brutal and angry cadences of gangsta rap, while the members of a feudal upper class mused over their own demise in Elizabethan English? (Hedges 1996)

That is, what if written English had been frozen in the forms that were used in the King James Bible, while the spoken language had moved on, and the gulf between the two varieties of English had restricted literacy to an elite upper class?

Suppose politicians in the United States could take something like "Thou shalt not suffer a witch to live" from the King James Bible and turn it into a rap slogan aimed at illiterate thousands in American inner cities and rural small towns, with complete confidence that its targets wouldn't be able to find that section of the Bible and read the sequence in context, or read commentaries and discussions of the section. Suppose that at the same time the elite classes in the United States would know so little about rap that they'd pay no attention to the slogan and its effects. Suppose politicians could take the loaded word "abomination," which figures so prominently in the Old Testament, reshape it in a dialect unfamiliar to upper-class Americans, and begin using it as a buzzword to whip up hatred against whatever they disapproved of. This is precisely the sort of problem that Arabic-speaking peoples struggle with in the real world today.

Hedges acknowledges that the image is an exaggeration for many privileged speakers of Arabic, but reports that it accurately reflects the linguistic circumstances of the poor throughout the Middle East, whose inability to read written Arabic and interpret it for themselves leaves them dangerously vulnerable. Amy Docker Marcus quotes the Arab poet and songwriter Nabeel el-Khadeer's lament that "Language is the weapon of our times." And Hedges makes it clear that although Arabic may seem far outside American concerns, it in fact affects Americans directly: He explains that the carefully crafted inflammatory slogans and buzzwords aimed at the poor by politicians are "almost incomprehensible to educated Arabs, only widening a dangerous gulf between an elite that looks to the West and *an enraged underclass from which suicide bombers and murderers of tourists can be recruited*" (Hedges 1996; emphasis added).

The situation in the mainstream cultures of the United States is different, right? There may be a little resistance to new Bible translations, but most Americans are literate, and are broad-minded about religious language. We may feel a sense of stylistic loss when the Christmas angels' "Fear not" is modernized into "Don't be afraid"; we may feel that rendering "Let not your heart be troubled" as

"Don't worry" throws away much of the beauty of the earlier version. I certainly feel that way. But nobody is ready to *riot* against such changes. We may be offended when people pepper their speech with "Jesus Christ" or "God damn" as their preferred casual curses, but we're not likely to attack them physically for that behavior. We may be disgusted when writers and artists take liberties with subjects that we personally consider sacred, but we're not interested in putting such people in prison for their actions. Right? Yes and no. As is true of so many language-related issues, it depends. It's not simple or straightforward.

Some examples of American attitudes toward religious language are as curious as any that an anthropologist might bring back from fieldwork at the outermost fringes. As when the local government of Kleberg County, Texas, voted unanimously in favor of saying "heaven-O" as the official government greeting, never mind the fact that "hello" has nothing whatsoever to do with hell or with the word "hell." (It's instructive, and at the same time bewildering, that this information appeared on page 25 of the December 13, 1997, issue of *TV Guide*, without a byline and with the disrespectful title "Then They All Got Back into Their Heavenicopter and Flew Back to the Mental Hospital.")

Annie Dillard, writing in *Holy the Firm*, describes the "set pieces of liturgy" as language that people have managed to address to their God "without getting killed."

And Stanley Fish makes a claim that is neither obviously absurd nor obviously poetic—but obviously important, linguistically and spiritually—when he writes that "Religious discourse . . . cannot be unconcerned with the substantive worth and veracity of its assertions, which are in fact *presupposed*" (Fish 1996, page 22). That is, we can't just dismiss someone's religious language casually, because unless there is an open statement to the contrary we have to assume that the speaker believes that its various propositions are true.

It's not an accident that Fish makes this claim in an article titled "Why We Can't All Just Get Along." Many Christians who agree with Stanley Fish may find themselves in the awkward position of having to use religious language which presupposes that all the world's billions of non-Christians are doomed to spend eternity in hell. That terrible claim is presupposed by numerous examples of religious language used in Christian sacred texts, sermons, hymns, and the like. It's made explicit in the recent manifesto of the Christian Evangelical denominations in the United States, published in the June 14, 1999, issue of *Christianity Today:* "We deny that anyone is saved in any other way than by Jesus Christ and his Gospel. The Bible offers no hope that sincere worshipers of other religions will be saved without personal faith in Jesus Christ." That's carefully worded, but its intended meaning is quite clear. (A typical response when I ask believers how they deal with this is "I try not to think about it" plus a swift change of subject.)

In a multilingual and multicultural America this particular presupposition can have complicated consequences. I have a Buddhist friend whose first visit to an American church was his last—because it included a statement from the minister, directly *to* my friend, that his deceased Buddhist parents were at that moment in hell and would remain there for all eternity. I've seen a number of Southern Baptist ministers, facing a point-blank outraged question like "Are *you* saying that all Buddhists and Jews will go to *hell?*" escape by answering with "I wouldn't presume to make a judgment of that kind." The preacher who talked to my friend either wasn't that adroit, or genuinely felt a religious obligation to say what he did; if the latter reason is the explanation, I'm grateful that I carry no such burden.

To understand how religious language in English affects people's lives in the United States today, we need to remember two things as we go along.

First: The effects that religious language has on an English-speaking population are effects of *contemporary* English, which brings with it all the presuppositions of contemporary English.

This point is far too often overlooked or forgotten. Scholars and theologians of the English-speaking world may be convinced that they know what the words of some religious sequence in English "really" mean, based on their understanding of what the corresponding sequences in ancient Aramaic or Hebrew or Greek "really" meant. I suspect that they're sometimes wrong, and not only because millennia have gone by since the words were first spoken. For all their expertise, they have no way of knowing what English body language— especially what intonation and tone of voice—should be assigned to the translations of religious utterances from their original languages.

Only English spoken by a machine (my answering machine, for example) carries no emotional meaning. Quoted English speech is most often read silently, but we hear it in the mind's ear with some pattern of intonation attached. "If you love me you will keep my commandments" means one thing, while "If you LOVE me, you will KEEP my COMMANDments!" means something else. Not even the most learned scholars—like the members of the famous Jesus Seminar, who presume to rule on which sayings attributed to Jesus he actually did or didn't say—know which of those two English utterances, let alone the multitude of other possibilities, was intended by the original non-English utterance. If the scholars are correct in the judgments they make about such things, that's admirable. But ordinary people, which includes most of us, are even more ignorant of theology and religious theory than of linguistics. We don't experience English religious language as an English way of saying some sequence of Greek or Hebrew or Aramaic that we're able to understand in the original; we understand it as the English of today.

Much time is spent in religious discourse in America, both spoken and written, struggling to explain that when Jesus said "Be ye therefore perfect as my Father in heaven is perfect" he didn't mean *perfect*. "Perfect" in the original language, we're told, didn't mean "perfect"; it meant something else, something more along the lines of "mature" or "whole" or "complete" but not exactly any of those either. This is little or no help to average devout Christians, who will continue to feel that they've been commanded to be perfect.

Second: The effects of religious language are in no way restricted to effects on believers, and that's not just because believers and nonbelievers share the same world.

I've asked many people who insist that they are *totally* nonreligious whether they find "The Lady is my shepherdess; I shall not want" offensive. Whether they are shocked by the crucified Santa Clauses that can be found on sale in Japanese gift shops at Christmas. (Bizarre as this seems, the sort of cross-cultural blundering it demonstrates can be seen in almost every gift shop—and truck stop—in America, where the symbols of different Native American religions appear scrambled and distorted in exactly the same fashion on objects of every kind.) If it makes any difference to them whether the gay lifestyle is called "something many people strongly disapprove of" or "an abomination." If they have any opinion about whether their dog has a soul, or about the point at which a fetus has a soul. I've asked them how they'd feel if they heard an emergency room nurse say to a frantic wife in the waiting room, "Mrs. Jones, the doctors have resurrected your husband and you'll be able to see him shortly." They are ordinarily amazed at how strong their reactions to my questions are and at how much these things do in fact matter to them. Finally, I've been intrigued by the number of professedly nonreligious young people I know who object to any sort of disrespectful use of the phrase "The Force."

In earlier chapters we've discussed the effects of naming some human state as a disease, as in the case of renaming menopause "hypoestrogenemia." The effects of such naming extend far beyond the individual menopausal woman and into the society around her and the society at large. Similarly, when the state of weighing more than the cultural ideal is called neither a normal variation in human shape nor a disease, but is named as a *sin*, the consequences permeate the culture. Not to mention the fact that the contemporary understanding of the sin in question—gluttony—is a distortion of what the term "really" meant. Gluttony is obsession with food. When that obsession takes the form of a constant preoccupation with staying rail thin, it is as much a form of gluttony as is overeating—but contemporary American English has lost track of that meaning, making it possible for one group of gluttons to feel virtuous while considering the sorry state of the other group to be evidence of immorality or moral weakness.

The same thing holds when alcoholism or other addictions, or homosexuality, or attempted suicide, are classified as sins. People behave very differently toward someone whose state is considered proof of moral weakness and wickedness (a sinner) than they do toward someone who is considered to be sick and in need of medical treatment (a patient); the insanity defense for murderers is the prototypical example of that fact. And people who believe their own state and behavior to be sinful behave differently in this world than people who are convinced that they're not personally responsible for their condition because they are its "victims."

Everyone who interacts with a *sinner*—family, friends, workplace associates, teachers, helping professionals, and on down the list—is affected by the acceptance of that word from the vocabulary of religious language and behaves in ways that are shaped by that word. It makes very little difference whether they are themselves believers; the effects of the words "sin," "sinful," and "sinner" on the person they're applied to bring about changes, including legal changes, and others respond to the circumstances that are created by those changes.

Western elite culture, the culture of the highly educated professional and the academic, is just as subject to the effects we've been discussing as the cultures of our less privileged and less educated citizens; the same thing is true of cultures that are still functioning in ways that Western society set aside centuries ago.

It's not always easy to disentangle religious language effects from the effects of other factors that tend to hide the religious aspect, but the religious ones are always there. We're going to look now at one of the most obvious and easily identified examples, that of the ongoing furor about the overwhelming "maleness," in linguistic terms, of Christianity and Judaism.

Case Study: The Controversy over "Inclusive" Language

If asked in public, most people in the United States will agree unhesitatingly that the Judeo-Christian God has no sexual gender, that

God is neither male nor female (nor neuter, for that matter), and that the entire concept of sexual gender has no more relevance with regard to God than being accordion-pleated or paginated would have. They're absolutely right about that. In the Judeo-Christian culture, to think otherwise—to worship a God who is understood to have the shape and form of a human being of one gender or the other—is to commit idolatry. Nevertheless, few controversies have so torn the Judeo-Christian churches apart and so roused Judeo-Christian passions in America as the ongoing struggle over the masculine/feminine domain in what is usually called "inclusive" language. (Strictly speaking, "inclusive" language means that the religious language must include ethnic groups other than whites, must include the aged and the handicapped as well as the young and able, and so on. But the dispute over male versus female linguistic items has almost taken over the term.)

English is one of the languages that makes a fuss about the specification of human biological gender; it's not possible in English to use a singular third-person pronoun without making a specific choice among masculine "he," feminine "she," or neuter "it." It's this characteristic of the language that is responsible for Rosemary Ruether's famous, flawless, and splendidly contradictory example, "God is not male; He is Spirit."

English speakers have been trying for centuries to escape from this bind by using "they, their, theirs, them" as singular third-person pronouns, as in "Every member of the congregation had their own hymnal." (Contrary to popular belief, this practice is not a recent development.) When they do that, however, they're told three things: first, that they're making a grammar error; second, that substituting "his or her" for "their" in such sequences is awkward and cumbersome and should be avoided; and third, that the *correct* way to express their meaning is "Every member of the congregation had his own hymnal"—because "everybody knows the word 'his' in that sort of sentence *means* 'his or her.'"

The first and second of these statements are subject to argument; they depend on what dialect is being used and on opinions about style. The third, however, is simply false. Research has more than amply demonstrated that people today interpret as *exclusively male* the so-called generic masculine items of English like the masculine pronouns and words such as "mankind," all of which are alleged in grammar books and style manuals to include their corresponding feminine meanings. When research subjects are given sets of sentences such as "Every doctor dreads his Board exams" and "The composer who doesn't play the piano is hampered in his work" and are asked to draw pictures to illustrate them, by overwhelming majorities they draw pictures of a male doctor, a male composer, and so on.

No evidence whatsoever exists that masculine vocabulary and imagery are any more genuinely "inclusive" in religious language than in nonreligious language. We have no reason to assume that if research subjects were asked to draw illustrations of sentences such as "Every sinner hopes that he will be forgiven" they would change their behavior and draw roughly as many female sinners as male ones. This is no problem in religious life for men, who find themselves everywhere included and represented. But the situation for women is different.

Theologian Elizabeth A. Johnson writes:

What results when the human reality used to point to God is always and everywhere male? The sacred character of maleness is revealed, while femaleness is relegated to the unholy darkness without. . . . This state of affairs has a profound impact on women's religious identity. (Johnson 1993, page 37)

It's ironic that this quotation, which so perfectly argues the religious language case for women, should bring us right up against another major problem of religious language today. For people of color the constant association of holiness with whiteness, and of wickedness with blackness—as in "the unholy darkness without"—causes great pain. The good and the holy in religious language is *always* light and white; we never hear that our sins might be washed as black as ebony.

Claudia Camp is even more specific:

Because the Christian traditions have for so long put "God" and "father" in the same category, this conjunction has had a real historical impact. "God is a father" is a literal statement within the discourse. (Camp 1993, page 33)

We've run up against the linguistic relativity hypothesis controversy again. If linguist Joseph Beaver is right that "grammar and attitudes have nothing to do with each other," then we're talking about nothing more than style and taste. If Benjamin Whorf was right, we're talking about something far more important. If, as Pinker would argue, all that's necessary to clarify matters for a woman who feels excluded from Judeo-Christian religious language is to *point out* to her that all those male terms are "generic," we have no problem; if Pinker is wrong, the problem is very serious.

Hymn-writer Brian Wren states it very well:

If our language about God is harmless, and has no effect on our thinking and behavior, then the fact that all our names and images of God are male is unimportant. . . . On the other hand, if language powerfully shapes our thinking and behavior, then the maleness of God-language . . . becomes a crucial issue. (Wren 1991, page 55)

Over the course of more than a quarter century of investigating religious language in American English, I've asked hundreds of churchgoing Christians—in privacy, and with my promise of complete confidentiality—what they *really* believe about God's gender. The response, a great deal of the time, has gone like this: "I know I'm supposed to believe that God doesn't have any gender, and that's what I always *say*—but really, I think God is male." In some cases the answer has ended with the astonishing "I think God is a man. Not a *human* man, of course—but a man." What does "a man, but not a human man" mean? I have no idea. I haven't had the opportunity to do this informal experiment with the Jewish or Islamic counterparts of these Christians, unfortunately; but if I had to guess, I'd guess that the results would be similar. I *have* had the opportunity to ask large numbers of people who claim to be nonreligious; when they don't fend me off with "I have no opinions about that, since it's all nonsense anyway," for the most part they agree that God is "really" male.

As this would predict, those who complain about the "generic masculine" in the English Bible, buttressed as it is by an endless proliferation of explicitly male terms like "Father" and "Lord" and "King" and "Son of God," meet with intense criticism from the public as well as from professionals in religion. Zondervan (a major American religious publisher) recently brought out a *very* mildly inclusive Bible. It used such rephrasings as "Child of God" rather than "Son of God" and "humankind" rather than "mankind"; it changed many singular verbs to plural so that the genderless "they" could be used instead of the gendered "he or "she." The result was such a firestorm of criticism that printing was hastily stopped, despite the financial loss for the publishing house.

It's one thing when such criticism comes from denominations which openly claim that God intends for women to be subordinate to men. That is at least in part a logically consistent position. I say "in part" because so long as Judeo-Christian theology insists that God has *no* sexual gender, it's illogical to choose any gender at all for language that refers to that God. You don't have to. It's possible to just say "God" everywhere, without any pronouns; the result is not always elegant, but it's entirely comprehensible—and entirely logical when everyone involved is insisting that the entity in question has no sexual gender. Here's an example:

> Thus, when God's Spirit "hovers over" the "face" of the earth, we learn
> that God's relation to creation was an intimate, loving one as a mother
> hen protecting her chicks, a metaphor God when on earth will repeat.
> (Spencer and Spencer 1998, page 23)

Ruether's "God is not male; He is spirit" could simply be "God is not male: God is spirit," and the contradiction would disappear. Even "Godself" for "Himself," if it were routinely used, would soon sound normal and ordinary. But doing that would mean deliberately changing existing religious texts, and the resistance to that—in the

United States just as in the Arab nations—is very strong and deeply entrenched.

Ordinarily, individuals who insist that the religious language of Judeo-Christianity *must not* be changed—either by doing without pronouns for the divine or by making it "inclusive"—also insist that (a) they know very well that God has no sexual gender, and (b) they know very well that men and women are equal in God's sight and should also be equal in the sight of man (by which they of course claim to mean everyone, both male and female, and transgendered).

Suppose we assume that they do in fact believe exactly what they claim to believe. If so, it requires cognitive and linguistic gymnastics of the most intricate kind, and a consistent strategy of reframing, as in the recent very clever editorial by David Neff in *Christianity Today* which claimed that the argument has nothing to do with sexual gender anyway. Gender, he argues, is a red herring. His title is "The Great Translation Debate," and his claim is that the entire inclusive language argument is not about gender at all, but about how to be "most faithful to the ancient text" (Neff 1997, page 16). Or as stated bluntly by Grant R. Osborne in "Do Inclusive Language Bibles Distort Scripture? No," which opens with this sentence: "Whether or not to use inclusive language in Bible translation is not a gender issue but a matter of translation theory" (Osborne 1997, page 33). That may be true for scholars like Osborne, but for the ordinary person in America it is a gender issue.

We need to be aware that even those who are most severe in their insistence that the Bible's language be translated with utmost fidelity make exceptions in some cases. For example, there is Jeremiah 20:7. In the King James Bible it reads, "O Lord, thou hast deceived me, and I was deceived; thou art stronger than I, and hast prevailed; I am in derision daily, everyone mocketh me." The New King James has it as "O Lord, You induced me, and I was persuaded; You are stronger than I, and have prevailed. I am in derision daily; everyone mocks me." Scholar Abraham J. Herschel gives the literal meanings of the two verbs in question as "wrongfully inducing a woman to consent to prenuptial intercourse" and "violent forcing of a woman to submit to extranuptial intercourse." He offers the translation "O Lord,

Thou has seduced me, and I am seduced; Thou hast raped me, and I am overcome." This would certainly make the clause about being mocked a good deal easier to understand. But even the liberal Jerusalem Bible, which starts out with "You have seduced me, Yahweh, and I have let myself be seduced," isn't willing to go that far; it continues with "you have overpowered me; you were the stronger. I am a daily laughingstock." Faithful translation may be the professed goal, but when the result would have Jeremiah accusing the Deity of having raped him, the literalists back down. Clearly, there are *limits* to this professed goal of "being most faithful to the ancient text."

Here are three more examples of commentary about inclusive language, to show you how varied and ingenious they can be, and how impassioned:

> Even if speakers/writers should self-consciously choose not to use the masculine pronouns for God, the fact remains that they are self-consciously choosing *not* to use them; they are *intentionally deciding* to go against internalized grammatical convention and the deep, unconscious habits of the society. . . . Thus the practice of avoiding the masculine pronoun when talking about God will never become habitual and routine; such practice must and will remain at the level of self-aware rebellion. (Hook and Kimel 1993, pp. 16–17)

> While women, in their own fashion, may sin as much as men, it is the pride and willfulness and violence of men that most radically disrupts the world's peace and order. Feminist reformers may have no trouble in recognizing this fact, but they seem not to notice that breaking the arrogance and power of men requires a God who is, among other things, the Judge of Nations, the Lord of Hosts, the "King of glory . . . mighty in battle." . . . God's lordship is the only plausible check on the predatory tendencies of wicked men and nations, from Pharaoh to Haman to Hitler. (Berke 1996, page 35)

> The most simple and compelling reason to reject gender-reimaging is that God, though not a man or a male, has used masculine terms in making His self-disclosure to humanity. (Berke 1996, page 37)

The second Berke quotation, if taken seriously, would lead us straight to the isolationist position held by Arab speakers toward the Koran, in which the words in the religious texts are perceived as *literally* the words of God Godself. And how would we then carry on the evangelical practice of translating the Bible into the many human languages in which there are no masculine pronouns?

It might seem that all we'd have to do is make sure that a new pronoun, an exclusively masculine pronoun, is added to those languages that don't already have one. However, we have no reason to believe that that would be any easier to accomplish in other languages than it has been in English. There have been nearly 100 attempts in recent history to give English a gender-neutral third-person pronoun to avoid the constant "he or she" problems, and every single one of those attempts has failed. This is typical linguistic pathology; everybody, in their daily speech, uses "they" as a way out of the quandary; everybody, when talking about what is "correct," says it's wrong to use "they" to refer to just one person.

It's easy to add a new name-for-a-widget to a language; we do that for English almost every time something new is invented or discovered. It's also easy to make changes that do nothing but substitute one widget (as long as it's not a sacred Widget) for another. The English Bible says that marriage means a man shall leave his father and mother and cleave to his wife. Bible translators Gene and Marie Scott translated that into Sharanhua as "For this reason a man shall have the same mosquito net as his wife"; the Sharanhua of Peru don't leave their parents' homes when they marry. (See Zoba 1997, "Your Sins Shall Be White as Yucca," for details.) This sort of thing has to be done all the time in translating the Bible. But adding a new pronoun to a language is different.

Pronouns carry powerful presuppositions about reality as the speakers of that language perceive it. It *matters* to English speakers whether something being spoken or written about is animate or inanimate, human or nonhuman, one or more than one, male or female or neither. Sentences that lack such information are totally unacceptable. Speakers of other languages are equally unable to imagine using pronouns that make distinctions differently—that divide up reality differently—than the way *they're* accustomed to doing it. Pronouns are one of our most powerful tools for specifying what things members of a culture must pay attention to, and there will always be strong resistance to their modification.

We're often told that all of this controversy is a tempest in a teapot because, since not one of us has ever perceived what we are trying to describe and discuss, all talk about the Holy One is *by definition* metaphorical. That's all very well in theory, but people don't understand beloved religious metaphors as "only figures of speech." Trained religious professionals such as clergy and monks and nuns may be able to ignore the symbol and worship only the Divine Reality behind it; very few ordinary people are able to do that. We may know *intellectually* that our Heavenly Father is an unimaginable disembodied genderless divine Something-or-other; but when we pray to that Heavenly Father the image in our minds and hearts is probably a very human-looking man, something like Abraham Lincoln or Paul Newman, or their equivalents in other ethnic groups.

We could easily test the hypothesis that speakers of American English really perceive the Christian God as having no sexual gender. We would only have to produce a new biblical movie in which God speaks from the burning bush—and the voice of God is neither Charlton Heston nor James Earl Jones but the voice of a *woman.* Diane Sawyer, perhaps, or Jessye Norman. We all know what would happen, however much we claim to understand and believe that God is genderless. The people in the audience would react with a shocked silence, perhaps a shocked gasp. And then, depending on how devout they were and what denomination they belonged to, they would either burst out laughing or stand up and march out of the theater in outrage.

Male . . . Female . . . and?

I have restricted the discussion in this section to the two traditionally recognized biological genders: male and female. That has religious-language precedent; the Bible says "Male and female created He them." There is today, however, a vigorously thriving academic and scientific field known as "gender studies." The field of gender studies proposes that it's an error to assume automatically that a human being is either male or female, with no other possibilities to choose from. It also claims that sexual gender is not necessarily a biological matter, but is at least in part the result of socialization. If the gender studies scholars and scientists are correct, the traditional categories—and the pronouns associated with them—are not enough. If English is not willing to move to a *genderless* third-person pronoun, they would tell us, then it will have to find additional pronouns to refer to those human beings who insist that neither male nor female pronouns accurately name *their* gender.

This book isn't an appropriate forum for taking up this argument. It will be obvious, however, that adding more categories for gender would only make the inclusive language arguments even more difficult and more passionate than they are when we have only "he" and "she" to deal with. It would be far simpler, far more logical—and unquestionably more consistent with the theological precept that God is genderless!—if we eliminated the biological gender distinction from our religious language altogether. We can be certain, however, given the ferocious opposition to making such a change even when only the male/female distinction is involved, that trying to do it for the sake of additional genders would be impossible.

The inclusive religious language controversy revolves around a metaphor, obviously. That metaphor—GOD IS A FATHER, which presupposes maleness and dominance—has been a source of comfort to humankind through the ages; it has also been, and is still, a source of conflict and division and turmoil. It can't be a definition, like "A bat is a mammal," and subject to scientific objective testing; it can *only* be a metaphor.

"Fine," says the practical person. "Since we know that, let's just get rid of it. Better yet, let's get *all* the metaphors out of religious language!" It can't be done. This is one area of human language in which metaphor is our only resource. We can perhaps talk about ethics, and about morality, without metaphor, but religious language without metaphor is impossible.

Other Metaphors
in Religious Language

Another part of life in these United States where religious language has profound effects, and where those effects extend beyond believers, is in our choice of a unifying metaphor around which we can organize our lives and our behavior. Because roughly half of our population is female, the metaphor of the Father won't serve that purpose, and trying to switch to the Parent would land us right back in the inclusive language mess. Something else has to be selected.

Christians (who are the majority religion in the United States) read in the New Testament that Jesus has commanded them to return good for evil; they read that it is the meek and the peacemakers who will inherit the earth; they read that the rich and the powerful will have great difficulty getting into heaven. (And much more of the same.) They sing hymns about "Gentle Jesus, meek and mild"; they memorize and love the Twenty-third Psalm with its description of the Lord as a shepherd. All admirable in theory; all downright pretty, like the Christmas cards where the lion and the lamb lie peacefully cuddled up together under a tree.

But when the time comes to choose a metaphor around which to organize their religious/spiritual lives, in the way that we've chosen the metaphor of the Football Game as an organizing mechanism for our business lives, no gentle shepherds need apply. Even the quickest glance around the shelves of a Christian bookstore will make it unmistakably clear that the dominant unifying religious metaphor for the ordinary religious person is the Warrior.

Warriors don't turn the other cheek, they don't return good for evil, they don't give the thief who steals their shirt their coat to go with it. Warriors get out there and do just one thing: *They fight to win.*

For the adults fulfilling this role, the script for this metaphor is clear. If they're in combat, if they're mentally ill, if they're fanatics, or if they're in contact sports, they may do some of their fighting physically. Otherwise, in a society such as ours that has legal penalties

(not always enforced, but at least on the books) against physical violence, they do their fighting verbally. Our culture honors and rewards them for this behavior. Unless they become famous or
accomplish something truly remarkable, as did Martin Luther King,
Jr., we call people who return good for evil "wimps" and "weaklings."

I have been flabbergasted by this my entire adult life, and awed by
it. It's particularly baffling to me that we see this in its most extreme
form in those devout persons who claim to believe that the Bible
must be taken absolutely literally; no one buys more books and tapes
and videos about "spiritual warfare" than the biblical literalist. Only
among such groups do we find the extraordinary current practice of
holding prayer meetings at which you pray for misfortunes or
tragedies to happen to those you oppose, like the groups whose admitted purpose was to pray for the death of President Clinton.

What are the effects of this metaphor on the culture at large? It has
turned us into a people who, while paying lip service to peace—and
reacting with horror to extreme violent events such as the Oklahoma
bombing and the sequence of school massacres—allow our lives to
revolve around violence. We are a people who spend large portions
of our disposable incomes supporting violent movies and books,
who allow our children to spend hours of their day playing violent
computer games, who do nothing more than shake our heads when
we learn that one product available to our children is a set of Serial
Killer trading cards, and who—inevitably—conduct our business by
the rules of football rather than the rules of the Bible, using ruthless
competition to win as our governing strategy. Those who profess to
take the Bible literally and want it applied literally in many areas of
human life—especially the area of sexual behavior—very rarely
want to extend that idea to business and economics, where it would
mean that they were forbidden to buy and sell real estate, forbidden
in most cases to lend money at interest, required to return good for
evil, and much more of the same kind. As Walter Wink puts it:

> The myth of redemptive violence is the simplest, laziest, most exciting,
> uncomplicated, irrational, and primitive depiction of evil the world
> has ever known. Furthermore, its orientation toward evil is one *into*

which virtually all modern children (boys especially) are socialized in the
process of maturation. (Wink 1998, page 53)

I agree with Wink's statement; I would add only that the "boys especially" in question are for the most part brought up by women; little girls must therefore be socialized to be willing to participate in this process. By "redemptive" violence, Wink is referring to the concept that violence is acceptable, even admirable, when its goal is to accomplish good, as in just wars.

The strength of the Spiritual Warrior metaphor is growing daily, and it has spread from the domain of actual combat to the more pervasive domain of all competition. It used to specify only that the Warrior must win; now it is understood to demand that everybody else except the Warrior must lose. That is, there can be only *one* winner, and that winner must leave an empty battlefield behind. We saw this in the recent Olympic Games when the Nike ads at Atlanta said, "You don't win silver. You lose gold." And our young people, who've come into this semantic controversy late in the battle—or in the third quarter—and are not being taught the relevant history, have lost track of the principle of the just war. That principle stipulates that violence must always be the *last* resort, carried out with heartfelt regret because everything else has been tried and has failed, and no other action appears to be possible. The Warrior metaphor has brutalized our sports and is brutalizing our lives, and it is a religious language phenomenon.

The most extraordinary section in Lakoff and Johnson's *Philosophy in the Flesh* (1999) is pages 563–564, where they claim that—having proved to their satisfaction that there cannot be a disembodied mind—they extrapolate from that to the claim that there cannot be a disembodied soul. That is, there cannot be a mind with an existence independent of the body; *therefore*, there cannot be a soul with an existence independent of the body. They do not even consider the possibility that a divine Creator would be able to construct something—something which human beings could refer to as "the soul"—and give it characteristics so different from the mind that it would be entirely capable of independence from the body.

They don't consider the possibility that their "embodied mind" is in fact a metaphor, which the soul transcends. Instead, they conclude on page 564 that "what is needed is an alternative conception of embodied spirituality that at least begins to do justice to what people experience." The Warrior is a good candidate for such a conception (and you couldn't ask for anything more "embodied"); there are just as many accounts of esctatic and mystical experiences occurring during combat and intensive competition as during meditation.

For some multilinguals, the Warrior metaphor of American English will introduce into religious conversations a kind of confusion and misunderstanding that we've grown familiar with throughout this book. There are cultures and languages in which the role of warrior has little or nothing to do with winning, and in which the warrior's role is to *avoid* combat.

I've been asked for an example from another culture and language that would be a "metaphor translation" of the Spiritual Warrior in American English, and I've done a great deal of searching; I've asked a number of my multilingual respondents for help in this regard. So far, I've been unable to find anything even remotely comparable to the American array of books and tapes and movies and organizations—as well as religious professionals, both in and out of church—that explicitly identify and endorse the Spiritual Warrior. That seems to be an exclusively American cultural phenomenon. It's possible to get tentative agreement about a proposed metaphor, just for discussion purposes; I've had moderately positive reactions to a proposal that the Gracious Gentleman is analogous in Confucianism to the Warrior in Christianity. But such discussions quickly become extremely uncomfortable; there is, for example, no corresponding Gracious Lady metaphor in Confucianism, and no inclusive language movement.

Beads on a Single String

What we know about religious language provides us with more information about how multilinguals manage when their two languages give them conflicting messages (like the Tibetan speaker of

English, whose most usual native word for "body" means roughly "a thing that you leave behind"). We have a multitude of choices as our examples; let's take the very large population of American Christians for whom the following three statements hold:

- They accept the Warrior metaphor while at the same time believing in a Bible that tells them to turn the other cheek and return good for evil.
- They are for the death penalty and against abortion, simultaneously.
- They use the commandment "Whoever kills any man shall surely be put to death" (Leviticus 24:17) as support for their position on the death penalty while ignoring the commandment that "everyone who curses his father or his mother shall surely be put to death" (Leviticus 20:9) and "the adulterer and the adulteress shall surely be put to death" (Leviticus 20:10).

—and much more of the same kind—all simultaneously.

Like the multilingual who picks and chooses among conflicting presuppositions of his or her various languages according to the circumstances, they navigate smoothly and skillfully among all these contradictions. The philosopher F.L.G. Frege gave us the perfect metaphor for this situation when he said that the propositions of any single religious faith are like the beads of a necklace or rosary: They're all on the same unifying string, making them recognizable as the propositions of a single faith—but each one is separate and complete unto itself, so that any one of them can be handled without any reference to the others. That is, you choose among them according to what it is that you are doing at the time and what your needs are for doing it.

Assimilation Is Conversion

In an article in the February 1997 issue of *Reason Magazine* titled "Assimilation, American Style," Peter Salins writes:

The greatest failing of the melting pot metaphor is that it overreaches. It exaggerates the degree to which immigrants' ethnicity is likely to be extinguished by exposure to American society and it exaggerates the need to extinguish ethnicity. . . . Perhaps a new assimilation metaphor should be introduced—one that depends not on a mechanical process like the melting pot but on human dynamics. Assimilation might be viewed as more akin to religious conversion than anything else. In the terms of this metaphor, the immigrant is the convert, American society is the religious order being joined, and assimilation is the process by which the conversion takes place. . . . Conversion is a mutual decision requiring affirmation by both the convert and the religious order he or she wishes to join. Converts are expected in most (but not all) cases to renounce their old religions. But converts do not have to change their behavior in any respects *other than those that relate to the new religion.* (Salins 1997, page 23; emphasis added)

That is, someone who has openly joined a Christian church in the United States must sit quietly and respectfully, without objecting, while a minister reads and preaches about turning the other cheek and following the Golden Rule, and even reads verses of the Bible commanding us not to charge interest and not to bring lawsuits—but once that person leaves the church, no one expects that the Shepherd will replace the Warrior in his or her life. Perhaps, if we treat assimilation like conversion, as long as those who assimilate observe all the rules of public life and public citizenship there's no reason *in theory* why they couldn't continue to maintain their ethnic heritage and their native language in the privacy of their homes. The assimilated multilingual individual would end up with a string of beads perhaps even less matched, even less a harmonious whole, than usual—but they would remain just one string of beads.

In theory, this sort of lip service model for assimilation is appealing; in religious life, it might even work. As always, the string of beads would have to be left at home when the multilingual went off to work.

A Final Note—Religion plus Music

Throughout this book I've repeatedly pointed out the importance for English of the melody attached to words by tone of voice and intonation of the voice—the tune the words are set to. In most forms of discourse that is as melodic as it's possible to be; only in musical comedies do adults burst into song in the middle of their conversations and other language interactions. We may sing lullabies to tiny kids, we may sing in the shower or in the car, but that's as far as it goes.

If you and I are sitting around talking about religious matters, we're still not likely to burst into song. But for churchgoing Americans, the singing of religious language in the form of *hymns*—not just listening, but actually singing along—will be a regular feature of life at least once a week. It would be remiss of me not to mention this, and not to point out that language set to music with a pleasing melody has a power that spoken language rarely can achieve. People will listen, and listen willingly, to sung words that they wouldn't tolerate for a minute if spoken—something that the writers of "protest songs" are well aware of. People (even totally nonreligious people) who would leave immediately if others started praying aloud at them will happily sit and listen to the singing of religious music. People who have little interest in a cause will unite around it because of the extraordinary attraction of a song—we only have to think of what was accomplished in our past by Julia Ward Howe's "Battle Hymn of the Republic."

Brian Wren has used this aspect of language, combined with his great skill in the constructing of metaphors, to remarkable effect. There is his hymn "Holy Weaver, Deftly Intertwining," in which he carries the metaphor GOD IS A WEAVER through the verses. There's "Joyful is the Dark," in which he turns the usual EVIL IS BLACK/ GOOD IS WHITE metaphor pair around, using phrases such as "the roaring, looming thundercloud of glory." In "Bring Many Names" he explores a set of metaphors, including not only

"Warm father God" but also "Strong mother God" and "Old, aching God, grey with endless care." Songs can build bridges that spoken words cannot, and that speakers can only long for and envy. There are many reasons for this in theory; in practical terms, the reason is simply that people are more willing to listen to another person sing than they are to listen to another person talk.

7

Why Not Have Just *One* Language That *Every*body Knows?

So what's the solution? "Thoughtfully planned bilingualism" says Einar Haugen, a linguist. . . . Haugen wants each of us to have a "native, homely, familiar everyday language in which we can live and love" as well as a second "language of wider communication" that will enable us to jet around the world.

(Vines 1996, page 27)

Remember Einar Haugen's proposal, mentioned previously on page 35?

Is Haugen right? Maybe. When the communication problems of a multilingual world are discussed, people often express agreement with him (or with some variation on his idea) and suggest that an obvious solution is staring us right in the face: Let's have a single language (traditionally called an "international auxiliary language," or IAL) that *everyone* would learn in early childhood, so that all human beings on this planet would have at least one shared medium for communication. What could be more logical, or more practical?

Suppose that, for purposes of discussing this idea, we call our hypothetical IAL "WorldSpeak." We'd need to call it something far less English and far more internationally neutral in form, and choosing the final name would have to be done with great care and attention, but WorldSpeak will do for our present purposes. The scenario that carries out this idea and makes WorldSpeak a genuine IAL—in two versions—is easily imagined.

In both versions, all children would acquire their native tongues in the usual way, along with whatever other language or languages were present as input in their language environment; this would involve no change from our present practice.

In both versions, all adults would know WorldSpeak, which would put an end to the need for translators and interpreters, either human or electronic, in every aspect of international interaction. Translation and interpreting would become activities done as *art* rather than as necessities. Monolingual persons would exist only in the increasingly rare circumstances of peoples truly cut off from modern education and technology. This would save huge amounts of time and money and effort, freeing up resources that could be used for other purposes. Not only because of the logistics-related savings, but also because we would have fewer of the expensive international misunderstandings that result from language differences. Professional translators and interpreters (other than literary translators), along with professionals involved in machine translation, would have to go through the sort of dislocation that occurs when any work role becomes obsolete in a society; they would find other ways to make their livings, in due time.

WorldSpeak Scenario A

When children started school, WorldSpeak would be a new "basic" subject with the status of reading and writing and math—from the very first day, everywhere in the world. This would establish a global pidgin. Then, once the first generation of WorldSpeakers had children of their own, every home on the planet would be a multilingual household. And human children would start acquiring WorldSpeak by being exposed to it in the home from birth, making WorldSpeak a worldwide *native* language. People would then take WorldSpeak courses in school just as they now take courses in their native languages, not to *learn* the language but to polish their comunication skills and learn "proper" grammar and usage,

WorldSpeak Scenario B

In this version every child would learn WorldSpeak as in Scenario A, but instruction would begin much later, probably as a required subject for two semesters in the final year of high school (or its equivalent in other societies). The core inventory of WorldSpeak skills—the ability to carry on a simple conversation, read and write nontechnical materials, and do survival math—would be a requirement for graduation and for getting a job. It would be taken for granted in the way that literacy is taken for granted in the industrialized world today. Whether an individual went on beyond that level of fluency would be a matter of individual taste and need.

People involved in global business or law or diplomacy, or in any of the sciences, would routinely take additional WorldSpeak courses as part of their university and professional education. People planning a vacation in a foreign country would brush up their World-Speak skills with a television or computer course, or by studying a "WorldSpeak for Tourists" book, the way people now brush up on their high school French before spending a week in Paris. There would undoubtedly be a horde of "WorldSpeak consultants."

Just as we now assume that any adult we meet will be able to read and write and do simple math, we would assume that he or she would be able to get by after a rough fashion in WorldSpeak. There would of course be times when our assumption turned out to be incorrect, just as today we sometimes run into an illiterate adult, but that would be rare. The degree of WorldSpeak fluency would vary from person to person. For some people, especially those who had grown up in households where parents chose to use the IAL regularly in the home, "knowing" WorldSpeak would mean native or near-native fluency. For others it would mean the sort of fluency a person today typically has after two semesters of a foreign language in high school if a moderate effort is made to maintain that level of fluency in adult life.

You'll see at once that Scenario A is the simpler and more efficient choice. Things would be a bit rocky for the first generation, and there would be unanticipated glitches to work out. But from then on, with WorldSpeak having become a native language for everyone, the process would go smoothly. Scenario A takes advantage of the scientific facts about language acquisition. We know that if we want our kids to have real fluency in Chinese they need to start learning Chinese as early in life as possible, preferably as infants in the home; the same thing would be true for fluency in the international auxiliary language. There is absolutely no question about this; once the transitional period was over, Scenario A would be simpler than Scenario B in every way and would yield superior results. However, it is by no means certain, or even probable, that Scenario A would be our choice.

Think about it, please, in terms of the questions that we have been exploring in previous chapers of this book: What would it mean for the human race if it were not only the case that monolingualism had disappeared from this earth, but also that every human being shared a single *native* language? We'd be rid of the expense and inconvenience associated with translating and interpreting, yes; international affairs could be conducted more efficiently and swiftly, yes. But what *other* consequences might there be? We'll come back to this issue later in the chapter.

Once the seemingly logical and overwhelmingly obvious decision has been made that an IAL would be a good thing and that efforts should be made to put one in place, you come to the hardest and most predictable question, the one that must be settled before any other steps can be taken:

> *Which* language is going to be the one that every human being will be expected to know?

The natural human reaction is an immediate "Well, *my* language, of course!" but we are well aware that it's not that easy. There are only two possible answers:

- We choose some existing natural language and see that every educated person knows it, in the way that every educated European person was once expected to know Latin.
- We choose a language that's not a natural language but has been *constructed* (often for the purpose of serving as an IAL, in the way Esperanto was intended by its designer). We could pick one of the hundreds of such languages that have already been proposed, or we could construct a new one (in which case one can only hope that linguists would be consulted).

In either case, we could modify the chosen language to produce an "international version" of it if we wished. The most likely modification would be to simplify the language in arbitrary ways, as was done for Charles K. Ogden's 850-word "Basic English" or the version of English called "Simplified English" that all airplane pilots and air traffic controllers are today expected to know. Finally, although they may seem unlikely choices to most of us, we must not rule out in advance the idea of a sign language, or of systems such as Morse Code, when making our decision. They might have advantages that don't come immediately to mind. (A system now exists for writing and typing sign languages, called SignWriting; it's cumbersome, but it works.)

Let's consider those two basic alternatives: natural language versus constructed language.

Choosing an Existing Natural Language as the IAL

It's disconcerting, because none of us has ever been allowed to make our wishes on the subject known, but it has to be admitted: *This is already under way.* In a very informal and disorganized fashion, the world has already chosen English (or, as speakers of many other languages would insist, has had English imposed upon it) as its global language. If that's the wrong choice, either because some other nat-ural language would be better for the purpose or because we should instead choose a constructed language, we need to recognize that in a hurry, while there may still be time to stop it.

A few years ago Pakistan set up a language study commission, which concluded that "there is no escape for any country in the world from learning English well, and thoroughly" (Reeves 1997). When South Africa ended white minority rule in 1994, its official languages were Afrikaans and English; the new government added nine African languages spoken in the country to the official language list. The result? "Faced with making preflight safety announcements in 11 languages, South African Airlines pared down to English. Sim-ilar decisions have given English near supremacy at universities, Par-liament, the post office and the telephone company" (Reber 1998). In a February 21, 1999, on-line review of Manfred Gerlach's book *Even More Englishes*, we read that it's a collection of papers "devoted to general problems of the world language" and that two papers in-vestigate "the form and functions of the world language" in South Africa and Nigeria.

"Speakers of other languages," writes Gordon Bilney from Aus-tralia, "won't necessarily think it's fair that they should have to learn English to get the most out of life in the 21st century; nor is it, but there's little choice." (Bilney 1998.)

There's no way to avoid it. We have to acknowledge that while American politicians are fretting about the perils of bilingual educa-tion—and making speeches warning us that without "English Only" laws we face possible secession attempts by Florida and New Mexico, as Canada faces possible secession by Quebec—English has already, literally, begun taking over the world.

Let's assume for a moment that this situation is going to continue. If English is to be the final Terran choice, attempts will undoubtedly be made to bring a degree of order into the process. In spite of the dismal track record of all "language academies" and "bureaus of lan-guage" throughout history, we will surely try again. As Barry New-man points out, with obvious uneasiness, "English no longer simply divides itself into regionally rooted dialects—or distinct 'Englishes' as some argue—but into a rabble of non-native registers . . . for spe-cific purposes. . . . What happens to this language is no longer our prerogative. English is no longer our possession" (Newman, 1993). Oops!

On May 16, 1996, an announcement was posted on the Internet by Macquarie Limited's Sue Butler, for a series of international con-ferences. Their unifying topic was "English as an Asian Language"(a later slip of the key said revealingly that English "*is* an Asian Lan-guage"), beginning with a conference on Thai English to be held in Bangkok and one on Philippine English to be held in Manila. Defin-itions of terms included these two very significant items:

> A national variety of English is a form or dialect of English which has a national distribution. It is acknowledged to be the form of English identified with the particular nation, having developed features which distinguish it from other varieties of English as a consequence of its separate history, geographical location and cultural context.

> Standard English should be defined as that accepted form of English which occurs in prestigious English-language newspapers, publishing and broadcasting in the specified country.

Separate history? Separate *cultural context*? A standard based on "prestigious" media output in "the specified country," never mind how English might be used in the *New York Times*? Oops!

It doesn't help matters that we have no accepted definition of Standard English that could be *proposed* as an international stan-dard. Existing definitions are of two kinds. In one group you'll find a multitude of safely vacuous variations on "Standard English is the language used by educated people." (That is, "We know Standard English when we see it or hear it.") The other group contains dan-gerously specific definitions that betray the ongoing public igno-rance of basic linguistic facts, a situation for which the public can't be blamed but which desperately needs repair. Consider, for exam-ple, this definition from the state of Virginia's House Bill No. 2437, passed not in 1900 but in 1997, with emphasis added by me:

Standard English includes the written and spoken language which is accepted by generally recognized authorities as grammatically correct in the United States and *shall not include any dialect, jargon, patois or vernacular based on the English language.*

Given this state of affairs, it's reasonable to wonder what will become of English as it spreads like some variety of linguistic kudzu into every corner of Earth; but that's something that we know, from experience, cannot be predicted. It's impossible to keep a living language from changing, although that won't keep the governments of Earth from trying.

Something of this kind perhaps happened at that point in the mists of prehistory when everyone in the known world spoke a single language—let's call it *Ur*. Although there were no media, prestigious or otherwise, there were surely standards. We can imagine one Early Human sneering at another's inferior way of speaking Ur. And then millennia went by, and instead of Ur there were French and Albanian and Chinese and Basque and English and Mohawk. But our world is not the world that Early Humans knew. In a world that has satellite television and the Internet, and telephones that will work in the middle of the most barren desert, human beings who are separated by geography are no longer isolated from one another *linguistically*. Only a planetwide catastrophe that restored *pre*historical conditions could once again make it even remotely possible for words to change gradually over time, in isolation, to such an extent that only highly trained specialists in historical linguistics would be able to tell that they had ever been the same. What happened to Ur (or conceivably to several "Urs") could not happen to International English.

Well, then, can we say that the whole issue of IALs is now moot? Is it settled that WorldSpeak will be some impossible-to-predict form of English? Should those of us lucky enough to already know one or more varieties of English just relax and be grateful that we happened to be born into an English-speaking language environment?

Nobody knows. The Englishing of Earth is something like the global warming of Earth. It may be happening; some experts say so. It may already be an accomplished fact; it may be too late to stop it;

some experts say so. In which case, instead of passing laws to protect English we should be doing our utmost to protect our remaining store of *other* languages! We know from the biological sciences how dangerous it is to reduce any pool of existing varieties to just one. Nothing we know in linguistic science gives us reason to believe that it would be any less dangerous for the world's language "gene pool" to be reduced to only English, even with a multitude of dialects.

Furthermore, before native speakers of English jump to any conclusions, they would be wise to ask native speakers of other languages how *they* feel about the idea that English should be the *lingua franca* (which meant "*French* language") for today's human race. And then they would be wise to back off a good long distance to spare their ears after asking. Many peoples in this world—perhaps almost all—deeply resent the idea that they should sit back and allow all international commerce and science and diplomacy, all international communication, to be conducted in English. A recent attempt by an Internet service to require all communication about soccer to be in English—a very *small* area of Earthly communication—provoked so passionately negative and furious a response that it was hastily canceled. Even nations whose dominant language *is* English are fighting to keep their own brand from going under; the *Sydney Morning Herald* for August 14, 1997, reported that a group of Australian researchers have "produced an Australian weapon to fight . . . American linguistic imperialism," in the form of a dictionary of Australian words and phrases to be substituted for American linguistic imports (Jopson 1997).

Consider the program now being proposed by the foremost linguist of France, Claude Hagège, in his 1996 book *L'Enfant aux Deux Langues*. H. Stephen Straight (reviewing the book in the March 1998 issue of *Language*) says on page 140 that Hagège "*openly addresses what may well be the most pressing question of educational policy today*: how to prepare French schoolchildren—and by extension schoolchildren across Europe and around the world—for the multilingualism that will pervade the 21st century" (Straight 1998, page 140; emphasis added). And then, to the question of which languages should be taught in French elementary schools:

Hagège heart-stoppingly responds—if I may coin an acronym—ABE, Anything But English. The world-wide popularity of English threatens to divert French school-children from the task of developing proficiencies in the many other languages of the European community and of the world. (Straight 1998, page 140)

Anything but English! It would fit nicely on a bumper sticker or a coffee mug, and it contrasts nicely with *English Only*. Hagège's proposal is that the French elementary schools offer German, Italian, Portuguese, Spanish, and (for speakers of minority languages in France) French, followed in high school by two additional languages. The goal is that each French youngster would know four languages: the native tongue, two additional European languages learned in early childhood, and one other language learned in adolescence. *Only at the high school level would English be one of the possible choices,* and even then it would have to compete with Russian, Arabic, Hungarian, Swahili, Chinese, Hindi, Japanese, and more. Hagège perceives this project as an urgently necessary measure for preventing the global linguistic takeover of English. It's quite clear; speakers of other languages may not be able to prevent it—it may be too late to stop the English juggernaut—but they resent it from the bottom of their hearts.

The fact that English appears to be the easiest solution to the problem of global Babel doesn't mean that it is necessarily the best solution. Perhaps a serious effort ought to be made to call it off. Native speakers of English, because they suffer from the same native-language bias as any other human beings, are the last group who should sit in judgment here. We have to ask ourselves: "What if my native language were Gaelic? Or Arapaho? Or Maori? How pleased would I be with English as an IAL?"

Innocent though we native speakers of English may be personally of any interference in the affairs of other nations and nationals, the political facts are real and have to be faced: For most of the world, English is the Superpower Language. It is the ultimate "colonial" language. It's the language of the Ugly American and the Snobbish Brit. It's the language callously imposed on the downtrodden immigrant or subjugated indigenous population. For the sake of *peace* in the world, perhaps we should set aside our natural preference and our gut feelings and consider other alternatives.

The first "other alternative" is that we should choose some other existing natural language instead of English. But how do we do that? Many, if not all, nations would insist that their language should be the one chosen, and would offer a strong case. The French would point to their literature, their history, the tradition of French *as* a lingua franca, and the fact that French uses the Roman alphabet; other European nations would present similar arguments. The Japanese (and other Asian nations) would point to their own proud literary tradition, their history, their position in the world, and the fact that their writing system does not carry the stigma of Western colonialism as the Roman alphabet does. The Hopi (and many other Native American nations and indigenous peoples around the world) would insist that it is precisely the apparent difference between their language and the more commonly used languages, not to mention the absence of a recent history of conquest, that would make Hopi the ideal choice.

And so it would go, with all this passionate wrangling being carried on through translators and interpreters. It's not a prospect that gives one hope, and it's the sort of thing that has led to wars in humanity's history. Perhaps we should abandon the idea of an existing natural language as IAL altogether. Which would bring us to—

Choosing a Constructed Language (Existing or New) as the IAL

The traditional hypothesis has been that because a constructed language is the language of *no* nation or ethnic group, it would be free of the political problems that all natural languages bring with them. Esperanto materials frequently claim (incorrectly) that this is true of Esperanto. A distinction is usually made between auxiliary languages (auxlangs), designed with international communication as a deliberate goal, and "conlangs," usually constructed for other purposes. (The Elvish languages showcased by Tolkien in his epic *Lord of the Rings* and the Klingon language constructed by linguist Mark Okrand for the *Star Trek* television series are conlangs rather than auxlangs.)

Constructed languages aren't a new idea, nor did they begin with Esperanto, and there have been hundreds of them. The first one for which we have any historical records was Lingua Ignota, a language devised by Hildegard of Bingen. We know almost nothing about it except that it existed and that—since it was constructed in an era when Latin was the recognized IAL—it was probably not meant to serve as an international tongue. The first for which we have any useful information came from one George Dalgarno of Scotland in 1661. The first that any number of people actually *used*, both in speech and in writing, so far as we know, was Volapük, the work of a German priest named Johann Martin Schleyer, in 1880. Volapük was so successful in Europe and the United States that by 1889 it was said to have 200,000 aficionados and 300 supporting groups. There were Volapük publications and international Volapük conferences. But the language was very difficult to learn, and it died almost as fast as it had become popular.

When the far less intimidating Esperanto, the creation of ophthalmologist Lazar (often called "Ludwig") Zamenhof, appeared in 1887, it quickly took over the territory that Volapük had been holding; it continues to this day to be the most successful of all proposed IALs. Estimates of the number of Esperanto speakers range from as low as 50,000 to about two million; if even the smaller of those numbers is accurate, it's an impressive total, far larger than the total number of speakers of many natural languages. Esperanto has a sizable literature, both original and in translation. It has a sturdy international support structure. It has been around long enough to undergo minor reform, and there are various proposed "new and improved" Esperantos. In the early 1900s, with the great linguist Otto Jespersen (himself the author of a constructed language called Novial) leading the charge, it appeared that a multinational committee and academy might actually give some version of Esperanto an official standing—but two world wars, and the dreadful internal power struggles within the IAL movement, put an end to that effort. Nothing on the same scale has been attempted since.

A language called Solresol, based entirely on the names for the seven units of the Western musical scale, was introduced by Francois Sudré, a French scientist. All its words were combinations of the syllables (do, re, mi, and so on) used to teach singing. Solresol had the unique advantage of being a language that could be sung and played and hummed and whistled as well as spoken, and for a while in the 1800s it had a considerable popularity. At one point, the French military even considered adopting it as an auxiliary means of communication.

For vast amounts of information about the few constructed languages that I've mentioned here, and many others not mentioned—some just now coming into existence as tiny hobby languages known only to their individual devisers—you need only call up your favorite Internet search engine, type in the search words "International Auxiliary Languages," and watch your screen fill with Internet addresses. You'll find links to scores of sites, including entire web pages devoted even to the most obscure of the languages. (There is a Solresol Web site, for example.) You'll find a site at which the biblical story of the Tower of Babel is presented with translations into a large number of constructed languages. You'll find instructions for subscribing to two Internet discussion lists, one for conlangs and the other for auxlangs, if this interests you. A complete and detailed history of everything you could possibly want to know about IALs over time, written by Donald J. Harlow (as Chapter 3 of his wonderful but hard-to-find *The Esperanto Book*), is available to you at www.webcom.com/-~donh/esperanto.html. The International Auxiliary Language Association (founded in 1924 by Alice Vanderbilt Morris) is long gone, but the movement for IALs is thriving and healthy.

The question is, would humanity be better off choosing one of these languages to serve as WorldSpeak? Would that be any more satisfactory than choosing an existing natural language?

Case Study: Two Example Languages

To make the various problems and issues more clear, let's take a closer look at two examples of constructed languages. One is Zamenhof's Esperanto, the prototypical and most successful auxlang; the other is a conlang constructed by me in the 1980s called Láadan.

The Case of Esperanto

By IAL standards, Esperanto is a smashing success. Many thousands of people speak and understand and read and write it. So far as I have been able to determine, it is the only constructed language for which there do exist a few individuals who can reasonably be considered native speakers; these are the "denaska" (from birth) Esperantists who have learned the language as infants because it was the only tongue their parents had in common and was therefore spoken in their home. When a document is published in a number of languages, it's not unusual to find an Esperanto version included in the set. Esperanto is frequently described today as a true "international language," and the general public appears to accept that description without question.

I have taught Esperanto to English speakers, both adults and children. Much of its vocabulary is transparent for those who know English, and they find its core grammar rules simple and easily remembered. How quickly students learn to speak and understand the language depends on such things as their opportunities to practice those skills and how inhibited they are; some learn very quickly, others have more difficulty. But I can say without hesitation that if you speak and read almost any Germanic or Romance language you can learn to *read* Esperanto easily in three or four hours. If you know one Germanic and one Romance language—English and Italian, for example, or German and French—you can almost read it on sight without any instruction whatsoever.

Here's a brief sample—a few sentences about the River Nile from a children's reader called *El Afriko*—that will show you why I can say that with such confidence:

Preskau 40 milionoj da homoj loĝas en la baseno de la rivero Nilo. Dum miloj da jaroj, la bonstato de tiuj egiptoj kaj sudananoj de-

pendis de la fluo de la Nilo. Dum sezonoj, kiam la pluvofalo en la su-
daj montoj estis granda, la "nilanoj" properis. Kiam la pluvofalo estis
malgranda, ili malsatis. (No author or date of publication shown;
page 16)

(Almost 40 million people live in the basin of the River Nile. For
millions of years, the wellbeing of every Egyptian and Sudanese de-
pended on the flow of the Nile. During seasons when rainfall in the
southern mountains was plentiful, the "Nile-people" prospered. When
the rain was scanty, they did badly.)

And here are a few verses of the Tower of Babel story (Genesis
11:1–9), which Zamenhof himself translated from Hebrew. (I've
followed current Internet practice and have used "sx" for "ŝ," "cx"
for "ĉ," "gx" for "ĝ.")

1. Sur la tuta tero estis unu lingvo kaj unu parolmaniero.
   (Now the whole world had one language and one way of
   speaking.)
2. Kaj kiam ili ekiris de la orienta, ili trovis valon en la lando
   Sxinar kaj tie ek logxis. (As men moved eastward, they found
   a plain in the land of Shinar and there they settled.)
3. Kaj ili diris unu al alia: Venu, ni fau brikojn kaj ni brulpretigu
   ilin per fajro. Kaj la brikoj farigxis por ili sxtonoj, kaj la
   bitumo farigis por ili kalko. (And they said one to another,
   "Come, we will make bricks and bake them with fire." And
   they made bricks for their stones and made tar for their
   mortar.)
4. Kaj ili diris: Venu, ni konstruu al ni urbon, kaj turon, kies
   supro atingos la cxielon . . . (And they said, "Come, we will
   build for us a city, and a tower that reaches to the sky . . . "
5. Kaj la Eternulo diris: Jen estas unu popolo, kaj unu lingvon
   ili cxiuj havas; kaj jen, kion ili komencis fari, kaj ili ne estos
   malhelpataj en cxio, kion ili decididis fari. (The Lord said,
   "They are one people, and they have one language, and they
   have begun to do this; it will be impossible to keep them
   from doing anything that they decide to do.")

Esperanto is obviously not being held back because it's difficult to learn or because materials are expensive and hard to find. Like many other well-designed IALs, its problems are primarily social and political rather than linguistic. Although Esperanto is international in the narrow sense that it incorporates features of more than one national language, it in no way meets the criteria for a global language. It is essentially pidgin Indo-European, without enough native speakers as yet to qualify as a creole. If the only language you know is Chinese or Yoruba or Navajo or Korean, or any one of thousands of other natural languages, Esperanto will look no more familiar to you than any other foreign language does. And because the national languages on which Esperanto is based are those of the imperial and colonizing nations of Europe, it carries the same unsavory political connotations for most of the world's peoples that English carries.

If you go to the Esperanto sites on the Internet (start with www.esperanto.net or www.esperanto.com, where you'll find links to all the rest), you'll be astonished at the abundance of material available, often with translations into dozens of other languages. You'll find free Esperanto courses on-line, for various levels; there's an on-line "Esperanto Yellow Pages." Any library of moderate size will have Esperanto teaching materials and publications. The Universal Esperanto Association has members in eighty-three countries and national affiliate organizations in fifty-five countries; there are hundreds of special-interest Esperanto organizations. (You can contact the Universal Esperanto Association at 777 United Nations Plaza, New York, New York 10017, or by e-mail to uea@inter.nl.net.) Esperanto is taught in schools all over the world. In Hungary it's one of the languages that students can study to satisfy high school language requirements; one major Hungarian university has offered an Esperanto degree since the 1960s. More than 100 international conferences are held in Esperanto every year, without any need for translators or interpreters. More than 100 magazines and journals in Esperanto are published regularly. Radio broadcasts in Esperanto are a regular feature in many countries.

Finally, the Esperanto community today demonstrates a new and welcome maturity with regard to the IAL issue by supporting forums on the subject that are not restricted entirely to Esperanto. Take a look at Mark Fettes' "Esperanto Studies and Interlinguistics" home page for an excellent example; you'll find it at http://magi.-com/~mfettes/studies.html. There is also an Esperantic Studies Foundation (3900 Northampton Street Northwest, Washington D.C. 20015-2951—or http://www.esperantic.org) which publishes a newsletter devoted to the subject.

Zamenhof included in his writing system a number of letters trimmed with typographic squiggles which the majority of keyboards and/or computer software either can't produce or can produce only with very complicated maneuvers that drastically slow down typing. The solution to this problem now in use on the Internet (and shown in the translation of the Tower of Babel story above) is to convert letter-plus-squiggle to letter-followed-by-x. This is an awkward and unsatisfactory remedy; people who know Esperanto find it distracting and annoying, and people new to the language have to struggle not to try to pronounce the "x" when they see it. It does, however, work as a temporary fix. And it's reasonable to assume that if Esperanto became our WorldSpeak we would quickly either produce software sophisticated enough to make all those "x"s unnecessary, or we'd agree—in spite of the outraged protests of Esperantists—to substitute symbols that are already available on our keyboards.

The Case of Láadan

I didn't choose Láadan as a case study example for some proposed inherent superiority to the other possible candidates. I chose it because I constructed it myself, which gives us three major benefits that I could not guarantee if I chose any other constructed language. First, I can vouch for the accuracy of my information about Láadan, instead of having to contend with a dense fog of rumors and myths. Second, I don't have to worry about lawsuits charging me with copyright and license violations. And third: Because Láadan has no "owner"—a decision that I had the power to make, and did make—no one would end up facing a lawsuit for trying to improve the language.

Zamenhof put together his vocabulary of root words for Esperanto by choosing forms that were common to many of the Indo-European languages, in particular the Romance and Germanic ones. His goal was to provide an auxiliary language for international communication, and his strategy was to make it look as familiar as possible to anyone who already knew an Indo-European tongue and as easy as possible for such a person to learn. The genesis of Láadan was very different.

In 1984, DAW Books published my science fiction novel *Native Tongue*, the first in a series of three (and soon to appear in a reprint edition from Feminist Press). My interest had been caught by a reformulation of the mathematical concept known as Goedel's theorem in Douglas Hofstadter's *Goedel, Escher, Bach: An Eternal Golden Braid*. The reformulation said that for any record player there would be records that it could not play without self-destructing. It occurred to me that you could extrapolate from that proposition and say that—provided the linguistic relativity hypothesis is true—for any culture there would be *languages* that it could not use without self-destructing. *Native Tongue* was a thought experiment in which a group of women linguists constructed a fictional language called Láadan as a deliberate subversive act intended to bring about social change. It was set in a fictional universe (mostly a fictional United States) where the validity of the linguistic relativity hypothesis was presupposed. Because linguistics is my own scientific discipline, I didn't feel that I could resort to the usual practice of just throwing in a few dozen allegedly Láadan words to serve as local color. I felt obligated to go through the process of constructing the language myself in order to write about it.

I had two goals for Láadan, and neither one was that it should be an IAL. In the real world, the goal was to fulfill my ethical obligations as a science fiction author trained in the scientific discipline of linguistics—just as, if I had been an astronaut writing a novel about space exploration, I would have considered myself obligated to provide accurate detail about spaceships and their operation. In the world of the novel, my goal was to construct a language designed to express the perceptions of human women; the hypothesis of the linguist women in the novel was that widespread use of Láadan would result in a major change—perhaps self-destruction—for the book's fictional male-dominated culture.

I started with the list of 100 core words known as the "Swadesh" list (for linguist Morris Swadesh, its author), which is what most linguists use when they begin fieldwork in a language not previously written down. It includes "woman" and "man" and "talk" and "go" and "sleep" and "eat"—the bare minimum of words that could be considered necessary for survival. But instead of going to existing languages for the shapes of those root words as Zamenhof did for Esperanto, I did the task mechanically, in four steps:

1. I chose a set of seventeen phonemes that struck me as most easily managed by speakers of all existing natural languages, plus a single high tone.
2. I set up a few simple rules for combining these phonemes.
3. I wrote out sets of possible syllable shapes that come from applying the rules to the phonemes.
4. I assigned the results to the words on my list.

After having just read my criticism of Esperanto for its use of graphic doodads that aren't on most keyboards, you're right to wonder why I gave Láadan a tone, thus creating exactly the same sort of nuisance—on a smaller scale, but the same problem nevertheless. The strategic reason was that adding just one tone (indicated on words by an accent mark) increased greatly the number of different syllables I could construct with only seventeen phonemes. It was a mistake, all the same. My graphics solution has been to type a high-toned vowel as a capital letter when no accent marker is available—so that Láadan becomes LAadan in e-mail messages, for example. That is just as awkward and annoying as the Esperanto letter-plus-x solution.

When I had the core vocabulary finished and had to decide how I wanted to expand beyond that, I relied on the novel's stipulation that the language was intended to express the perceptions of human women. I took the King James version of the Bible as my diagnostic probe because it is the most "masculine" document, linguistically, that I know of, and I started translating long sections into Láadan. This worked very well as a method for finding out where the English lexical gaps are in terms of expressing women's perceptions.

For example, nothing in the traditional story in Luke of the birth of Jesus in Bethlehem expresses what his mother would certainly have felt—after having given birth on the floor of a stable with the assistance only of an elderly husband—when *three kings* suddenly showed up and had to be dealt with as guests. I've had babies, and I've had unexpected company, and I can all too easily imagine Mary's perceptions of that situation, which is portrayed every year in Christmas pageants all over the world without the slightest attention to its grotesque awfulness for the just-delivered woman. The words that would name guests of that sort, and express perceptions of that situation, aren't available in English; to make the perceptions clear, a woman using English would have to resort to the tactic known as "going on and on and on," making it unlikely that anyone would listen to or read her words. I filled some of the gaps for which examples like this provided a linguistic spotlight by adding items to Láadan's vocabulary; and I gave the language ample—and extremely simple—ways to increase the vocabulary so that others could continue with that task.

Zamenhof tried to make his constructed language as much like other Indo-European languages as possible, for the excellent reason that that would make it easy for speakers of many Indo-European languages to learn and use it. There are things he did that have been criticized, such as having an obligatory marker on direct objects, but no one can deny that he did very well. The survival and wide use of Esperanto to this day demonstrates that.

For Láadan, on the other hand, I tried to choose features that were common to as many different human languages as possible—features that might plausibly be characteristic of what many linguists call Universal (that is, Global) Grammar, the grammar of Terran. (Including a marker on direct objects, something about which I am in agreement with Zamenhof because it offers more flexibility for varying the order of words in sentences.) At the same time, because the characters in my novel were trained linguists, I could plausibly assume that they'd be aware of the social problems associated with national languages, and I tried to keep Láadan as free of "nationalistic characteristics" as I could. I tried to keep the playing field for learning Láadan—its learnability—as level as I could make it while still maintaining its independence from existing languages.

My metaphor for construction was the patchwork quilt, which is an appropriate choice in the context of a "women's language." From among the languages with which I had some familiarity I borrowed scraps that I felt would be useful for expressing the perceptions of women easily and conveniently. For example, I borrowed from Navajo its wonderful pejorative marker, which is a single phoneme ("lh") that you can add to a Navajo word to give it a negative slant.

To understand what that would be like, we can arbitrarily choose the obsolete English morpheme "*ge-*" (pronounced "guh") and declare it to be the English pejorative marker. Because native speakers of English have all the rules for combining English syllables into words safely filed away in their long-term memories, they would know where and how to add "ge-" to English words. We could then have the following pair of sentences, the first of which is a neutral statement and the second of which carries the message that anyone saying or writing it has a negative attitude toward a Congressman:

A. "Let me tell you the story I heard today about my Congressman."
B. "Let me tell you the story I heard today about my geCongressman."

I wish English did have a pejorative marker like that, instead of relying as it does on intonation; the English writing system is very convenient but it provides so little information about intonation that it's hard to figure out anything about the writer's emotions and attitudes in sequences of written language. Women who took a look at the grammar and dictionary of Láadan (Martin 1988) agreed with me about the usefulness of the pejorative, and they wrote to me to propose that the language should also have an *anti*pejorative—another small chunk that could be added to words to give them a *positive* slant.

When I constructed Láadan, I had advantages that many who try such a project don't have. I had a Ph.D. in linguistics, I had been trained by linguistics professors of the highest caliber, and I had decades of experience as a professional linguist working with languages from more than one language family. I had available to me the contemporary linguistic knowledge about the set of characteristics that seems to be shared by all human languages. I had the benefit of many articles and papers written on the subject of how to avoid the language-construction mistakes of the past. I had personal knowledge of what it feels like to deal with language bias. I did my best to make good use of all those things. And what happened? In spite of all those advantages, in spite of my genuine and well-informed efforts to do things properly, I made serious mistakes.

I was hurrying. I had a novel to write, and a family to support with money that I wouldn't receive until the novel had been turned in to the publisher. I was working all alone, and this was before I had access to the world's linguistic community on the Internet. I had many other tasks to work on at the same time; I couldn't give the project anything remotely like my full attention. I say these things not to excuse my errors but to explain them. It's safe to assume that a linguist or linguists hired for the specific task of constructing a proposed WorldSpeak, with today's linguistic community only a keystroke away for advice and discussion, would do an enormously better job than I did.

The methods I chose meant that I had to sacrifice the learning advantages that Zamenhof had had with speakers of English and of most European languages. I considered that sacrifice more than justified by the fact that it would free me from the political baggage Esperanto carries. The words of Láadan resemble no natural language other than coincidentally. They have to be learned from scratch and memorized, no matter what your native language might be, and a paragraph of the language will look equally unfamiliar to speakers of all languages. As a brief sample, here are the first few verses of the Twenty-third Psalm written in Láadan:

Lahila nayahá letha. Aril loláad ra le themath, rahath. Dórúu Ba leth mewoliyen woduneha. Dódoth Ba leth mewowam wowiliha. Dónetháa Ba óotha lethath.

(The Lord is my shepherd. I shall not want. He maketh me to lie down in green pastures. He leadeth me beside the still waters. He restoreth my soul.)

You will not be surprised to learn that the pronouns of Láadan, like the pronouns of many other human languages, make no gender distinctions. A single pronoun includes both males and females. All the examples of "he" in the original verses, therefore, are translated in the Láadan version by a pronoun that applies equally to males or to females.

Unlike Esperanto (and unlike linguist Mark Okrand's Klingon), Láadan did *not* become an international success. Not in the novels, and not in the real world. Not even as a "human interest story." In the more than a decade since its grammar and dictionary were published, and during which I have done hundreds of interviews with various media, not one reporter has ever contacted me and said, "Hey, I hear that you made up a language that's supposed to express the perceptions of women, and I want to write a story about that!" It exists nonetheless to serve two useful purposes. It's an example of an "artificial" language carefully constructed by a trained linguist whose deliberate intention was to avoid the political problems of languages like Esperanto. And it exists (along with the fragments we have from Hildegard of Bingen's project) as an answer to the irritating question, "How come no woman has ever made up a language?" (It may be that hundreds of women over the course of history have constructed languages; if that is so, however, all the records of those languages have disappeared.)

Ironically, Láadan—an experiment that escaped to some extent from the laboratory—acquired its own political problems, some comical and some distressing. They were problems I hadn't anticipated and had taken no precautions against. One major reason for this development was the mistaken idea that because Láadan was designed to express the perceptions of women it was a language to be used only *by* women. Many languages exist which appear to be focused toward ease in the expression of male perceptions; it has never been suggested that they are therefore only for use by men.

I want to close this section by showing you a few entries from the Láadan dictionary, because I know no more efficient way to make clear what "expressing the perceptions of women" means. Here are ten examples; you'll notice that most of the definitions would have to be described as "going on and on and on."

widazhad   Pregnant late in the term of the pregnancy and eager for it to come to an end at long last.

rahéena   Non-heart-sibling; one so entirely incompatible with another that there is no hope of ever achieving any kind of understanding or anything more than a truce, and no hope of ever making such a one understand why; does not mean "enemy."

rathom   non-pillow; one who lures another to trust and rely on him or her but who has no intention of following through; a "lean on me so I can step aside and let you fall" person.

hahodib   To be in a state of having deliberately shut off all feeling.

doroledim   Say you have an average woman. She has no control over her life. She has little or nothing in the way of a resource for being good to herself. She has family and animals and friends and associates that depend on her for sustenance of every kind. She rarely has time for adequate sleep or rest. She has no time for herself, no space of her own, little or no money to buy things for herself, no opportunity to consider her own emotional needs. She is at the beck and call of others. For such a woman, the one and only thing she is likely to have a little control over is food. When such a woman overeats, the verb for that is "doroledim."

ramimelh   To refrain from asking, with evil intent; especially when it's clear that someone badly wants the other to ask.

radíidin   Nonholiday; a time allegedly a holiday but actually so much a burden because of work and preparations that it is a dreaded occasion; especially when there are too many guests and none of them help.

áazh Love for someone who was at one time sexually desired but who is desired no longer.

azháadin To menopause uneventfully.

bama Anger which is not futile and which is for good reasons, but when there is no one on whom you can blame what you're angry about.

If you are a man, and your reaction to one or more of those ten words is "But surely nobody would ever want or need to talk about *that!*" that is precisely the point. You might want to ask a woman how she feels about the matter before making a final judgment.

Before we leave this topic, it's necessary to mention that little or no attention has been given, so far as I can determine, to the question of what, exactly, someone who constructs a language is doing. That is, what kind of a mental "activity" *is* it? Is it like writing a novel or composing a symphony? Is it like doing mathematics? What is the mind up to when it carries out such a task? We can be certain of one thing: No "language constructor" (a lexical gap again), no matter how vivid his or her imagination, no matter how superb his or her intellectual skills, can come up with a language that goes beyond the specifications for a human language. Those specifications, whether innate in the Chomskian sense (or in the sense of the various reformers of the innateness hypothesis) or embodied in the sense proposed by Lakoff and Johnson, are part of our humanness; only by stepping outside our human bodies could we discover what *else* a language might have and/or do.

Shall We Start Over?

Times have changed; computers have changed; we are much more sophisticated about languages and matters linguistic than we once were. What about starting over right now and constructing a new version of WorldSpeak from scratch, making *sure* that we don't make any of the mistakes of the past?

We could load a giant computer system with samples of all the languages of the world, and have it extract all the things they have in common and compile the result into a database. We could give that completed database to a top-notch team of linguists and anthropologists (and their computers) to work with; we could give the team ample resources in time and money and information. If we did that, could the team construct a "Mainstream Standard Terran" language that every human being could look at and listen to without anguish while still treasuring and maintaining his or her native tongue? I'm certain that it could be done—but it's almost inconceivable that such a thing would happen.

Consider the furor that takes place right now over such comparatively minor "global" efforts as multinational trade agreements. Consider the frantic efforts being waged by politicians in the United States to legislate "English Only" and those being made by French politicians to keep French pure. Consider the desperate situation of many natural languages, whose speakers would rightly view the new IAL as just one more threat to their existence.

I can think of only one thing that would make us likely to set up a "WorldSpeak Construction Project." Suppose this planet were suddenly faced with a valid threat of invasion and colonialization by intelligent extraterrestrials. That event, and only that event, would unite us as Terrans against a common enemy, and we might suddenly see a crucial necessity for a single shared medium of communication. For the war effort, we would probably be willing to accept many things that we would refuse to accept in any other circumstances. Until I see that happening, my expectations for an IAL will remain very low.

Can a Language Be Owned?

I've said that the problems of IALs, even IALs that are put together in ways that make them relatively easy to learn and use, have often been social rather than linguistic, and I've mentioned some of those problems above. IALs have tended to reflect the cultures of those who construct or choose them—as the evidence for the strong link between language and culture would predict—and therefore to bring along with them all the political problems associated with those cultures. Because IALs are a hobby limited to people with unusual interests, as compared to people interested in postage stamps or baseball or gardening, they've frequently been constructed with little regard for how difficult they might be to learn and use. (In science fiction conlangs, for example, the emphasis tends to be more on how fancy the language is than on its usefulness for the ordinary person.) But the most counterproductive problem in terms of making a language successful in the real world is the problem of turf wars, which have been the downfall of IAL after IAL, and which need to be discussed separately because of their potential effects.

The turf war question is simply this: *Can a language be owned?* Nobody—no individual or group or corporation or government—owns English or Chinese or Farsi; the very idea is ridiculous. But what if someone sits down and creates a language (or a modified version of an existing language) in the same way that a person would write a novel or compose a symphony? Then what? Does that language belong to that individual?

The lengths that would-be Esperanto reformers went to in their attempts to get Zamenhof to endorse their proposals boggle even the broadest mind. Without question, the coups and countercoups and Machiavellian intrigues of (and against) Esperantists, and their endless public wrangles over who controlled the language, caused the downfall of the movement as a whole. It all became so absurd that no rational adult wanted anything to do with it.

An organization for promotion of English internationally—the British Council—bought and still holds the rights to Basic English, which is the major example of a modified existing language proposed as an IAL. A company called the Science News Service bought the rights to Interlingua, a language constructed by the International Auxiliary Language Association under the direction of linguists André Martinet and Alexander Gode. James Cooke Brown constructed Loglan and claims copyright ownership and control for it; he has been in court rather recently in a fight over whether a reform group now using the name Lojban can be legally prevented from using that name. (Lojban is described as a language specifically created as a mechanism for testing the linguistic relativity hypothesis.)

And then of course there's the matter of the Klingon language. According to Donald Harlow, Klingon's first few words were created by Scotty, chief engineer of the starship *Enterprise*. But when the Klingons caught the public imagination, and *Star Trek* episodes in which they appeared turned out to be wildly popular, Paramount sat up and took notice—and hired linguist Marc Okrand to create an entire Klingon language. The resulting *Klingon Dictionary* and its audio version and sequel have been smash best-sellers; the dictionary alone has sold hundreds of thousands of copies. There is a Klingon Language Institute housed at a university, with its own academic journal; there are two competing projects for translating the Bible into Klingon.

I'm exceedingly grateful to Klingon for the inroads it's made into the typical American loathing for foreign language learning. People who are multilingual because they know one natural language plus Klingon are more likely to be willing to learn yet another language, and I'm all for that. But I have major reservations about Klingon as an IAL, and I suspect that Mark Okrand would agree with me. For many and curious reasons, Klingon would be an inappropriate choice for WorldSpeak. The idea of an allegedly extraterrestrial language being taught as the Terran IAL is bizarre enough all by itself. The idea of trying to run a world with a language specifically designed to express the perceptions of a warrior race is equally strange, despite its convenient fit with the Warrior metaphor that organizes so much of American life; a language designed for the Diplomat metaphor would be better suited to the task. In addition, Klingon has features that were linguistics in-jokes, and its writing system is difficult and inconvenient. Klingon is definitely a fixer-upper as an IAL. But anyone who decided to propose and publish an "improved" version of Klingon would be in far more serious trouble than IAL reformers have ever found themselves in up to now. They would be in court facing not just Marc Okrand but the corporate might of *Star Trek* and Paramount.

Láadan (like Klingon or Elvish) wasn't intended as an IAL, but nothing in principle would prevent it from serving as one. I didn't want any turf wars; I went out of my way to make it very clear that I didn't consider myself its owner or its chief of staff or anything of the kind. It was part of a scientific experiment that I took absolutely seriously, into which "marketing" would have introduced an impossibly wild variable, and so I made no effort to market it. I constructed it, and then I turned it loose and observed what happened, without interfering. But that's not the usual practice. People who "create" a language tend to take the position that they own it and have complete control over it.

It may be that as a philosophical matter this question is not only trivial but silly. So you whipped up a little hobby language during your summer vacation, and now you want to claim that it's yours alone and nobody else is allowed to play with it. So what? Who cares? So a giant media conglomerate won't let you play with *its* language, in the same way that McDonalds Corporation will sue you if you try to call your coffeeshop Cafe McDonalds. So what? Who cares if the squabbles of obscure language hobbyists result in a legal precedent that establishes as law the principle that a language can be owned in exactly the same way that a copyright or trademark or patent can be owned?

We would be wise to care. We would be wise to pay cautious attention to these developments, because ownership of WorldSpeak would be a *gold mine*. There would be textbooks and audio programs and videos and standardized tests and computer programs and libraries of original and translated literature. There would be magazines and newspapers and scholarly journals, both print and electronic. There would be WorldSpeak versions of every significant document in international government and trade and diplomacy. The money to be made in signs alone, to go up on streets and buildings and bridges all over the world, would be huge, as would the profit from the WorldSpeak *instructions* that would have to go into the boxes for every widget sold around the world. Every language item now used in international meetings and conferences would have to be republished or re-produced using WorldSpeak. Think of the money to be made from the licensing rights to put WorldSpeak slogans and catch phrases on toys and lunchboxes and bumper stickers and coffee mugs!

Anyone sharp enough to purchase the rights to an IAL that succeeded as WorldSpeak would be wealthy in a way that would make Bill Gates' fortune seem modest. And I would be very surprised if there are no investors right this minute busy buying up the rights to all the Internet domain names that might plausibly turn out to include the ultimate IAL, such as www.worldspeak.com, www.earthish.com, and www.terran.com. Just in case. I'd buy those domain names myself, right this minute, if I could afford it.

Should We Be Sorry?

All the constructed languages have failed to establish themselves as *world* languages, although the progress of Esperanto over the past century—especially outside the United States—is impressive. The international organizations of our governments and the summit meetings among world leaders still require the expensive and awkward presence of professional interpreters and translators; they haven't profited by the excellent example of international Esperanto conferences. Large multinational businesses headquartered in the United States are beginning to insist that their managers and executives learn Japanese or Russian or Chinese or Spanish, and their counterparts elsewhere are insisting that their staffs be competent in English—but not one appears interested in demanding expertise in any constructed language. A booming business exists in machine translation systems that can convert documents into rough—extremely rough—equivalents of other languages, ready to be polished by human beings into final form. (You can look at one of those on the Internet at the aptly named http://babelfish.altavista.digital.-com/cgi-bin/translate.) No sign of a humanity-uniting ET invasion has appeared on the horizon so far. The movement for an international auxiliary language is the concern of only a small percentage of humankind, and that percentage doesn't appear to be very effective at ramrodding their own tastes through to wide acceptance.

Should we be sorry about this?

I'm not sure we should. It may be that a truly international auxiliary language, whether acquired in infancy or learned largely as a second and "foreign" language, wouldn't be a good thing after all. Even if the practical reasons in its favor (the savings in resources), as well as the romantic reasons, can be supported. Perhaps the Tower of Babel was a good strategic move.

The human race has not yet sat down and seriously considered these three crucial questions:

1. Would the existence of a global language spoken by every human being mean that all human beings would then share a single global culture encoded in that language?

All the popular literature about proposed IALs seems to take it for granted that there can be such a thing as a language that is culture-free, in the way that sequences of numbers and symbols in mathematical formulas are allegedly culture-free. But the first thing human beings do when they learn an IAL is start giving it cultural trimmings—organizations and institutes and newsletters and badges and so on. Esperantists around the world wear a tiny pin in the shape of a green star as a way of identifying one another. The success of the Klingon language, otherwise incomprehensible in the context of American attitudes about foreign language learning, has been due to the passion many Americans feel for the Klingon culture portrayed on *Star Trek*. It's not the language itself that fascinates them, but the culture for which the language is the medium. I do not for one moment believe that there could be a "pure" language free of culture. And we have not even *thought* about what a Terran culture, as opposed to a French or Chinese or Iroquois culture—or Southeast Texan culture—might be like.

2. Would it mean that the perceptions of all human beings would be shaped in significant shared ways by that language?

In every human language there are things that are easy and convenient to talk about, and things that are cumbersome and inconvenient to talk about. Things that can't easily be talked about tend to be forgotten and neglected, or restricted to a handful of fanatics who are willing to make the effort. Whether the linguistic relativity hypothesis is valid or not, WorldSpeak would have this feature, too, and we don't know which parts of life it might foreground and which parts it might shove into obscurity.

3. If the answer to either question is yes, is that all right? Do we want that?

Perhaps; perhaps not. We don't know the answers to those questions within the boundaries of single nations, much less for humankind as a whole.

We have no way of knowing, for instance, whether one consequence of having a shared worldwide native language would be the eventual death of all our *other* native languages. Perhaps the global culture that would be attached to a successful WorldSpeak would have such a seductive beauty and elegance (or such a down-home allure) that human beings would happily abandon other cultures and their languages for it. We don't know.

We are still at the primitive linguistic stage where educated people feel comfortable responding to communication breakdowns with "Oh, it's *only* se*man*tics!" Until we can do better than that, until we can get past the stage of basing language policy on folklore and whim and politics and budgets, until we come to respect the power language has, we might be wise to continue to make haste slowly.

The various proposed IALs are moving along now at a snail's pace, with most of them having the status of eccentric hobbies. English is spreading like wildfire, but so clumsily that speakers of other languages—including constructed languages—are beginning to wake up and resist, perhaps in time to stop the takeover. A global culture is building for some segments of the population, as evidenced by the Internet and by such phenomena as the Global Nomads. It's all very disorganized and inefficient, which holds the process back and often results in two steps back for each step forward. This may well be an international blessing in disguise.

Before we risk the possibility, however, slim, that we might be turned into a global *nation* by the power of a single shared language, we must remember one very significant fact: The most brutal and vicious and intractable and endless of all wars is a *civil* war.

8

Language and the Brain

There is clearly a very strong species-specific language instinct, or what Chomsky would call a language acquisition device, a LAD. But equally one needs a LASS, as Jerry Bruner puts it, which is a language support system; people who speak language and who encourage the use of language, and so forth.

(Oliver Sacks, quoted in Mcintyre 1995, page 95)

Well, yes—but then, on the other hand, no!

I agree with Dr. Sacks that both a LAD and a LASS are needed for the acquisition of language, but he's much braver than I am. Even for that very limited claim—that language learning requires both nature and nurture—I would hesitate to use the word "clearly," because almost nothing in the current literature on this subject can be considered clear. Even when the statements seem to be uncontroversial, they still cannot accurately be described as "clear."

In fact, any prudent individual writing on "language and the brain" today finds the abundant deniability resources of English extremely seductive. The temptation is to write everything in Hyperdeniability Mode, something like this:

Numerous hypotheses have been put forward, and a variety of proposals have been made. It has been claimed that X, but that has been contradicted forcibly by the claim that Y and the evidence for Z. No final decision among these competing and contradictory theories appears to be possible at this time. [Blah, blah, blah . . .] What is said below, therefore, should not be construed as constituting the taking of a position of any kind.

English allows me to do this. You'll notice that it even allows me to avoid admitting that I am the one who insists on remaining free to deny that I've said what I am about to say. I'm tempted, but I'm not going to do it that way. The buck will stop here, but with two preliminary warnings.

First: I have never dissected a single brain, and I could not interpret a brain scan even at gunpoint; I cannot, therefore, speak or write with personal authority about human brains in neurophysiological terms.

Second: When we hear or read anything about the human brain any less concrete than a specification of its physical weight and size—and when we read anything *whatsoever* about the human mind—that information must be taken with a large grain of salt. When something of that kind strikes you as plausible, the rational course is to assume that it's valid as a metaphor and use the metaphor for whatever it turns out to be worth—but leap to no other conclusions without solid supporting evidence. Lakoff and Johnson tell us in *Philosophy in the Flesh* that there's no way to even talk about the mind, or the mind as "part of the brain," except in metaphors.

Independent of these metaphors, we have no conception of how the mind works. Even the notion *works* derives from the Mind As Machine metaphor. (Lakoff and Johnson 1999, page 248)

With those two warnings in place, I will do my best to sort out the troublesome issues and make clear what the questions are and why there is so much confusion. This badly needs doing. Nonspecialists who are interested in "language and the brain" today can buy and read half a dozen fat books, all current, all by qualified experts, only to find that each one says all the others are wrong and offers interminable arguments to that effect. I had a student in a linguistics course once whose major was engineering; a few weeks into the course, tried past endurance, he shouted, "If engineers did engineering the way you linguists do linguistics, every bridge in *America* would fall down!" He was probably right.

We try hard, I must point out. The subject of linguists' scientific investigation is nothing like chemicals or rocks or beetles, items that can be measured and weighed and poked at. It's not like planets and stars, items that in spite of being enormously inconvenient for human investigation can nevertheless be examined with sufficiently powerful telescopes and probes and the like. Rather, it is located somewhere—or perhaps somewhen, and more probably both—in the human brain and/or mind. If Karl Pribram's model of the brain as a hologram is correct, it is perhaps located *every*where—and everywhen—in the human brain and/or mind. Our access to the brain is very limited; as for access to the mind, we don't know where the mind *is,* or even whether it makes any sense to talk about it as having a location. Nevertheless, we linguists press on, determined to do our work as science rather than as speculation, and we should get credit for that.

In the context of this chapter, we're looking for answers to many questions; the six below represent what seems to me to be the barest minimum.

1. How is a single native language learned? What goes on in the brain and mind?
2. How does the learning of an additional native language or languages take place? What goes on in the brain and mind?
3. How does the learning of one or more additional languages—not as native tongues but as foreign ones—take place? What goes on in the brain and mind?

For those first three questions, we also want to know whether the answers are different for infants (as opposed to older children and adults) and whether there's a "dose-related" difference that makes learning one language substantially and significantly different from learning four or learning fourteen.

4. What physiological effect(s) and psychological effect(s) do these learning processes have on the brain and mind?
5. Is the answer to #4 different for monolingual versus multilingual persons?
6. Is there some separate language "faculty" or "organ" that is responsible for all this?

These questions are the subject of ongoing research in the cognitive sciences and in their applications in fields like medicine, education, law and law enforcement, and more; now that we ask computers to produce and understand roughly natural speech, they're important in computer science and robotics and engineering. The answers we have at the moment are, in my opinion, only in the most preliminary and tentative stage, although they are sometimes presented in the literature in a very authoritative style.

Much is being written right now about the metaphor and model in which knowledge (loosely speaking) takes the form of connections laid down between and among neurons, with the claim that connections frequently activated become strong and that unused connections disappear. Because this model is biological instead of mechanical, the disappearance in question is literally by death—the death of the unused neurons. One way of thinking about that would be to say that it's as if the newborn brain is a huge assemblage of dots, and learning is a matter of connecting those dots by drawing lines between them; the more you go back and forth over the line you draw, the harder you bear down with your pencil, the less likely it is that that line will fade away or be erased. That's different from imagining switches that are to be turned on or off; on the other hand, you can't help thinking about what happens when you go over a line so many times and with such force that you poke a hole in the paper.

Overview

Linguists and neuroscientists, cognitive scientists of all kinds, are split into factions, each of which considers the others to be not just plain vanilla wrong but stubbornly and perhaps indefensibly wrong. (I won't be discussing all of those factions here; if I tried to do that, I'd inevitably fail, because by the time the book appeared there'd be at least three new ones.)

One major division is between those who believe that human infants are born with some sort of innate language learning "equipment" or "ability" and those who disagree with that idea. That split has an additional branch, growing out of Lakoff and Johnson's claim in *Philosophy in the Flesh* that innateness is no more relevant in this context than gender and pagination are in the context of God-talk. The innateness versus noninnateness split, they contend on page 507, "makes very little sense given what we have learned about human brains." Another contentious split exists over whether or not language learning—innate, noninnate, or other—is a special and unique kind of learning. New factions and new proposed theories continue to appear; for example, an entire volume has just been published promoting the "emergentist" approach to the subject, which is neither explicitly for nor explicitly against innateness but suggests a compromise. (See MacWhinney 1999.)

My own votes are for the innateness hypothesis and for language learning as unique; I find the evidence from research on sign languages particularly compelling, because it is our first real evidence of children constructing a language from scratch, on their own. (See Aguilera-Hellweg, 1994.) This puts me squarely in one of the factions and will be obvious as you read. I would plead for moderation among the opposing camps, however, since all of us at this point are surely wrong to some degree.

Human infants are born unable to speak or sign or understand any language. However, their brains and minds are in *some* sense prepared in advance to recognize languages and to work out their rules from raw language data. By "raw data" I mean data that come to the infant in the form of ordinary daily speech and experience rather than as systematic, organized language lessons or instruction. Except in the case of very severe mental retardation or trauma or physical incapacity, children go on to acquire native command of the language or languages they're exposed to in their language environment, whether those are sound languages or sign languages. Children do this in spite of the fact that the data provided to them are often limited or defective, and vary greatly from one environment to another. They go through a uniform series of stages that Steven Pinker has labeled, charmingly, "Syllable Babbling, Gibberish Babbling, One-Word Utterances, Two-Word Strings, and then All Hell Breaks Loose" (Pinker 1994, page 269).

Suppose that from birth you provide your infant with carefully designed daily English lessons taught by a well-qualified native speaker of English. You can then expect that by roughly the age of twelve months the child will begin to use a few words of English, and that by roughly the age of five years the child will speak English as an adult does. The five-year-old may say "wabbit" for "rabbit" and will not have an adult vocabulary or an adult's communication skills— but the child will know all the basics just as well as the adult does. The child will be able to make statements, ask questions, issue commands and threats and promises and verbal attacks, carry on a conversation, argue with other people, indicate past and future time, specify singular and plural, indicate negatives—all the basics. The child won't be able to recite the rules he or she uses in doing all the these things, of course. But adults can't recite those rules, either, unless they're trained linguists—and even then, we don't know how accurate the rules are. As any linguistics student can tell you, the alleged rules, and their forms, keep changing.

It's important not to let yourself be confused by the fact that you, the educated adult, are able to recite all sorts of grammar rules you were taught in English classes. If you try to state the rule you use to do something as simple as forming a yes/no question such as "Did you see a football game today?" you'll discover that you can't do it. As a linguist, my formulation of that rule for practical everyday purposes is "Move the first auxiliary verb into a position immediately to the left of the surface subject of the sentence," which isn't the sort of rule taught in English classes. Nevertheless, and regardless of whether my suggestion for the rule is correct or not, you do *know* that rule, whatever its exact form may turn out to be, and so does every English-speaking small child. Each time you form a yes/no question accurately, you demonstrate that knowledge, as does the child. I once asked one of my linguistics professors why we don't state the rule as "Move the surface subject of the sentence into a position immediately to the right of the first auxiliary verb in the sentence," and got a startled look, followed by an explanation that was more elegant but boiled down to "We don't do it that way because we've never done it that way." None of this keeps us from proving, by using the rule, that we really do know what it says.

Suppose that from birth you provide your infant with carefully designed daily lessons in both English and Chinese, taught by well-qualified native speakers. Perhaps you offer the two languages on alternate days; perhaps you offer one language in the morning and the other in the afternoon, every day. The child who gets these lessons will have the same experience as the child discussed previously, but in both English and Chinese. There may be a slight delay in beginning to talk, and the process of mastering the basics may be completed a little later, but that's also true of individual children who learn only one language. That's why we use the phrases "roughly twelve months" and "roughly age five."

(The average timetable holds for all human children and for all languages, but there is a considerable amount of individual variation. There are children—entirely normal children who go on to normal language competence and performance—whose first word comes as early as seven months or who don't master the basics until as late as age eight. There are, however, no children whose first words occur at two months or who don't master the basics until age twelve and who still go on to demonstrate normal language abilities.)

The difference between the two kids in terms of their language development is that the child who gets lessons in both Chinese and English will go through a stage in which Chinese and English are slightly mixed up—but that stage is brief and will be over by roughly age five.

However, in both cases—English only, or English and Chinese—if the idea of language lessons for an infant never enters your head and you simply use language around the child in the ordinary way, *the same thing will happen*. With or without lessons, talking in the language(s) used in the child's environment will begin at roughly twelve months and the basics will be under control by roughly five years. This remains true in an environment where three or more languages are regularly and routinely spoken by the older children and adults, whether you are sufficiently maniacal to provide lessons in three or more languages or you do nothing of the kind. As stated earlier, if there is an upper limit to the number of languages this is possible for, other than that imposed by the number of waking hours in the child's day, we don't know what it is.

These facts are the same all over the world. There are no human languages for which the average timetable is different in any significant way. If we wanted to support the claim often made by English-speaking Americans that Russian or Navajo is *inherently* harder to learn than French, we would have to accept the idea that infants who learn Russian or Navajo are more intelligent (or in some other way better equipped at birth to learn languages) than infants who learn French. No evidence exists for such a claim.

This is very different from what happens with other skills that we might want to teach to children. With *very* rare and unpredictable exceptions, children in our society who aren't given lessons won't be able to play the violin, or figure-skate, or play tennis, or do algebra—even if the other people around them do those things every day. And when lessons are provided for those other skills, there will be extreme variation in what happens. Some children will become experts and others will do badly. Some, in spite of major efforts, will never manage to learn. Some will learn quickly and others will learn slowly, even when intelligence and motor dexterity are essentially the same. The various subparts of the skills will be learned in different orders. And so on. This variation is one of the reasons why many linguists insist that whatever it may be that human beings use for learning languages natively—a language "faculty" or a language "organ" or a language "instinct" or a language something else—it is a *separate and different* thing from whatever it is they use for the kinds of learning that typically take place as a result of structured lessons and training. (Language is of course not the only skill that children learn without formal lessons.)

Suppose that, as some schools of linguists contend, infants are born with no innate mental equipment for acquiring native languages—and nevertheless manage to do it according to the same timetable and in the same fashion and with the same final results, everywhere in the world. This accomplishment then looks almost magical. If children are born with some sort of advance mental preparation, however, native language learning remains an awesome performance, but a scientific rather than magical explanation seems to me to be more possible. The major controversy among those of us who accept the idea that something about language learning is innate is over what that advance mental preparation is *like.*

I think it's safe to say that newborn children already have available, as part of their mental equipment, a set of specifications for what human languages can contain and what human languages can do. Some of these may be *either/or* specifications; others are specifications with a range of values from minimum to maximum. Children don't face the task of working out the grammar of the language spoken around them from scratch, therefore. Their task is instead the less difficult job of eliminating from the universal set of possible grammar specifications all those that don't *belong* in the grammar of the language or languages they're learning.

Consider, for example, the set of basic orderings of subject and verb and object—three items that are present in every human language—in sentences. Although more than one ordering will always be possible, every language has one that it considers more basic than the others. In English, for example, that basic ordering is subject and then verb and then object, as in "The rabbit ate the lettuce," although "The lettuce, the rabbit ate" is possible in the proper context.

For the sake of discussion, let's think of the set of ordering possibilities as if it were six on/off switches. (Understand, please, that

that's strictly a metaphor—we have no evidence for a claim that anything in the brain is actually in a physical form that could be recognized as an on/off switch.) We could then say, figuratively speaking, that there would be one Most-Basic-Ordering Switch for "subject, then verb, then object," one for "subject, then object, then verb," and so on.

By roughly age five, the kids will have to have done three things with regard to this aspect of language:

1. Discovered which order is most basic in the language (or languages) they're hearing and observing around them.
2. Strengthened the "on" position for that switch by repeatedly activating the neurons and neuronal connections that are responsible for it.
3. Allowed the other switches to decay (metaphorically speaking, moved them to the "off" position) by failing to activate the neurons and neuronal connections responsible for them.

What the child who is learning two or more languages natively has to do is slightly different. There may be fewer switches in the set of six to be turned off; and it will be necessary, by roughly age five, to know which switches that are turned on correspond to which of the languages learned. Children can do this with ease.

The ability to learn languages in the way outlined above—from raw data, without formal instruction or study—starts to decline as the child grows older, at varying rates depending on the individual. For many (if not most) people, very little of this ability remains by adulthood. It may be that they then do have to learn foreign languages by using the same strategies and abilities and mental equipment that they use for any other kind of learning.

What we see happening in adult foreign language classes bears that out. There is no uniform worldwide pattern in results. Even large groups of people who go through identical courses in a language show great variation afterward. Some work very hard and never learn much; others seem to "pick up languages" with little effort. Some, no matter how hard they try, always have a strong foreign accent, while others sound much more native. Some learn well enough to get by in a year or two while others may need five or six years of classes to achieve the same level of skill. That is, we see the same sorts of patterns that we see when people take classes in geometry or tennis. There doesn't seem to be any evidence for a universal adult "language acquisition device" that would correspond to the one infants are equipped with.

The model of language learning I've described here makes it possible to understand why adults find it easier to learn languages that are very much like languages they already know. Consider the subject and verb and object ordering in sentences again. The child is born with all six relevant "switches" for that part of the grammar present. If one language acquired in infancy requires Switch 3 to be turned on and another requires Switch 5, learning that requires no extra effort for an infant or very young child. But in an adult whose only native language requires Switch 3 to be on, all the other switches in the set have long since been turned off. When that adult tries to learn a language requiring Switch 3, the learning task is only to conclude, "Oh, I see; it's just like my native language." But an adult whose native language requires only Switch 5 doesn't have that advantage and must memorize the information controlled by Switch 3 as if it had never been encountered before.

This model also explains why it is that the more languages you learn after you reach adulthood, the easier it is to learn yet another one. The more languages you learn, the more your mental arrangements for language learning will resemble the astonishingly effective ones you were born with—metaphorically speaking.

The physical form (using that term very loosely) of the "language acquisition device" in the brain is a mystery, and the scientific papers discussing it are often equally mysterious. We know what the device has to do when the child uses it. It has to create and test hypotheses about the language being learned, and then use the results—with modifications as needed—to build the grammar. The child tries chunks of sound and body language in an effort to communicate with the people in its environment, and concludes from the results that the chunks are or aren't part of the language being learned. It makes perfect sense to say that a child who has tried to say "cookie" and has been rewarded for that by actually getting a cookie is likely to remember the successful chunk of language and try it again. Because that makes sense, there was a time when scholars (called "behaviorists") claimed that language acquisition was simple trial-and-error learning, much like the way research animals will learn to press a lever if you reward them when they do that by accident. However, we can be absolutely certain (for once!) that can't be right. There's no way a system like that could account for the *uniformity* in language learning by human children.

It used to be suggested that the LAD was like an old-fashioned computer, for which every decision was either entirely right or entirely wrong, and which could never in even the most trivial way go beyond the bare data put into it by human beings. A more recent proposal has been that the LAD is instead like a *neural net*. A neural net is a computer setup which is able to decide that a particular conclusion is probably somewhat more likely to be correct than some other conclusion and can constantly modify such judgments, not only on the basis of actual data encountered but also by extrapolation from those data.

Lakoff and Johnson propose in *Philosophy in the Flesh* that the uniformity in language learning can be explained by the uniformity of human infant experience throughout humankind; perhaps that's correct. Perhaps uniformity of experience—being held, being carried, being fed, eating, sleeping, and so on—is sufficient explanation, and would let us dispense with the Language Acquisition Device. It's an interesting hypothesis. It seems to me to imply that instead of *universal grammar* there is *universal culture*—a core of human experience that is part of the definition of being human and from which human language is developed by the "embodied mind." If so, given the link between language and culture, I'm not at all sure that anything very different is being proposed.

It may be that all these metaphors, and Pribram's hologram metaphor as well, are wrong. It may be that the brain handles language learning in a way so very special that we have no accurate image with which to describe it yet and no mechanism for talking about it. For the moment, I will continue to assume the innateness hypothesis.

Now, just having the inborn language device, whatever its form and methods, isn't enough to guarantee a native language. We know for sure, without question, that children can't learn a language without regular exposure to that language in use by others who already know it. No normal human being would be cruel enough to test that concept by raising some kids with no exposure to language at all, just to see what would happen. But it has been tested. There have been enough tragic examples of children in very abnormal circumstances—children whose input of language during childhood was drastically limited, sometimes almost nonexistent—to provide such a test. We know that these children may learn to use language to some degree when they're taken from the deprived environment and placed in better circumstances, but they never achieve normal language competency. However, we don't know what the *minimum* amount of language data input is; kids can manage with an astonishingly small amount.

In the United States (and many other countries and cultures) the typical situation is that the adult who is most responsible for the care of a child during infancy and the toddler years talks to the child in a variety of language usually called "Motherese" (but by no means restricted to mothers). In Motherese the basic vowel sounds of the language are pronounced with an exaggerated clearness, for example. And conversations often include a kind of reinforcement of language that people would never use with older children or adults. Like this:

1.
CHILD: Doggie hungry!
ADULT: Right! The doggie is hungry!
CHILD: Doggie want lunch!
ADULT: Yes, the dog wants its lunch!
CHILD: Mama feed doggie!
ADULT: You think it's time for Mama to feed the dog.
(And so on.)

Much emphasis has been put on the importance of Motherese in the popular press lately. It has even been used—misused—in stories claiming that children in day care facilities will be held back in life because they don't have their mothers doing this sort of thing at them all day long. There are many cultures (and families), however, in which adults rarely speak to infants and small children, and where Motherese would be viewed as an absurd way to deal with kids; nevertheless, children in those environments learn to speak their native languages just like children elsewhere. It's fashionable to insist that learning can't take place without *active* practice and participation by the learner; it's fashionable, but it's wrong. Much learning can take place passively, with the learner paying very close attention but taking no overt action. In cultures where this is the favored method, people routinely observe a skill in use for long periods of time, and then one day simply begin using it themselves, competently.

In a perfect world, human children from the very first day of their lives would have abundant language input from the adults around them—whether that input came from family members or from other caregivers, either of whom would serve the purpose. Few actions are more likely to help youngsters grow up to be successful and happy adults in our society than providing them with abundant opportunities to practice the skills needed for human language interactions of every kind. This gives kids an extra advantage in today's technological world, where efficient and effective communication of information has become the single most valuable skill. However, we have plenty of evidence that children are perfectly capable of acquiring their native languages without that sort of treatment and attention. They must have exposure to language data; but it doesn't *have* to be abundant, it doesn't *have* to include the "Motherese" material, and the data don't even have to be very good.

As stated elsewhere in this book, it was once taken for granted that children who acquired more than one language natively would have somewhat slower language development overall, sometimes coupled with temporary problems related to language in the early school years—but this has been proved to be false. Multilingual children, like any other children, can experience problems at school as a result of all sorts of factors, but there's no cause-and-effect relationship between those problems and multilingualism itself.

We've now come to the end of those things that we can be reasonably certain about, and are moving into areas where we are still only able to speculate. Such as: What happens *inside* the brain and mind when a native language—or more than one native language—is learned? What happens *to* the brain and mind? How is that different from what happens when languages are learned later in life, with varying degrees of fluency but not natively? How much do we actually know about such things?

We know very little, and what we know is based on tenuous evidence, often evidence gathered from people whose brains were very different from normal brains due to illness or injury. Reports about brain research appear regularly in the media because brain research is perceived as "sexy." Unfortunately, such reports tend to do little more than increase the general confusion, which is why many scientists behave in a way that gets them accused of being elitists determined to keep their knowledge away from the public.

Well, that's *approximately* what happened.

Let's look at a recent sequence of research relevant to our discussion in this chapter, and some media reports on that research. Here's a portion of a news release that appeared on the Internet in the summer of 1997 (with emphasis added by me):

> In a study that sheds new light on how the brain organizes language, researchers at Memorial Sloan-Kettering Cancer Center report in the July 10 issue of the British journal *Nature* that *the organization of the brain's language-production region in bilingual individuals is directly related to whether they learned a second language as toddlers (simultaneously with their native language) or as young adults.* . . . "A second language acquired during the teenage years, which is late in developmental life, is represented in the brain *in a separate location* from the native language," explains senior author Joy Hirsch, PhD.

The *Wall Street Journal* ran a story about this study in its July 10, 1997, issue, written by science reporter Ron Winslow and titled "How Language Is Stored in Brain Depends on Age." "Toddlers who learn a second language along with their native tongue," Winslow wrote, "store this capability in a single sector in the brain, the researchers discovered. But if the second language is acquired later . . . the brain designates a separate area for processing it." The *New York Times*, on July 15, ran a story by Sandra Blakeslee headlined "When an Adult Adds a Language, It's One Brain, Two Systems," reporting that "a new study has found that second languages are stored differently in the human brain depending on when they are learned."

The impression that even careful readers would get from the news release and the two newspaper stories is that in the current stage of knowledge about language and the brain we are able to think of the brain as if it were a cupboard, and that we know where languages are "stored" in that cupboard. We can visualize it: Here's the spot on the shelf where little Mary stashed the English and Turkish she learned before the age of three in her multilingual household; here are the two *different* spots on the shelves where Johnny stashed first the English he learned as an infant and then the Turkish he learned when his family moved to Turkey after he turned sixteen. Scientists can, figuratively speaking, go to those cupboards, open their doors, and poke at the stored languages. The news reports even identify locations for us, referring to "Broca's area" and "Wernicke's area." It's all very impressive, and confidence-inspiring. We know so much! Surely, if we want to know more, we just have to go check it out.

The problem is that the news stories—from a distinguished medical facility and two distinguished newspapers—are misleading. We can reasonably assume that the researchers involved have been tearing their hair out in frustration over these accounts.

Here's what actually happened.

Sloan-Kettering had twelve bilingual patients—six who had learned both languages as toddlers, and six who had learned a second language as teenagers—scheduled for brain surgery. All had to undergo fMRI (functional magnetic resonance imaging) brain scans. The fMRIs, which allow you to see what parts of the brain are active by tracking the flow of blood to various locations, are done to provide the surgeons with individualized brain mapping; this increases the doctors' chances of carrying out surgery without damaging the parts of the brain most responsible for particular functions in that patient. Graduate student Karl Kim, Dr. Hirsch, and their associates asked the twelve patients to talk to themselves silently during the fMRIs about things they had done the day before, first in one of their languages and then in the other. (Talking aloud would have interfered with the fMRI procedure.) The scans were then compared, with particular attention to the two locations in the brain known as Broca's area and Wernicke's area, both of which are known to be involved in language processing.

For all twelve patients, activity in Wernicke's area showed no differences, but there was an interesting difference in the amount of activation in Broca's area. The six patients who learned both languages at the same time in infancy all showed increased activation of just one region in Broca's area. In the six who had learned one language in infancy and the other language in their teens, two separate regions in Broca's area showed activation. In addition, evidence obtained through other Sloan-Kettering patients who weren't involved in this specific study supports the idea that for *each* additional language learned in the teenage years or adulthood, a separate region in Broca's area would be activated in this same fashion.

That's what happened. Now, what does it tell us? First I need to mention some facts that the news stories didn't bother with or simply trampled into the ground:

1. Twelve research subjects make a very small study. It's typical of brain research that only a handful of subjects are involved, for the obvious reason that getting access to human brains is difficult and expensive. In this study there was the serendipitous fact that the fMRIs had to be done anyway for medical reasons, and the research task was one that could be done at the same time without creating problems. In most areas of human research, studies involving only six to twenty subjects wouldn't be looked at as remotely respectable. An exception is made for brain studies; but brain researchers are well aware, when publishing results based on twenty brains, that if they

had been able to get access to twenty-one or twenty-two they might have found something entirely different.

2. Talking to yourself silently, in your mind, is *not* identical to talking out loud. It's called "covert subvocalization," and we can't be certain that conclusions based on covert subvocalization can be extended to ordinary spoken language.

3. Broca's area is described, in the news stories and elsewhere, as devoted to speech production and grammar. (Wernicke's area is usually described as devoted to interpreting the meaning of language.) But Broca's area—the area where the difference was found—is also deeply involved in controlling *motor* activities that are part of language. Wendy K.Wilkins and Jennie Wakefield (1995, page 170) write that Broca's area is specialized for "the hierarchical structuring of information in a format consistent with a temporally ordered linear sequence reflective of that structure," which, translated, is the *outlining* of information. Nothing that we know about Broca's area leads to the conclusion that languages are "stored" there. We don't know with certainty that the idea of language "storage" has any validity. How the media got this "storage" idea I can't say; presumably something one of the researchers said during an interview—in an attempt to explain specialized information to nonspecialists—was misinterpreted, and the misinterpretation was then shared and passed on to the public.

In summary, what we actually did learn as a result of this study is that we have one more piece of evidence for two things that were already well known: (1) that there appears to be some sort of neurological difference in language processing between monolingual persons and multilingual persons; and (2) that there appears to be some sort of difference between language processing in people who become multilingual in infancy or early childhood and those who become multilingual later in life. *None of this is news.* That doesn't mean that the results of the study aren't important. Evidence in the field of language and the brain is so slim that every additional scrap is precious—but that doesn't make it news. And it's not in any way surprising, given what we believe that we already know. Its primary value is that it *supports* what we already know.

The news release and the newspaper articles caught *my* attention because I was involved in trying to sort out the answers to my question about whether my multilingual respondents feel like "a different person" when using one or another of their languages. Suppose that when I looked at my database of questionnaires I had found that all those who answered with a yes had learned their additional language(s) as adults, and that all those who anwered with a no had learned their languages simultaneously in very early childhood. Or, somewhat less plausibly, the other way around. *That* would have been extremely interesting! I would have wanted to pursue the matter. But as is usually the case with such things, it didn't turn out that way. I found no correlation whatsoever between the distribution of yes and no answers and the ages at which my respondents learned their languages.

The model of language learning described in this chapter does answer the "how" questions in the sense that we can describe the process and its outcomes, as demonstrated in the outside world by human behavior, in considerable detail, for all human children. Our answers to the questions about what goes on "in the brain and mind" are still only metaphorical, however.

It does appear to me that language learning before adulthood is a different process from other kinds of learning, although this idea continues to be controversial. If it's correct, it follows that there is a language acquisition device of some kind that's responsible—but only logically, and only metaphorically.

It's *possible* that every neuron in the brain is involved in language learning and that the process is distributed and duplicated throughout the entire brain; it's possible that our perception of certain areas as being "specialized" for language is a misunderstanding. We have examples of young children who, despite having lost huge portions of their brains to surgery or trauma, develop normal language abilities. At the moment, specialization seems plausible, especially after puberty—but we could be wrong. The brain (and presumably the mind as well) has such an enormous capacity that it doesn't have to conform to our ideas about scientific economy and careful stewardship of resources. We just don't know. Not yet.

When I was studying linguistics in the late 1960s and early 1970s, one of the things my professors talked about was the problem of how meaning is assigned to sentences by the human beings trying to understand them. The profs explained that to a human being it seems that the language-processing part of the brain would have to *prevent* meaningless sentences from occurring—but that that's just a human prejudice. The brain *could* just produce any old string of stuff that happened to come along and then throw out the bad ones at the very last minute, in a fashion that scientists would consider disorderly and unscientific. It's like mail order companies that send out every item of merchandise in the same large container. When you get a wristwatch in the mail in a box that would hold a large clock, it strikes you as a waste of resources. But the companies have learned that it's actually cheaper in the long run to throw everything into identical boxes in a single operation than to maintain an inventory of different-sized containers and spend time sorting things out to fit them. It may be that the brain uses principles like that, instead of acting in a way that seems more "brainlike" to us as observers heavily indoctrinated in the prejudices of Western science.

Is there anything we can do about any of this? Now we are truly in uncharted territory. Our past experience with trying to teach languages, or trying to interfere in any other way with the learning and development of languages, indicates that our abilities along these lines aren't impressive. As to whether we *should* do any of the few things we're able to do—that question is the subject of this book.

Conclusion

It is all too easy to underestimate the power of language, the power of linguistic science, and the power that is represented by *mastery* of a language. We have an unquestioning respect for the body of knowledge in fields such as physics and astronomy and medicine, and we're awed by people who can routinely make use of such knowledge. But we take the daily use of language for granted. Why? For the very simple reason that everybody, including tiny children, can do it.

If speaking a language were like brain surgery, learned only after many long years of difficult study and practiced only by a handful of remarkable individuals at great expense, we would view it with similar respect and awe. But because almost every human being knows and uses one or more languages, we have let that miracle be trivialized into "only talk." We forget, or are unaware of, the power that language has over our minds and our lives; we use that power ourselves as casually as we use the electric power in our homes, with scarcely a thought given to its potential to help or to harm. We make major decisions about language on the most flimsy and trivial—and often entirely mistaken—grounds. We allow the most basic concepts of language science to remain the cognitive property of a handful of specialists who write and speak about it in a jargon incomprehensible to the rest of us; at the same time, we worry little if at all about the growing ignorance of linguistic science among even highly educated people—including those who teach "language courses" in our schools and universities. After all, it's "only talk."

I have tried in this book to show you how unwise and how dangerous such attitudes and practices are, and how important it is for us to refuse to accept them any longer. I have tried to restore some of the sense of wonder that human language is entitled to. I have tried to make it clear that the ability to know and use a language deserves both respect and awe, and that the ability to know and use more than one is even more praiseworthy. I have explained that not only is there no *threat* to English in the United States from other languages, but it is the other languages of this country that are in danger. I have done my best to point out the implications for humankind of the loss of languages, as well as the possibility that we will find ourselves on this planet with only one language left to us if we're not careful.

I have tried to make a case for the proposition that linguistics should be taught in every school system just as chemistry is; I have offered the daring proposal that it would be more valuable in the curriculum than football. And I have tried to sketch the outlines of some of the unacknowledged motivations behind our current language policies in the United States, especially those that seem completely irrational, such as postponing foreign language courses until after the ability to learn foreign languages has begun to decline.

We go on as we are at our peril.

The End

Appendix

The Multilingual Questionnaire Database

I. The Questionnaire

Instructions

Please answer the questions below for me; feel free to use separate sheets of paper if you prefer. E-mail responses are welcome. Questionnaire results are for use in a book that I am writing. Please be sure to let me know if you prefer to remain anonymous—otherwise, you will be given credit for any information that I quote or paraphrase. Feel free to take as much time as you need; I would much rather have your responses later than not at all, and you should not feel rushed. Thank you for your help; if you have questions, don't hesitate to write or call. I'm at 501–559–2273.

Suzette Haden Elgin

*Identifying Information, for My Records and
for Analyzing the Data*

1. Please give me your name, mailing address, e-mail address, and phone number. (Your addresses and phone numbers will be kept confidential.)
2. How old are you?

3. What is your level of education? (Elementary school, high school, college, graduate school, trade school, etc.)
4. Please list any degrees or training certificates that you have received.
5. What kind of work do you do?
6. Do you have any special linguistic qualifications? That is, are you a translator or interpreter, a foreign language teacher, a speech therapist, or anything of that kind? Do you have any language disability? Please explain.

Information About Your Languages

1. What is the language that you learned first?
2. What is your second language? How old were you when you learned it?
3. Please list any other languages you know, with the age that each was learned.
4. Which language do you consider to be your native language? (If more than one, please list all of them.)
5. Which linguage do you consider to be your second language?
6. Please list all languages that you speak comfortably. If you have studied any of them formally—that is, taken classes in them or studied them on your own—please indicate that for me.
7. What languages do you understand easily? (Please indicate any in which you've taken classes or have studied on your own.)
8. What languages do you read easily? (If you've studied them, please indicate that.)
9. What languages do you write easily? (If you've studied them, please indicate that.)
10. Are there other languages that you can "get by" in or have knowledge of? Please list them and explain.
11. When you use any of the languages, do you feel like you are a DIFFERENT PERSON than when you use your native language? If so, could you tell me a little about that?

12. Are there situations in which—even if everyone present knows both or all of the languages—you prefer to use one language rather than another? If so, please explain.

13. Are there situations in which—even if everyone present knows both or all of the languages—you prefer NOT to use a particular language? If so, please explain.

14. Which language or languages do you use at home?

15. Which language or languages do you use at work?

16. Which language or languages do you use socially?

17. Is there a language you use for other purposes? Please explain.

18. What language or languages would you like for your children to learn? Why? (If you don't have children, please answer as you would if you did.)

19. Is there a language you'd rather your children did NOT learn? Why? (If you don't have children, please answer as you would if you did have them.)

20. Are there any languages that you once knew, but have now forgotten? Can you tell me a little about that?

21. Is there anything else you'd like to add about your languages, your feelings about languages, or any related subject?

NOTE: The two questions that follow might be time-consuming for you to answer, and I don't want to impose on you. If you'd rather not bother with them, I will understand. If you can help me with them, however, I would find the information extremely valuable. If you want to choose just one or two of the items instead of dealing with all of them, that's fine. If examples occur to you that have not occurred to me, I would be most grateful to have them. Once I have seen the data I will probably need to come back to you individually and ask a follow-up question or two; I am interested in how bilinguals/multilinguals deal with possible conflict (cognitive dissonance) when their two or more languages express these concepts in drastically different ways. For any that you do answer, I'd be grateful for a literal translation of the items in languages other than English, so that I know what I'm dealing with. If you prefer to send this sort of material by snail mail, I am at PO Box 1137, Huntsville, Arkansas 72740–1137, USA.

22. I am especially interested in metaphorical differences between languages for a number of key areas, both when expressed overtly as metaphor (like English "to pass away" for "to die") and when the metaphor is the literal meaning of the word (as with English "breakfast" for the first meal after the night's fasting). For this purpose, I would be very interested in knowing what words and/or phrases your languages (other than English) use for any or all of the following: to have (or get) an abortion; to die; to be born; to get sick; to be well/healthy; to make a piece of art (or create art); to set up a government; to sin; to get angry; to fall in love; the law of gravity; energy; science.

23. I am also exploring the differences in what are called "unifying metaphors" in bilingual/multilingual speakers and contexts. For example, American English speakers can get almost any project under way by saying, forcefully, "Wagons—HO!" which brings up in consciousness the metaphor of wagon trains setting off across the plains, etc. I would like two pieces of information. First, can you identify a comparable unifying metaphor in your other language or languages? Second, do you feel that any one of the set of such metaphors you use is more powerful and compelling than the other(s)?[1]

Thank you.
Suzette Haden Elgin

PS: If you have suggestions for other persons who might be willing to participate in this project, I'd be delighted to have their responses as well. And I am of course interested in any comments or criticisms you may have.

II. The Respondents

NOTE: The languages listed below are those in which the respondent has indicated a perception of fluency—from native fluency at one extreme to

---

[1]With regard to this question, a generational split exists. People of my own generation (roughly sixty or older) answered the question without hesitation. Younger respondents, however, reported that "Wagons—HO!" was not a unifying metaphor for them; many said they'd never heard it.

the ability to carry on conversations comfortably at the other. Many respondents listed a number of other languages (sometimes many other languages) in which they were literate or could "function as a tourist" or had a variety of other competencies, but which they did not consider themselves able to speak and understand comfortably.

It appeared to me in a number of cases that the respondent was being overly modest about his or her multilingual competencies. In such cases, I have nevertheless reported the response as it was given. (The only exception is that I have added English after making certain that it should be added. Some respondents, though obviously at ease with English, did not list it as one of their languages.) It goes without saying that the respondents' perceptions of their own fluency must be respected. But it's important to know that there are respondents who reported living and working for long periods of time, using a particular language daily for everyday affairs, and who still did not include that language as one they spoke and understood comfortably. This is a clear demonstration of the confusion about what it means to "know a language," as discussed in the Introduction. In my opinion, the multilingual competencies of many respondents are understated below.

I would like to express my deep gratitude to the many respondents who provided me with lengthy responses to Questions 22 and 23, and to those who sent me supplementary pages expanding on their answers to other questions; I know this represented a substantial expenditure of time and energy on their parts:

1. Abichaker, Toufic; Arabic, French, English, Spanish, Italian, German
2. Anderson, Myrdene; English, Norwegian, Saami
3. Andruski, Jean; English, French, German, Mandarin Chinese, Russian
4. Anonymous; Sesotho, English, Zulu, Afrikaans
5. Anonymous; eight fluent languages—requested that I not list them because the distinctive nature of the set would betray identity
6. Anonymous; English, Mandarin Chinese, Cantonese
7. Anonymous; Latvian, English, French
8. Anonymous; English, Spanish
9. Anonymous; Spanish, English

10. Anonymous; German, French, English
11. Anzali, Soheila; Azerbaijani, Farsi, German, English, Turkish
12. Arouca, Karen; Portuguese, English, Spanish, Italian
13. Aylward, Renata; English, Spanish
14. Bauer, Laurie; English, French, Danish, German
15. Bemore, Caroline; Navajo, English
16. Blalock, Lucy Parks; Lenape, English
17. Boihang, Lesedi; Setswana, Xhosa, Zulu, English, Afrikaans
18. Boon, Glendia M.; American Sign Language, English
19. Bregman, L. D.; English, Afrikaans
20. Brewer, Keri; English, American Sign Language
21. Brodine, Ruey; English, Italian
22. Brown, Gordon; English, French, Swedish, Spanish, German
23. Browne, E. Wayles; English, Serbo-Croatian, Russian, Polish, Slovenian
24. Combon, Marlis; German, Spanish, Italian, English, French
25. Chiarenza, Anna Caterina; Italian, German, English
26. Chomphosy, Bounlieng; Lao, Thai, English
27. Chong, Steve; Cantonese, English, Malay
28. Chung, Karen Steffen; English, German, Spanish, Mandarin Chinese
29. Cook, Diana; English, French, Spanish
30. Cyr, Danielle E.; Quebec French, English, Swedish, Italian, German
31. Mark de Clark; English, Afrikaans, Zulu
32. Derzhanski, Ivan A.; Bulgarian, Russian, English, Hungarian, German, French, Italian, Spanish
33. Dorian, Nancy Currier; English, German, French, Scottish Gaelic (East Sutherland variety)
34. Doty, Margaret Ann; English, Italian, German
35. Eck, Karen; English, French
36. Eikamp, Rhonda; English, German
37. Eldredge, Linda G.; English; Signed English for the Deaf; American Sign Language
38. Eroz, Betil; Turkish, English
39. Estival, Dominique; French, English
40. Faris, Michael A.; English, Polish, Polish Sign Language

41. Fidelholtz, James L.; English, Spanish, German, Polish

42. Frishberg, Nancy; English, American Sign Language

43. Furiye, Atsushi; Japanese, English

44. Gladstone, Kate; English, Hebrew, French, German, Russian

45. Gluckman, T. J.; English, German, French

46. González, Luis Alberto; Spanish, English

47. Gregory, George Ann; English, Spanish, Choctaw

48. Gu, Peter Yongqi; Mandarin Chinese, English, Hebei Chinese

49. Halford, Richard; English, Afrikaans

50. Haraghey, Marjolijn; Dutch, English, German, Afrikaans, French

51. Hardman, M.J.; English, Spanish, Jaqaru, Aymara

52. Herrarte, Caroline; English, Spanish

53. Herzfeld, Anita; Spanish, English, German

54. Hilgendorf, Suzanne K.; English, German

55. Iturrizaga, Dimas Bautista; Jaqaru, Spanish, English

56. Joergensen, Mikala; Danish, English, German, French

57. Julian, Jane; English, Hebrew

58. Kaspy, Lior; Hebrew, English, Arabic

59. Kernberger, Carolyn; English, Spanish

60. Khoza, Zangie; Tsonga, Swazi, English

61. Kirchner, James; English, Czech, German

62. Kondo, Chikako; Japanese, English

63. Kronenberg, Kenneth; English, German

64. Langent, Moeketsi; Sesotho, English, Afrikaans

65. Lattey, Elsa; German, English, Spanish

66. Lenstrup, Marie; Danish, English, German, Swedish, Norwegian

67. Li, Wen-Chao; Mandarin Chinese, English

68. Llanes, Jose R.; Spanish/English

69. Luk, Ching Man; Cantonese, English

70. Maduell, Mariana; English, Spanish, Italian

71. Maesfranckx, Patricia; Dutch, English, German, Swedish, French

72. Mahdi, Waruno; Indonesian, English, German, Russian, Dutch

73. Mamathuba, Elelwani Charity; Venda, English, Afrikaans

74. Martinez, Alejandro G.; Spanish, English

75. McIntire, Marina L.; English, American Sign Language

76. Meynard, Yves; French, English

77. Mohamed, Rahima; English, Afrikaans
78. Morrison, Dave; English, American Sign Language
79. Murphy, Linda; English, French
80. O Se, Gavin; English, German, French, Irish
81. Palmer, Chris; English, French, German
82. Parkman, Victoria; Russian, Ukrainian, English
83. Páteris, Lehtla; Latvian, Russian, German, English
84. Pomerantz, Ori; Hebrew, English
85. Rasmussen, Allysse Suzanne; English, Spanish, American Sign Language
86. Rebsch, Debby; German, English
87. Reighard, John; English, French, Italian, German, Portuguese, Spanish
88. Resende, Rosana; Portuguese, Spanish, English
89. Robertson, Michael; English, Italian
90. Rose, Alex; English, French
91. Schaufele, Steven; English, French, German, Italian
92. Schober, George; English, German
93. Seck, Maguette; Wolof, French, English
94. Siley, Delphine; French, English
95. Sosa, Juan Manuel; Spanish, French, English, Portugeuse
96. Sotello, Susana; Spanish, English
97. Stallings, Fran; English, Japanese
98. Stenson, Nancy; English, Irish, French
99. Swan, Pamela; Japanese, English, Spanish
100. Troen, Carol R.; English, Hebrew, French
101. Trudel, Jean-Louis; French, English
102. True, Sean; English, Spanish
103. Umans, Meg; English, Spanish, German, French
104. van der Goot, Auke; Frisian, Dutch, English, French, German
105. van Wyk, Karin; English, Afrikaans
106. Verspoor, Cornelia M.; English, Dutch, French
107. Vlijm, Chantal; Dutch, English, French, German, Spanish
108. Vonarburg, Elisabeth; French, English

109. Walling, Espy Rodriguez; Spanish, English, French
110. Whiteley, Colin; English, Spanish, French, German, Catalan, Portuguese, Italian
111. Wilson, Mark A.; English, German
112. Yamamoto, Masayo; Japanese, English
113. Yanjin, Yao; Chinese (Mandarin and Shanghai), English
114. Zeviar, Churyl; English, French, American Sign Language
115. Zoeppritz, Magdalena; German, English, French

III. The Languages of Respondents

Name of Language	Number of Speakers
Afrikaans	9
American Sign Language (ASL)	2
Arabic	7
Aymara	1
Azerbaijani	1
Bulgarian	1
Cantonese (Chinese)	3
Catalan	1
Choctaw	1
Czech	1
Danish	3
Dutch	1
English	115
Farsi	1
French	40
Frisian	1
German	39
Hebei (Chinese)	1
Hebrew	4
Hungarian	1
Indonesian	1

Name of Language	Number of Speakers
Irish	2
Italian	13
Japanese	5
Jaqaru	2
Lao	1
Latvian	2
Lenape	1
Malay	1
Mandarin (Chinese)	6
Navajo	1
Norwegian	2
Polish	3
Polish Sign Language (PSL)	1
Portuguese	5
Russian	7
Saami	1
Scottish Gaelic	1
Serbo-Croatian	1
Sesotho	2
Setswana	1
Shanghai (Chinese)	1
Signed English for the Deaf	1
Slovenian	1
Spanish	35
Swazi	1
Swedish	3
Thai	1
Tsonga	1
Turkish	2
Ukrainian	1
Venda	1
Wolof	1
Xhosa	1
Zulu	3

Bibliography and References

Books

Aitchison, J. 1998. The Articulate Mammal: An Introduction to Psycholinguistics, 4th ed. New York: Routledge.

Asher, R. E., ed. 1994. The Encyclopedia of Language and Linguistics. Oxford: Pergamon Press.

Auer, P., ed. 1998. Code-Switching in Conversation: Language, Interaction, and Identity. New York: Routledge.

Bain, B. 1996. Pathways to the Peak of Mount Piaget and Vygotsky: Speaking and Cognizing Monolingually and Bilingually. Rome: Bulzoni Editore.

Beinfield, H., and E. Korngold. 1991. Between Heaven And Earth: A Guide to Chinese Medicine. New York: Ballantine Books.

Bérubé, M. 1996. Life as We Know It: A Father, a Family, and an Exceptional Child. New York: Pantheon Books.

Bodmer, F. 1944. The Loom of Language. (Edited by L. Hogben.) New York: W. W. Norton.

Bolinger, D. 1972. Intonation. Harmondsworth: Penguin Books.

Cantoni, G., ed. 1996. Stabilizing Indigenous Languages. Flagstaff: Northern Arizona University. [A Center for Excellence in Education monograph.]

Carson, D. A. 1998. The Inclusive-Language Debate: A Plea for Realism. Grand Rapids, MI: Baker Books.

Cherry, K. 1987. Womansword: What Japanese Words Say About Women. New York: Kodansha America.

Claiborne, R. 1983. Our Marvelous Native Tongue: The Life and Times of the English Language. New York: Times Books.

Cook, V., and M. Newson. 1996. Chomsky's Universal Grammar, 2nd ed. London: Blackwell Publishers.

Crawford, J. 1992. Hold Your Tongue: Bilingualism and the Politics of English Only. Reading, MA: Addison-Wesley.

Crystal, D. 1992. An Encyclopedic Dictionary of Language and Languages. London: Penguin Books.

_____. 1994. Dictionary of Language and Languages. New York: Penguin.

_____. 1998. The Cambridge Encyclopedia of Language, 2nd ed. Cambridge, UK: Cambridge University Press.

_____. 1998. English as a Global Language. Cambridge, UK: Cambridge University Press.

Edwards, J. 1995. Multilingualism. London and New York: Routledge.

Ekman, P. 1985. Telling Lies: Clues to Deceit in the Marketplace, Politics, and Marriage. New York: W. W. Norton.

Elgin, S. H. 1984. Native Tongue. New York: DAW Books. (And forthcoming from Feminist Press, New York, in October 2000.)

_____. 1987. Native Tongue II: The Judas Rose. New York: DAW Books.

_____. 1988. A First Grammar and Dictionary of Láadan. Madison, WI: Society for the Furtherance of Fantasy and Science Fiction (SF3).

_____. 1993. Genderspeak: Men, Women, and the Gentle Art of Verbal Self-Defense. New York: Wiley.

_____. 1994. Native Tongue III: Earthsong. New York: DAW Books.

_____. 1996. How to Disagree Without Being Disagreeable. New York: Wiley.

_____. 1997. How to Turn the Other Cheek and Still Survive in Today's World. Nashville, TN: Thomas Nelson.

Ferré, F. 1961. Language, Logic, and God. New York: Harper and Row.

Festinger, L. 1957. A Theory of Cognitive Dissonance. Evanston, IL: Row, Peterson.

Frantzis, B. K. 1993. Opening the Energy Gates of the Body. Berkeley, CA: North Atlantic Books.

Friedrich, P. 1986. The Language Parallax: Linguistic Relativism and Poetic Indeterminacy. Austin: University of Texas Press.

Gannon, M. J. 1994. Understanding Global Cultures: Metaphorical Journeys Through 17 Countries. Thousand Oaks, CA: Sage.

Gill, S. and I. Sullivan, 1992. *Dictionary of Native American Mythology.* New York: Oup.

Grimes, B. F. 1992. Ethnologue: Languages of the World, 12th ed. Dallas, TX: Summer Institute of Linguistics.

Grosjean, F. 1982. Life with Two Languages: An Introduction to Bilingualism. Cambridge, MA: Harvard University Press.

Hagège, C. 1996. L'enfant aux deux langues. Paris: Editions Odile Jacob.

Hakuta, K. 1986. Mirror of Language: The Debate on Bilingualism. New York: Basic Books.

Hall, E. T. 1959. The Silent Language. New York: Doubleday/Anchor.

_____. 1969. The Hidden Dimension. New York: Doubleday/Anchor.

_____. 1977. Beyond Culture. New York: Doubleday/Anchor.

_____. 1984. The Dance of Life: The Other Dimension of Time. New York: Doubleday/Anchor.

Harlow, D. The Esperanto Book. Available on-line: http://www.webcom.com/~donh/eaccess/eaccess.book.html.

Herschel, A. J. 1975. The Prophets. New York: HarperCollins.

Hofstadter, D. 1979. Goedel, Escher, Bach: An Eternal Golden Braid. New York: Basic Books.

Hull, P. 1990. Bilingualism: Two Languages, Two Personalities. University of California Psychology Department, dissertation.

Johnson, E. A. 1993. She Who Is: The Mystery of God in Feminist Theological Discourse. New York: Crossroad.

Johnson, K. 1996. Second Language Learning. London: Blackwell.

Kaptchuk, T .J. 1983. The Web That Has No Weaver: Understanding Chinese Medicine. New York: Congdon & Webb.

Kelly, K., ed. 1988. Signals: Communication Tools for the Information Age, New York: Harmony Books/Crown.

Key, M. R., ed. 1980. The Relationship of Verbal and Nonverbal Communication. The Hague: Mouton.

Klitzman, R. The Trembling Mountain. New York: Plenum.

Kouritzin, S.G. 1999. Facets of First Language Loss. Mahwah, NJ: Lawrence Erlbaum Associates.

Labov, W., and D. Fanshel. 1977. Therapeutic Discourse: Psychotherapy as Conversation. New York: Academic Press.

LaFleur, W. R. 1992. Liquid Life: Abortion and Buddhism in Japan. Princeton: Princton University Press.

Lakoff, G. 1987. Women, Fire, and Dangerous Things: What Categories Reveal About the Mind. Chicago: University of Chicago Press.

Lakoff, G., and M. Johnson. 1980. Metaphors We Live By. Chicago: University of Chicago Press.

———. 1999. Philosophy in the Flesh: The Embodied Mind and Its Challenge to Western Thought. New York: Basic Books.

Lee, P. 1996. The Whorf Theory Complex: A Critical Reconstruction. Philadelphia: John Benjamins.

Lucy, J. A. 1992. Language Diversity and Thought: A Reformulation of the Linguistic Relativity Hypothesis. Cambridge, UK: Cambridge University Press.

Lyovin, A. V. 1997. An Introduction to the Languages of the World. Oxford: Oxford University Press.

MacWhinney, B., ed. 1999. The Emergence of Language. Mahwah, NJ: Erlbaum.

McNeill, D. 1992. Hand and Mind: What Gestures Reveal About Thought. Chicago: University of Chicago Press.

Meyer, W. E. 1980. Aliens & Linguists: Language Study and Science Fiction. Athens: University of Georgia Press.

Niemeier, S., et al., eds. 1998. The Cultural Context in Business Communication. Philadelphia: John Benjamins.

Nishimura, M. 1997. Japanese/English Code-Switching: Syntax and Pragmatics. New York: Peter Lang Publishing.

Obler, L. K., and L. Menn. 1982. Exceptional Language and Linguistics. New York: Academic Press.

Ogden, C. K. 1930. Basic English: A General Introduction with Rules and Grammar. London: Paul Treber.

O'Grady, W., and M. Dobrovolsky, with M. Aronoff. 1989. Contemporary Linguistics: An Introduction. New York: St. Martin's Press.

Pinker, S. 1994. The Language Instinct: How the Mind Creates Languages. New York: William Morrow.

Reuther, R. 1993. Sexism and God-Talk: Toward a Feminist Theology. Boston: Beacon Press.

Rheingold, H. 1988. They Have a Word for It: A Lighthearted Lexicon of Untranslatable Words and Phrases. Los Angeles: Jeremy P. Tarcher.

Rosenberg, C. E., and J. Golden, eds. 1992. Framing Disease: Studies in Cultural History. New Brunswick, NJ: Rutgers University Press.

Rossi, E. L. 1986. The Psychobiology of Mind-Body Healing: New Concepts of Therapeutic Hypnosis. New York: W. W. Norton.

Sampson, G. 1998. Educating Eve: The "Language Instinct" Debate. London: Cassell.

Schiffman, H.F. 1998. Linguistic Culture and Language Policy. New York: Routledge.

Schneider E. W., ed. 1997. Englishes Around the World I and II: Studies in Honor of Manfred Goerlach. Philadelphia: John Benjamins.

Scollon, R., and S. W. Scollon. 1994. Intercultural Communication. London: Blackwell.

Searle, J. 1969. Speech Acts. Cambridge, UK: Cambridge University Press.

Seligman, S. D. 1990. Dealing with the Chinese: A Practical Guide to Business Etiquette. London: Mercury Books.

Shopen, T. 1979. Languages and Their Status. Cambridge, MA: Winthrop.

Smith, H. 1965. The Religions of Man. New York: Harper & Row/Perennial Library.

Spencer, A. B., and W. D. Spencer, eds. 1998. The Global God: Multicultural Evangelical Views of God. Grand Rapids, MI: Baker Books.

Valdman, A., ed. 1998. French and Creole in Louisiana. New York: Plenum.

Vance, J. 1958. The Languages of Pao. New York: Ace Books.

Van Dijk, T. A., ed. 1985. Handbook of Discourse Analysis. London: Academic Press.

Van Wolferen, K. 1989. The Enigma of Japanese Power: People and Politics in a Stateless World. New York: Knopf.

Watzlawick, P., et al. 1967. Pragmatics of Human Communication: A Study of Interactional Patterns, Pathologies, and Paradoxes. New York: W. W. Norton.

Wierzbicka, A. 1996. Semantics: Primes and Universals. Oxford and New York: Oxford University Press.

Whorf, B. L. 1956. Language, Thought, and Reality: Selected Writings. (Edited by J. B. Carroll.) Cambridge, MA: MIT Press.

Wilkinson, S., and C. Kitzinger, eds. 1995. Feminism and Discourse: Psychological Perspectives. London: Sage.

Wink, W. 1998. The Powers That Be: Theology for a New Millennium. New York: Doubleday/Augsburg Fortress.

Wren, B. 1991. What Language Shall I Borrow? God-Talk in Worship: A Male Response to Feminist Theology. New York: Crossroad.

_____. 1989. Bring Many Names: 35 New Hymns by Brian Wren. Carol Stream, IL; Hope.

Yamada, H. 1997. Different Games, Different Rules: Why Americans and Japanese Misunderstand Each Other. Oxford: Oxford University Press.

Articles

Allman, W. T. "The Mother Tongue." U.S. News & World Report, November 5, 1990, pp. 60–70.

Anderson, M. C. "Gained in Translation." Archives of Family Medicine, September 1992, p. 33.

Andrews, J. "Culture Wars." Wired, May 1995, pp. 130–138.

Aronson, L. Review of African Nomadic Architecture: Space, Place, and Gender, by Labelle Prussin (Smithsonian Institution Press and the National Museum of African Art, 1995). Women's Review of Books, September 1996, pp. 8–9.

Barinaga, M. "New Insights into How Babies Learn Language." New Scientist, August 1, 1997, p. 641.

Barr, B. "Inclusive Language, Women's Ordination, and Another Great Awakening." Christian Century, April 13, 1998, pp. 366–368.

Begley, S. "Your Child's Brain." Newsweek Magazine, February 19, 1996, pp. 55–62.

Berke, M. "God and Gender in Judaism." First Things, June/July 1996, pp. 33–38.

Berreby, D. Review of R. A. Harris, The Linguistics Wars. The Sciences, January-February 1994, pp. 45–49.

Bilger, B. "Keeping Our Words." The Sciences, September-October 1994, pp. 16–20.

_____. "In Their Own Words." Oklahoma Today, May-June 1994, pp. 34–43.

Bilney, G. "Why we've gotta speak Bill's language." (Review of D. Crystal, English as a Global Language.) Sydney Morning Herald, July 25, 1998.

Blackhall, L. J., et al. "Ethnicity and Attitudes Toward Patient Autonomy." Journal of the American Medical Association , September 13, 1995, pp. 820-825.

Blakeslee, S. "When an Adult Adds a Language, It's One Brain, Two Systems." New York Times, July 15, 1997.

Bower, B. "My Culture, My Self: Western Notions of the Mind May Not Translate to Other Cultures." Science News, October 18, 1997, pp. 248–249.

_____. "Brains show signs of two bilingual roads." Science News, July 12, 1997, p. 23.

Brimelow, P. "Leaks in the Melting Pot." Forbes Magazine, October 6, 1997, pp. 46–47.

Brooke, J. "Indians Striving to Save Their Languages." New York Times, April 9, 1998.

Buchanan, M. "Fascinating Rhythm." New Scientist, January 3, 1998, pp. 20–25.

Buruma, I. "What Keeps the Japanese Going?" New York Review, March 17, 1988, pp. 39–43.

Butler, Sue. "English as an Asian Language." (Conference announcement, May 15, 1996). [On-line.] Available e-mail: sue@dict.mq.edu.au.

Button, G. "The Great Performer." Forbes Magazine, October 21, 1996, pp. 74–82.

Camp, C. "Metaphor in Feminist Biblical Interpretation: Theoretical Perspectives." Semeia 61 (1993), pp. 3-36.

Carrese, J. A. "Western Bioethics on the Navajo Reservation: Benefit or Harm?" Journal of the American Medical Association , September 13, 1995, pp. 826–829.

Cohn, C. "Slick'ems, Glick'ems, Christmas Trees, and Cookie Cutter: Nuclear Language and How We Learned to Pat the Bomb." Bulletin of the Atomic Scientists, June 1987, pp. 17–24.

Cotton, P. "Chaos, Other Nonlinear Dynamics Research May Have Answers, Applications for Clinical Medicine." Journal of the American Medical Association, July 3, 1991, pp. 12–18.

Cowan, R. S. "Less Work for Mother?" Invention & Technology, Spring 1987, pp. 57–63.

Crawford, J. 1996. "Summing Up the Lau Decision: Justice Is Never Simple." In Revising the Lau Decision: Proceedings of a National Commemorative Symposium. [On-line.] Available http://ourworld.compuserve.com/homepages/JWCRAWFORD.

_____. "Seven Hypotheses on Language Loss: Causes and Cures." In Cantoni 1996, pp. 51–68.

Day, R. "Temporal order judgments in speech: Are individuals language-bound or stimulus-bound?" Haskins Laboratories Status Report on Speech Research SR-21/22 (1970), pp. 71-87.

_____. "Digit-Span Memory in Language-Bound and Stimulus-Bound Individuals." Haskins Laboratories Status Report on Speech Research SR-34 (1973), pp. 127-139.

_____. "On Learning Secret Languages." Haskins Laboratories Status Report on Speech Research SR-34 (1993), pp. 141-150.

Davany, S. G. Review of S. McFague, Models of God: Theology For an Eco-
logical Nuclear Age (Fortress Press 1987). Religious Studies Review, January 1990, pp. 36–40.

DellaFlora, A. "Language and Experienced Reality." Albuquerque Journal,
June 14, 1998.

Devor, N. G. "A Service for Isaac." Christian Century, April 20, 1988, p. 391.

Diamond, J. "The Language Steamrollers." Nature, October 9, 1997, pp.
544-545.

Dorfman, A. "If Only We All Spoke Two Languages." New York Times, June
24, 1998.

Dorian, N. C. "Linguistic Models and Language Death Evidence." In Obler
and Menn 1982, pp. 31-48.

Dubow, C. "Great Doing Business with You, Grigori, and Thank You for
Not Killing Me! A Guide to Russian Business Etiquette." Forbes FYI, Fall
1998, pp. 141–148.

Duncan, J., and J. Laird. "Warning: Placebos Can Be Dangerous to Your
Health." Psychology Today, April 1981, pp. 26–27.

Dyson, E. "Intellectual Value." Wired, July 1995, pp. 137–141 and 182–184.

Ervin, S. M. "Language and TAT Content in Bilinguals." Journal of Abnormal Social Psychology 68, 1964, pp. 500–507.

Estrich, S. "Language Gap." Washington Post, January 1, 1997.

Fayez, J. A., et al. "The Climateric, Part I: Conquering Osteoporosis, Vasomotor Instability, and Urogenital Deterioration." Female Patient, April
1987, pp. 62–74.

Ferguson, D. "Lost Languages Threaten Tribal Cultures." Tulsa World, August 1, 1993.

Fernandez, E. "Cooléate, Man, Here Comes el Nuevo Creole." Village Voice,
October 7, 1986.

Fish, S. "Why We Can't All Just Get Along." First Things, February 1996, pp.
18-26.

Fishman, J. "What Do You Lose When You Lose Your Language?" In Cantoni 1996, pp. 80–91.

Fitzgerald, F. T. "Patients from Other Cultures: How They View You, Themselves, and Disease." Consultant, March 1988, pp. 65–77.

Foster, R. P. "The Bilingual Self: Duet in Two Voices." Psychoanalytic Dialogues 6(1), 1996, pp. 99–121.

_____. "The Bilingual Self—Thoughts from a Scientific Positivist or Prag-
matic Psychoanalyst: Reply to Massey." Psychoanalytic Dialogues 6(1),
1996, pp. 141–150.

Fox, B. "Morse users send out an SOS." New Scientist, January 20, 1996, p. 19.

Furuiye, A. "Prospects for Multi-Heritage People." [On-line.] Shijo-Tsushin #9, February 1997, pp. 1–2.

Garvin, G. "Loco, Completamente Loco." Reason, January 1998. [On-line].

Geary, J. "Speaking in Tongues: As Telecommunications, Tourism and Trade Make the World a Smaller Place, Languages Are Dying at an Alarming Rate." Time International Edition, July 7, 1997, pp. 1–7.

Gilchrist, B. G. "The Limits of Self-Determination." Toward Freedom, June-July 1996, pp. 9–10 and 22.

Goldin-Meadows, S., and C. Mylander. "Beyond the Input Given" The Child's Role in the Acquisition of Language." Language, June 1990, pp. 323-355.

Goleman, D. "The Self: From Tokya to Topeka, It Changes." New York Times, March 7, 1989.

_____. "Making Room on the Couch for Culture." New York Times.

Gonzalez-Mena de Lococo, V. "The Salient Differences Between Chicano Spanish and Standard Spanish: Some Pedagogical Considerations." The Bilingual Review, May-August 1974, pp. 243–251.

Grosjean, F. "Individual Bilingualism." In Asher 1994, pp. 1656–1660.

Halstead, L. S. "Post-Polio Syndrome." Scientific American, April 1998, pp. 43–47.

Hamadeh, G. "Religion, Magic, and Medicine." Journal of Family Practice, 25: 6 (1987).

Harvey, M. "Re: Reaching Out to Ethnic Audiences." Storytell, July 18, 1997. [On-line].

Headden, S. "One Nation, One Language?" U.S. News & World Report, September 25, 1996, pp. 38–42.

Hedges, C. "In the Balkans, Three Languages Now Fight It Out." New York Times, May 15, 1996.

_____. "A Language Divided Against Itself." New York Times, January 29, 1995.

Heyneman, M. "The Mother Tongue." Parabola, Fall 1992, pp. 8–12.

Hickock, G., et al. 1996. "The Neurobiology of Sign Language and Its Implications for the Neural Basis of Language." Nature 381, pp. 699–702.

Hinton, L. "Languages of the Elders May Be Silenced." Oakland Tribune, October 31, 1995.

Honan, W. H. "To Masters of Language, a Long Overdue Toast." New York Times, December 31, 1997.

Hook, D. D., and A. F. Kimel, Jr. "The Pronouns of Deity: A Theolinguistic Critique of Feminist Proposals." Scottish Journal of Theology 46, (1993) pp. 297–323. (Also published in pamphlet form with minor revisions, with no publisher or date shown.)

Immergut, D. J. "Bridging the Web's Language Gap." Wall Street Journal, November 12, 1996.

Iyer, P. "Nowhere Man." Utne Reader, May-June 1997, pp. 78–79.

Jabbour, H. D. "A Condescending Attitude." Plain Truth, March 1991, p. 16.

Javier, R. A. "Vicissitudes of Autobiographical Memories in a Bilingual Analysis." Psychoanalytic Psychology 12, 1995, pp. 429–438.

Jenner, G. "Building a Babel Machine." New Scientist, June 8, 1996, p. 48.

Johnson, R. C. "Voila! Free Translations." Electronic Engineering Times, April 8, 1996, p. 95.

Joseph, J. E. Review of Lee 1996. Language, September 1998, pp. 634–646.

Judge, A.J.N. "Guiding Metaphors and Configuring Choices, Part II." [On-line.] Available http://www.uia.org. (1991)

_____. "Misapplication of International Legal Norms in Socially Abnormal Situations." [On-line.] Available http://www.uia.org. (1994)

Juri, C. "Ever Heard of Spanglish? It's No Problema Amigos." Austin American-Statesman, December 26, 1997.

Kaalgard, R. "Interview: Larry Ellison." Forbes ASAP, June 7, 1993, pp. 71–74.

Kalbfleisch, J. "Probing the spoken word." Montreal Gazette, September 3, 1994.

Kandolph, C. "Our Story: The Haug/Kandolf Family." [On-line.] Available http: www.nethelp.no/Cindy/biling-fam.html.

Kaplan, R. D. "Travels into America's Future." Atlantic Monthly, August 1998, pp. 37–61.

Kay, J. H. "The Once and Future Kitchenless House." New York Times, February 23, 1989.

Kim, Karl, et al. "Distinct Cortical Areas Associated with Native and Second Languages." Nature, July 10, 1997, pp. 171 ff.

Kitasei, H. H. "Japanese Sacrifice Themselves to Save Their Institutions." Oakland Tribune, April 5, 1998.

Kleiner, K. "Language Deaths 'Bad for Us All.'" New Scientist, March 6, 1995, p. 15.

Knudsen, E. "Capacity for Plasticity in the Adult Owl Auditory System Expanded by Juvenile Experience." Science, March 6, 1998, pp 1531–1533.

Kristof, N. D. "Dung! What an Unusual Name!" New York Times, December 12, 1995.

Kuhl, P. K., et al. "Cross-Language Analysis of Phonetic Units in Language Addressed to Infants." Science, August 1, 1997, pp. 684–686.

Kuntz, G. "My Spanish Standoff." Newsweek, May 4, 1998, p. 22.

Lakoff, G. "Metaphor & War." East Bay Express, February 22, 1991, p. 1 and pp. 13-18.

Landers, C. "News and Views: From the Worlds of Translation." ATA Source, Summer 1996, page 5.

Laurence, L. "What's Happening to Me?" Ladies Home Journal, April 1994, pp.73–78.

Linthicum, L. "Indian Languages in Danger of Vanishing in Melting Pot." Albuquerque Journal, June 14, 1998.

Marcus, A. D. "War of Words: Arabic Emerges as a Weapon in Mideast Struggles." Wall Street Journal, March 13, 1997.

Martelle, S. "Arabic Spoken Here." Teaching Tolerance, Spring 1997, pp. 47–51.

Massey, C. "Cultural and Conceptual Dissonance in Theoretical Practice: Commentary on RoseMarie Pérez Foster's 'The Bilingual Self: Duet in Two Voices.'" Psychoanalytic Dialogues 6(1), 1996, pp. 123–140.

Mcintyre, T. "Oliver Sacks: The Bedside Interview." Whole Earth Review, Summer 1995, pp. 90–100.

Mitchell, K. Description of Yamada 1997, on Linguist List; March 18, 1998. [On-line.] Available e-mail: KKM@OUP-USA.Org.

Nanas, E. "Studying Japanese Is a Waste of Time." New York Times, March 3, 1989.

Nash, J. M. "Fertile Minds." Time, February 3, 1997, pp. xx–56.

Nathan, G. S. Personal communication, March 26, 1998. [On-line; e-mail.]

Navarro, M. (In Landers 1996.)

Neff, D. "The Great Translation Debate." Christianity Today, October 27, 1997, pp. 16–17.

Newman, B. "Lithuanian Linguists Resist New Attacks on Native Tongue." Wall Street Journal, April 12, 1993.

_____. "How the World Remakes English." Globe and Mail, March 24, 1995.

Osborne, G. R. "Do Inclusive Language Bibles Distort Scripture? No." Christianity Today, October 27, 1997, pp. 33–38.

Parshall, G. "A 'Glorious Mongrel.'" U.S. News & World Report, September 25, 1995, p. 48.

Peavy, F. "Questions for the Ganges." Whole Earth Review, Summer 1995, pp. 49–51.

Pederson, E., et al. "Semantic Typology and Spatial Conceptualization." Language, September 1998, pp. 557–589.

Peters, B. Review of Semantics: Primes and universals, by A. Wierzbicka (Oxford University Press, 1996). Language, March 1998, pp. 180–183.

Pollack, A. "Happy in the East (^_^) Or Smiling :-) in the West." New York Times, August 12, 1996.

Pressley, S. A. "Oaks Students Learn Their Language Roots." Tulsa World, November 8, 1993.

Prince, A., and P. Smolensky. "Optimality: From Neural Networks to Universal Grammar." Science, March 14, 1997, pp. 1604–1610.

Radetsky, P. "Silence, Signs, and Wonder." Discover, August 1994, pp. 59-68.

Ravitch, D. "Shi Taiad." Forbes Magazine, September 22, 1997, p. 138.

Reber, P. "Language Barriers." Columbia Missourian, July 12, 1998.

Reeves, R. "English Poised to Become World's Universal Language." Albuquerque Journal, April 25, 1997.

Rodriguez, R., and P. Gonzales. "Value of Being Bilingual Downplayed in Workplace." Albuquerque Journal, October 7, 1997.

Rosenberg, C. E. "Framing Disease: Illness, Society, and History." Hospital Practice, July 15, 1992, pp. 179–221.

Rubenstein, E. S. "Leaks in the Melting Pot." Forbes Magazine, October 6, 1997, pp. 46–47.

Salins, P. D. "Assimilation, American Style." Reason Magazine, February 1997, pp. 20–26.

Schiffman, H. F. "Linguistic Culture and Language Policy." [On-line.] Available http://ourworld.compuserve.com/homepages/JWCRAWFORD.

Schmitt, E. "House Approves Measure on Official U.S. Language." New York Times, August 1, 1996.

Seidenberg, M. "Language Acquisition and Use: Learning and Applying Probabilistic Constraints." Science, March 14, 1997, pp. 1599-1603.

Selzer, R. "The Art of Surgery." Harpers Magazine, January 1976, pp. 75–78.

Shopen, T. "Cape York Creole." In Shopen 1979, pp. 153–207.

Slobin, D. I. "Verbalized Events: A Dynamic Approach to Linguistic Relativity and Determinism." Unpublished paper presented at LAUD Symposium 1998, in Duisburg, Germany.

Sowell, T. "The Multiculturalism Cult." Forbes Magazine, May 20, 1996, p. 82.

Straight, H. S. Review of L'Enfant aux deux langues, by Claude Hagège (Editions Odile Jacob, 1996). Language, March 1998, pp. 139–142.

Swadesh, M. "Toward Greater Accuracy in Lexicostatistical Dating." International Journal of Anthropological Linguistics 21, 1955, pp. 121–127.

Swigart, L. "Women and Language Choice in Dakar: A Case of Unconscious Innovation." Women and Language, Spring 1992, pp. 11–20.

Vines, G. "Death of a Mother Tongue." New Scientist, January 6, 1996, pp. 24–27.

Ward, G. C. "India." National Geographic, May 1997, pp. 7–57.

Warren, R., and R. Warren. "Auditory Illusions and Confusions." Scientific American, December, 1970, pp. 30–36.

Wertheim, M. "The Way of Logic." New Scientist, December 2, 1995, pp. 38–41.

Whitney, G. "In World Cup Games, Words Get Lost and Gained in Translation." Wall Street Journal, July 14, 1994.

Wilkins, W. K., and J. Wakefield. "Brain Evolution and Neurolinguistic Preconditions." Behavioral and Brain Sciences 18, 1995, pp. 161–226.

Willeto, P. "Diné College Struggles to Synthesize Navajo and Western Knowledge." Tribal College Journal, Fall 1997, pp. 11–15.

Winslow, R. "How Language Is Stored in Brain Depends on Age." Wall Street Journal, July 10, 1997.

Woodward, C. Quoted in e-mail on Linguist List, 8/14/96. [On-line.]

Zimmerman, J. "A Babel of Tongues." U.S. News & World Report, November 24, 1997, p. 39.

Zwingle, E. "A world together." National Geographic, August 1999, pp. 6-33.

Items Without Byline

"Word for Word/Officially English: A Law to Learn 'Em a Thing or Two About the American Language." New York Times, July 18, 1996.

"Bilingualism: Si or No?" Oakland Tribune, October 22, 1997.

"We Don't Need No Stinking English." Time, September 18, 1996, p. 38. [Sidebar.]

"Speaking in Tongues." Time, June 2, 1997, p. J11.

"Classic Health Risk Factors May Not Apply to Latinos." Family Practice News, July 1, 1992, p. 21.

"ASAP Interview: Larry Ellison." Forbes ASAP, June 7, 1993, pp. 71–74.

"Quotation of the Day." New York Times, April 29, 1986.

Review of Polite Lies: On Being a Woman Caught Between Two Cultures, by Kyoko Mori. Publishers Weekly, November 3, 1997, pp. 71–72.

"The Bilingual Brain." Discover, October 1997, p. 26.

"Bilinguals Devote Distinct Areas of the Brain to Native and Second Languages." (Press release, Memorial Sloan-Kettering Hospital, July 10, 1997.) [On-line.]

"An Instinct for Language," interview with Steven Pinker. New Scientist, June 25, 1994, pp. 28–31.

"Speaking in Tongues." Time Magazine, June 2, 1997, p. J11.

"Dinner Conversation: She Wants Her TV! He Wants His Book!" (Dialogue between Neil Postman and Camille Paglia.) Harper's Magazine, March 1991, pp. 44-55.

Index